THE ACHIEVEMENT OF T. S. ELIOT

The Achievement of

T. S. ELIOT

AN ESSAY ON THE NATURE OF POETRY

F. O. MATTHIESSEN

With a chapter on Eliot's later work
by C. L. BARBER

Third Edition

A GALAXY BOOK
New York   Oxford University Press   1959

For

KENNETH *and* LAURETTE MURDOCK

What does the mind enjoy in books? Either the style or nothing. But, someone says, what about the thought? The thought, that is the style, too.

CHARLES MAURRAS

We begin to live when we have conceived life as tragedy.

W. B. YEATS

PREFACE TO THE FIRST EDITION (1935)

My DOUBLE AIM in this essay is to evaluate Eliot's method and achievement as an artist, and in so doing to emphasize certain of the fundamental elements in the nature of poetry which are in danger of being obscured by the increasing tendency to treat poetry as a social document and to forget that it is an art. The most widespread error in contemporary criticism is to neglect form and to concern itself entirely with content. The romantic critic is generally not interested in the poet's work, but in finding the man behind it. The humanistic critic and the sociological critic have in common that both tend to ignore the evaluation of specific poems in their preoccupation with the ideological background from which the poems spring. All these concerns can have value in expert hands, but only if it is realized that they are not criticism of poetry. In combating the common error, my contention is that, although in the last analysis content and form are inseparable, a poem can be neither enjoyed nor understood unless the reader experiences all of its formal details, unless he allows the movement and pattern of its words to exercise their full charm over him before he attempts to say precisely what it is that the poem means. The most fatal approach to a poem is to focus merely on what it seems to state, to try to isolate its ideas from their context in order to approve or disapprove of them before having really grasped their implications in the poem itself. Consequently, my approach to Eliot's poetry, and to poetry generally, is through close attention to its technique. I agree with Mallarmé that 'poetry is not written with ideas, it is written with words,' as well as with the assertion that what matters is not what a poem says, but what it *is*. That does not mean that either the poem or the poet can be separated from the society that produced them, or that a work of art does not inevitably both reflect and illuminate its age. Nor does it imply that a poet is necessarily lacking in ideas, or that the content of his work, the material he chooses to write about, and the interpretation he makes of it, is without cardinal significance in determining his relation to life and to the currents of thought in his time. But even that significance is obscured, if not distorted, by the criticism that pays heed solely to the poet's ideas and not to their expression, that turns the poet into a philosopher or a political theorist or a pamphleteer, that treats his work as a specimen of sociological evidence, and meanwhile neglects the one quality that gives his words their permanence, his quality as an artist.

In my evaluation of Eliot's poetry I have not been concerned with tracing the development of his thought, nor with his criticism except in so far as it throws light on his own poetical theory and practice, though the evolution both of his critical tenets and of his conception of the relation of the individual to society would make a good subject for another book. In order to give my book as close a unity as possible, I have consciously made an experiment in its organization. I have tried to write the whole as one connected essay, with each section closely interweaving with what goes before and what follows. Indeed, the division into chapters is simply a convenience, in order, through their titles, to stress some points that I am most interested in establishing. My desire for a sustained condensed effect has also caused me to make use of notes for some passages of more technical analysis, as well as for longer illustrations. These notes are intended to be integral elaborations of the text, but those readers who, like myself, are irritated at the distraction of being repeatedly referred to the back of the book, are asked to postpone that act at least until the end of each chapter. For unless the essay stands clearly on its own feet, without aid from the notes, it will not stand reading at all.

PREFACE TO THE 1947 EDITION

IN THE dozen years since I undertook this book much more criticism of Eliot has been written, most notably by Cleanth Brooks in *Modern Poetry and the Tradition* (1939), and several other studies are now projected, including one by Delmore Schwartz. My own views of the poet have inevitably undergone some change, but though I may now see limitations of which I was not conscious in my first absorption in Eliot's earlier work, I am even more impressed by the contemplative depth in his subsequent production. My growing divergence from his view of life is that I believe that it is possible to accept the 'radical imperfection' of man, and yet to be a political radical as well, to be aware that no human society can be perfect, and yet to hold that the proposition that 'all men are created equal' demands dynamic adherence from a Christian no less than from a democrat. But the scope of my book remains what it was before. I have not written about Eliot's politics or religion except as they are expressed through his poetry.

If I were writing the book now, I doubt that I would use the same compressed method of presentation, and I should certainly not introduce so many notes. But those notes still seem useful for their original purpose of providing a running commentary on my sub-title, on my conception of 'the nature of poetry.' I have therefore left most of them untouched, and the only revisions of my earlier text are designed to simplify some of its more cumbersome sentences, in which, as I can now see, I was flagrantly thinking out my material as I wrote it.

The first six chapters are still meant to stand as a whole, as an estimate not so much of particular poems as of Eliot's poetic method. I have now added two chapters on his chief work of the past decade. That on his Quartets first appeared in *The Kenyon Review* (Spring 1943). That on his Plays has just been written.

F. O. M.

October 1946

PREFACE TO THE THIRD EDITION (1958)

THIS BOOK has developed as Eliot has developed. The first six chapters, which the late F. O. Matthiessen published in 1935, are an essay on the nature of poetry as it had been re-defined by the literary revolution of which Eliot was a leader. In the next two chapters, published in 1947, Matthiessen dealt with the plays written up to the war and with the great new achievement of 1935-43, *Four Quartets*. The criticism written during the war and since, and the verse plays produced in 1949 and 1953, constitute a whole new stage of development, to which I have tried to do justice in the chapter which is added in this edition.

The book Matthiessen published in 1935, the first important book of a great American scholar and critic, grew out of his encounter with Eliot and Eliot's work when the poet was Norton lecturer at Harvard in 1932-33. Matthiessen had been reading Eliot's poetry with excitement and pleasure for some years, but he found himself launched on a book in 1933 because his realization of the scope of Eliot's achievement kept growing as his criticism, his lectures, his conversation, and his poetry illuminated each other. Matthiessen's method is to use Eliot's prose to define the qualities of his poetry, and his book quotes revealingly from the essays published in the various collections, from a wide range of still uncollected pieces, from unpublished lectures and notes, as well as, occasionally, from conversation. Quoting Eliot on Eliot can be a merely passive business, but Matthiessen is active: he is locating Eliot's achievement as well as describing it, and his essay has the vitality of discovery: a new major writer's position is just being made out and the whole landscape is being reordered in consequence. In writing about Eliot, he found for the first time an opportunity to express many of his own interests in art and society. The observations about Eliot's American heritage, particularly his relation to Henry James and Hawthorne, anticipate much that was worked out at large in *American Renaissance* (1941), a book which has become, as Henry Nash Smith has observed, 'a landmark in the interpretation of our literature.' Many of the remarks on the place of suffering and tragic insight in Eliot's conception of poetry also point forward to Matthiessen's intensive work on James during the war, notably *Henry James: The Major Phase* (1944).

Matthiessen did not read or write in a departmental way. The political concerns characteristic of literary discussion in the thirties are reflected in his book, and it is remarkable how firmly he holds a balance based on a long and broad view. His own liberal-socialist convictions were opposite to Eliot's conservatism; but he was like Eliot in combining an unfailing· respect for the integrity of works of art with a steady awareness of their complex involvement in the historical process. In following Eliot's thinking about art and culture, Matthiessen makes clear its range and organic unity as no other treatment that I know of has done; and he arrives also at some important statements of his own. The other thing that he does superlatively is to read passages from the poems. He does not provide a running commentary on the whole body of the work, a service that has since been performed with distinction by several other critics, notably Elizabeth Drew and George Williamson. Instead, his method is to illustrate general observations about features of Eliot's technique and sensibility by considering representative passages. In doing so, he keeps always a sense of the whole quality of the poetry, its roundness; and he is concerned with it both as an experience of beauty and as a human statement.

A critic's fundamental instrument is the whole of himself. Matthiessen was a person who strove for unity of being with a heroic intensity. His suicide in 1950 came as a profound shock to his many friends and devoted students, as well as to the whole intellectual community; his death was felt as the defeat of a hero. Thirty-four contributors joined in a collective portrait edited by Paul M. Sweezy and Leo Huberman and published first as a special issue of *The Monthly Review* and then as a book by Henry Schuman (New York, 1950). From the time when at Yale he united the roles of leading campus citizen and devoted student of the arts, to the last years when his day might include early morning work on his book on Dreiser, a seminar at Harvard on Henry James, a stormy committee session about university policy, and a convivial evening with Harry Bridges, his life embraced interests which are usually mutually exclusive. And his passionate and decisive temperament required a thoroughgoing commitment in every relation: in the History and Literature Department at Harvard, where he was the heart and soul of the board of tutors; in the affairs of Rhodes Scholars and his Yale honor society; in the publication with Professor Kenneth Murdock of *The Notebooks of Henry James;* in the financing of a non-Communist journal of socialist opinion, *The Monthly Review;* in the studies and the troubles of his students, many of whom became his friends; in following the work of the painter Russell Cheney, through whom he developed an informed taste in painting; in a religious life as a communicant in the Protestant Episcopal Church.

Matthiessen described his ideal of wholeness of life in writing about his experience while teaching abroad in 1947 at the Salzburg Seminar and in Prague. His richly human, well-written journal, *From the Heart of Europe,* was published just as the Communist coup in Czechoslovakia gave the lie to his generous hopes for a middle way there between West and East. The note which he left at his death, after speaking of exhaustion produced by severe depression, added in a final paragraph: 'How much the state of the world has to do with my state of mind I do not know. But as a Christian and a Socialist believing in international peace I find myself terribly depressed by the present tensions.' A number of editorials and statements in the press at the time of his death drew partisan morals by ascribing it entirely to his political concerns. What he himself wrote—his 'How much . . . I do not know'—shows that he preserved, even under the greatest stress, the dignity of his disciplined intelligence. Both his criticism and his political action were distinguished by the way he recognized the necessity of relating private and public experience while respecting the complexity of the relationships between them. One of the lines of poetry which Matthiessen made particularly meaningful to his students was the statement of Eliot's Becket that 'action is suffering and suffering is action.' His own action, in criticism, in politics, perhaps most effectively of all in his ever-generous teaching, involved suffering and so was informed with understanding and compassion. His nature was such that he had to suffer, and to act, violently. It often cost him a desperate effort, but until the end he managed to suffer and to act for others, for the subject in hand. The lasting value of his interpretation of Eliot reflects the resources for understanding which were won by living in this way.

C. L. Barber

Amherst, Massachusetts
May, 1958

ACKNOWLEDGMENTS (1935)

I WANT to thank the subject of my essay not only for his generous permission to quote from some unpublished lectures, but also for the great benefit of conversation during his recent year at Harvard. I am also thankful that my first introduction to Eliot's poetry came through my friends, the poets Phelps Putnam and Maxwell Evarts Foster, who made me listen to it read aloud, thus enabling me to feel from the outset its lyric sound and movement, instead of letting me begin by losing the poetry in a tortuous effort to find a logical pattern in its unfamiliar structure. I am particularly indebted to my friend and colleague Theodore Spencer, with whom I have discussed these matters ever since our first meeting nine years ago. I am afraid that he will find here more than one of his remarks, unacknowledged, but I hope not garbled. I want also to thank Walter and Esther Houghton, Perry and Elizabeth Miller, Eleanor McLaughlin, Louis Hyde, Russell Cheney, W. Ellery Sedgwick, Harry Levin, and César Lombardi Barber, fellow discoverers. I am grateful to David W. Prall for having turned his trained eye on the last two chapters; and many pages have benefited from the vigorous onslaught of Russell Davenport, who takes exception to much that I have said here and elsewhere, or am likely to say in the future. Among other contemporary critics I am most conscious of my obligations to the work of I. A. Richards and Edmund Wilson, not simply for their own remarks on Eliot, but, more importantly, for stimulus and challenge during the past several years.

I want also to thank Harcourt, Brace and Company for permission to quote extensively from Eliot's work.

CONTENTS

CONTENTS

BIOGRAPHICAL NOTE

THOMAS STEARNS ELIOT was born in St. Louis, Missouri, on September 26, 1888, the seventh and youngest child of Henry Ware Eliot and Charlotte Chauncy Stearns. The Eliot family, which is of Devonshire origin, goes back in America to Andrew Eliot (1627-1704), who, emigrating in middle life from East Coker, Somerset, was enrolled as a member of the First Church of Beverly, Massachusetts, in 1670. Apparently a cordwainer by trade, he was frequently chosen as Selectman, and finally as Town Clerk. He was a juror against the Salem witches at the same time that Hawthorne's ancestor was one of the judges who condemned them, but afterwards made a public recantation and greatly reproached himself for his delusion. The poet's direct ancestors were for several generations mainly merchants of Boston, though the Rev. Andrew Eliot, D.D. (1718-78), a strong Congregationalist and an enemy to Episcopalianism, was minister of the North Church, and was elected president of Harvard but declined to leave his congregation. The poet's grandfather, the Rev. William Greenleaf Eliot, D.D. (1811-87), a second cousin of Charles William Eliot, had gone out to St. Louis directly after his graduation from the Harvard Divinity School in 1834, and had established the first Unitarian church in that city. A man of great activity in public service throughout a long career, he was a balanced but firm opponent of slavery, and was instrumental in keeping Missouri in the Union. He likewise founded and helped to build Washington University (which would have been called Eliot University except for his objection), and became its Chancellor in 1872. Among his extensive writings, which were mostly of an ethical and philanthropic nature, was a sermon on 'Suffering Considered as Discipline.' From his large family of children two of his four sons entered the ministry; the youngest became a lawyer. His second son, Henry Ware Eliot (1841-1919), who was named after one of the foremost figures in New England Unitarianism, graduated from Washington University in 1863, and became connected with the Hydraulic Press Brick Company of St. Louis, of which he later was president. He was married in 1868 to Charlotte Chauncy Stearns (1843-1930), the daughter of a commission merchant and trader of Boston, and the descendant of Isaac Stearns, who had come out with John Winthrop in 1630 as one of the original settlers of the Bay Colony. The poet's mother was a woman of keen intellectual interests, whose published work comprised a full-length biography of her father-in-law and a dramatic poem on the life of Savonarola.

T. S. Eliot prepared for college at the Smith Academy in St. Louis (a department of Washington University), as his only brother had done eight years before him; and spent one final year at Milton. Entering Harvard in the autumn of 1906, he was thus in the same class with John Reed, Bronson Cutting, Stuart Chase, and Walter Lippmann. He was an editor of the undergraduate literary magazine, *The Harvard Advocate,* to which he contributed a few poems, was elected Class Odist, and belonged to various literary and social clubs. Among the members of the Harvard faculty those who most clearly left their influence upon him were Irving Babbitt and George Santayana. After completing his college course in three years Eliot continued his study of philosophy in the Harvard Graduate School. The year 1910-11 was spent in Paris, reading French literature and philosophy at the Sorbonne. He returned to America in the autumn of 1911, and passed the next three years again at Harvard, extending his study of metaphysics, logic, and psychology to include also Indic philology and Sanskrit. In the year 1913-14 he was appointed as an assistant in Philosophy at Harvard. At the end of that year he was awarded a travelling fellowship, and was in Germany during the summer before the outbreak of the War. In the following winter he was at Merton College, Oxford, reading Greek philosophy. About this time he began to contribute reviews to *The International Journal of Ethics;* and two technical essays, one on Leibniz and one on Leibniz and F. H. Bradley, were published in *The Monist* in 1916. His first mature poems to appear in print were 'The Love Song of J. Alfred Prufrock' in Harriet Monroe's newly established journal, *Poetry,* April-September 1915; 'Preludes' and 'Rhapsody on a Windy Night' in Wyndham Lewis's *Blast,* July 1915; and in Ezra Pound's *Catholic Anthology*—so called because it collected in that same year work of such diverse poets as Yeats and the Imagists—there were included, in addition to 'Prufrock,' 'Portrait of a Lady,' 'The *Boston Evening Transcript*,' 'Hysteria,' and 'Aunt Helen.'

He had been married in the spring of 1915, and during the next year was, according to his own report, 'teaching French, Latin, lower mathematics, drawing, swimming, geography, history, and baseball' at the Highgate School near London. Shortly thereafter he changed his occupation to banking and 'dealt with documentary bills, acceptances, and foreign exchange' in Lloyds Bank, Ltd. In 1918 he registered for the U.S. Navy, but was not taken into service owing to poor health. He became an assistant editor of *The Egoist* from 1917 to 1919, and a frequent contributor to *The Athenaeum* during 1919 to 1921, the brief period of J. Middleton Murry's editorship. His range of contributions to a great many other magazines gradually extended from *Lloyds Bank Economic Review* to *Vanity Fair.* In 1923 he became editor of a quarterly review, *The Criterion,* which he continued to conduct until shortly before the outbreak of the Second World War. He is now a director of the publishing house of Faber and Faber. In 1927, as a result of his growing interest in the English Church and State, he be-

came a British subject. In September 1932 he returned to
America for the first time in eighteen years, having accepted
the appointment of Charles Eliot Norton Professor of Poetry
at Harvard for 1932-3. Since that time he has lived for the
most part in London, though he has made a number of trips
back to this country, working for a period at the Institute
of Advanced Studies at Princeton and teaching at the University of Chicago. In 1947, he was awarded the Order of
Merit and the Nobel Prize for Literature; in 1955, the
Hanseatic Goethe Prize. His first wife, who had been in ill
health since the early 1930's, died in 1947. He married Miss
Valerie Fletcher, his private secretary, in January, 1957.

Eliot's poetry has been published in volume form as follows: *Prufrock and Other Observations*, 1917; *Poems*, 1919;
Ara Vos Prec, 1919, which is a collection, with additions, of
the two ·previous volumes, and which, with the exception
of one inferior poem that Eliot has not reprinted, is repro-
duced in *Poems*, 1920; *The Waste Land*, which won the
Dial award, 1922; *Poems*, 1909-25, which included all his
previous work and added 'The Hollow Men,' 1925; *Collected
Poems*, 1909-35, which added, among others, *Sweeney Agonistes*, 1927, *Ash Wednesday*, 1930, 'Burnt Norton,' 1934,
and the choruses from *The Rock*, 1934; *Murder in the Cathedral*, 1935; *The Family Reunion*, 1939; *Four Quartets*,
1943; *The Cocktail Party*, 1949; *The Complete Poems and
Plays*, 1952; *The Confidential Clerk*, 1953. Appearing concurrently with his poetry, Eliot's most important criticism
has been included in: *The Sacred Wood*, 1920, collected
chiefly from *The Athenaeum*, *The Egoist*, *Art and Letters*,
and *The Times Literary Supplement* (London); *Homage to
John Dryden*, 1924, three essays which had originally been
written for *The Times Literary Supplement*; *For Lancelot
Andrewes*, 1928, the contents of which had appeared variously in *The Times Literary Supplement*, *Theology*, *The
Dial*, and *The Forum*; *Dante*, 1929; *The Use of Poetry*,

1933, Eliot's eight Norton lectures; *After Strange Gods*, 1934, three lectures delivered in the spring of 1933 at the University of Virginia; *Essays Ancient and Modern*, 1936; *The Idea of a Christian Society*, 1940; *Notes towards a Definition of Culture*, 1948. The bulk of the first four of these volumes was included, along with several additional pieces, in *Selected Essays*, 1917-32, reissued in 1950 as *Selected Essays, New Edition*, with four pieces from *Essays Ancient and Modern* which were not in the original collection. A new collection, *On Poetry and Poets*, was published in 1956 to bring together other pieces which had appeared separately, in most cases during and after the second war. Mr. Donald Gallup's *T. S. Eliot, A Bibliography*, is an exhaustive listing through 1951 which reveals how extensively Eliot has contributed to books and periodicals.

I

TRADITION AND THE INDIVIDUAL TALENT

It is part of the business of the critic . . . to see literature steadily and to
see it whole; and this is eminently to see it *not* as consecrated by time, but
to see it beyond time; to see the best work of our time and the best work
of twenty-five hundred years ago with the same eyes.—Introduction to *The
Sacred Wood.*

IN *After Strange Gods: A Primer of Modern Heresy*, T. S.
Eliot stated that his aim was to develop further the theme
of 'Tradition and the Individual Talent,' which is probably his best-known essay. Nearly thirty years have now
elapsed since it was written—and over thirty since his first
notable poem, 'The Love Song of J. Alfred Prufrock'—a
detail which underscores the fact that it is no longer accurate
to think of Eliot's work as new or experimental. Indeed,
with younger readers 'Tradition and the Individual Talent'
is now as much of a classic as Matthew Arnold's 'The Study
of Poetry'; and putting those essays side by side one can
observe that Eliot's is equally packed with trenchant remarks
on the relation of present to past, as well as on the nature of
poetry itself.

It is illuminating to go further and juxtapose the whole
range of these writers' achievements. For, by so doing, one
becomes aware of the extent to which Eliot's criticism has
quietly accomplished a revolution: that in it we have the
first full revaluation of poetry since *Essays in Criticism* appeared in 1865. Arnold's observations on the historical course
of English poetry, his classification of the romantics of the
age just before him, his dismissal of Dryden and Pope as
authors of an age of prose, his exaltation of Milton, and his
depreciation of Chaucer on the score of lacking 'high seriousness'—all of these views, sensitively elaborated, not only

[3]

persuaded his generation but also, as Eliot has remarked, largely remain as the academic estimates of to-day. It is worth noting that A. E. Housman, who professed not to be a critic, also held most of them in his widely read lecture of 1933, 'The Name and Nature of Poetry.' Housman's enthusiasms remained those of the time when he was an undergraduate: he could see nothing in the seventeenth-century metaphysicals but perverse over-intellectualization, and he almost paraphrased Arnold's remarks on the school of Dryden. Moreover, when one goes through the names of the principal English critics since Arnold's death and since the brief plunge into the dead alley of aestheticism in the 'nineties, it is apparent that such representative work as that of Saintsbury, Whibley, or Bradley, or even that of W. P. Ker, was historical rather than critical, in the sense that it was engaged with description and categorization, filling in the outlines traced by Arnold, and only incidentally, if at all, raising any new questions. In America, Irving Babbitt, also indebted to Arnold (more, perhaps, than he recognized), was concerned with the relation of the artist's thought to society, but not at all with the nature of art.[1] In the years just before the First World War, the speculations of T. E. Hulme and Ezra Pound brought a new quickening of life which prepared the way for Eliot's own development; but there was no detailed intensive re-examination of the quality and function of poetry until the publication of *The Sacred Wood* in 1920.

It could not be wholly clear then, but it has become so now, that the ideas first arriving at their mature expression in that volume definitely placed their author in the main line of poet-critics that runs from Ben Jonson and Dryden through Samuel Johnson, Coleridge, and Arnold. In fact, what has given the note of authority to Eliot's views of poetry is exactly what has made the criticism of the other writers just named the most enduring in English. They have not been merely theorists, but all craftsmen talking of what they knew at first hand. When Dryden writes about Chaucer, or Coleridge about Wordsworth, or Eliot about Donne, we may not agree on all points, but we take them seriously since we can observe at once their intimate understanding of what they are saying. With the generation of readers since the First World War, Donne has assumed the stature of a centrally important figure for the first time since the seventeenth century; and his rise has been directly connected with the fact that Eliot has enabled us to see him with fresh closeness, not only by means of his analysis of the method of metaphysical poetry but also because he has renewed that method in the rhythms and imagery of his own verse.

When Eliot is thought of in connection with Arnold, probably the first thing that comes to mind is his reaction to the famous statement that the poetry of Dryden and Pope was 'conceived and composed in their wits, genuine poetry is conceived . . . in the soul'; his brief retort about poetry 'conceived and composed in the soul of a mid-century Oxford graduate.' In addition, one has the impression of deft, if inconspicuous sniping, kept up over quite a few years. What Eliot has attacked principally is not the conception of poetry as criticism of life; indeed, no one lately has taken that phrase very seriously except in so far as it throws light on Arnold's own poetry. The main offensive has been against certain jaunty inadequacies in Arnold's thought and, in particular, against his loose identification of poetry with religion. And yet, in his most recent remarks about Arnold, Eliot has recognized him as a friend, if not as a master; as one whose work at its best, both in verse and in criticism, has more to say to us than that of any other poet of his time.

Consequently, in any effort to gauge Eliot's achievement, to indicate just what traditions have entered into the shaping of his talent, it is important to remind oneself of the actual closeness of these two writers in the qualities of mind which

THE ACHIEVEMENT OF T. S. ELIOT

they value. It might almost be either who remarks that 'Excellence dwells among rocks hardly accessible, and a man must almost wear his heart out before he can reach her.' For certainly there is in each a full understanding of the unremitting discipline for the critic in learning 'to see the object as it is'; an equal insistence on the current of fresh ideas in which a society must move as a primary condition for the emergence of mature art; an equal veneration for French intelligence; and, again and again, a similar scoring, not by logic, but by flexibility, resilience, and an intuitive precision. In addition, in more than one notable passage, such as those which reflect on the lonely relation of the thinker to society, there is almost an identical tone. When Arnold realizes that in a sense the critic's goal is never reached, that it is kept in sight only by unending vigilance, he says: 'That promised land it will not be ours to enter, and we shall die in the wilderness: but to have desired to enter it, to have saluted it from afar, is already, perhaps, the best distinction among contemporaries; it will certainly be the best title to esteem with posterity.' And Eliot takes up the echoing theme:

It is not to say that Arnold's work was vain if we say that it is to be done again; for we must know in advance, if we are prepared for that conflict, that the combat may have truces but never a peace. If we take the widest and wisest view of a Cause, there is no such thing as a Lost Cause because there is no such thing as a Gained Cause. We fight for lost causes because we know that our defeat and dismay may be the preface to our successors' victory, though that victory itself will be temporary; we fight rather to keep something alive than in the expectation that anything will triumph.

Although Eliot relates to the central values stressed by Arnold to a degree which has not heretofore been recognized, it would be misleading to slur over the equally marked divergences between them. The chief difference

separating in quality both their criticism and verse is suggested in Eliot's remark that 'Arnold's poetry has little technical interest.' With Arnold, in so far as you can make such
a division, the emphasis is on substance rather than on form.
Such emphasis led him into his attempted definition of poetry as criticism of life, a phrase which would apply equally
well to a novel as to a poem, and which wholly fails to suggest the created vision of life which constitutes the essence
of all art. The same emphasis also runs through Arnold's
essays, where he gives us estimates of the value to the human
spirit of poetry and of individual poets, but, although he
frequently refers to 'the laws of poetic beauty and poetic
truth,' no detailed or even incidental examination of the
precise nature of those laws emerges. With Eliot, the emphasis is on form. His essays on various Elizabethan dramatists, for example, are not concerned with the full-length
rounded estimate, but with close technical annotation of
detail. It is possible that he may sometimes regret his too
sharp reversal: 'The spirit killeth, but the letter giveth life';
and yet it represents the intensity of his dissatisfaction with
the copious expansiveness of Arnold's age, with Swinburne
and Tennyson far more than with Arnold himself. In
thoughtful reaction, Eliot's method is spare and economical.
He watches with the trained eye of the hawk, and then
swoops on the one point that will illustrate the quality of
the whole. His brief essays present in clearest outline the
segment of the curve from which the complete circle can be
constructed.

It is this preoccupation with craftmanship that has enabled him to relish so fully the virtues of Dryden. But Dryden's power has been, so to speak, simply one of Eliot's incidental discoveries. The principal elements entering into his
revaluation of poetry can be most briefly described in terms
of the poets who have left the deepest and most lasting mark

on his own work: the seventeenth-century English metaphysicals, the nineteenth-century French symbolists, and Dante.[2] Such a combination of interests, which he possessed even before his earliest published work, might at first glance seem not only unlikely but exotic for a young man of New England stock, born in St. Louis and educated at Milton and Harvard. But actually they are not so. They relate organically to his background, though an adequate demonstration of that fact would require a still unwritten chapter of American intellectual history,[3] and might even surprise Eliot himself. Yet it is not to be forgotten that the symbolist movement has its roots in the work of the most thoroughly conscious artist in American poetry before Eliot, Edgar Poe; and that, therefore, in Eliot's taste for Baudelaire and Laforgue as well as for Poe, the wheel has simply come full circle. It is increasingly apparent that the renaissance of the New England mind, from Emerson and Thoreau to Emily Dickinson, felt a deep kinship with the long buried modes of thought and feeling of the seventeenth century; in fact, Emily Dickinson's poetry, especially, must be described as metaphysical. I do not suggest that Eliot is directly indebted to any of these writers; indeed, he once remarked to me both of his sustained distaste for Emerson, and of the fact that he had never read Miss Dickinson.

It must be noted, however, if only by way of parenthesis, that there is one author who grew out of the New England tradition to whom Eliot is greatly indebted. When he first began to write he could find among living artists of the older generation no poet who satisfied him, but, as Ezra Pound has remarked, it was Henry James, as well as Conrad, who taught them both 'that poetry ought to be as well written as prose.' In Eliot's case James taught him even more than that. In his tribute shortly after the novelist's death,[4] Eliot spoke of him as 'the most intelligent man of his generation,' by which he meant that, undistracted by 'ideas,' James had maintained a point of view and had given himself wholly to the perfection of his craft, and that he had reflected on the novel as an art 'as no previous English novelist had done.' In addition, Eliot was fascinated by the way in which James did not simply relate but made the reader co-operate; by the richness of his 'references'; by the way, for example, in *The Aspern Papers,* he managed to give the whole feeling of Venice by the most economical strokes. Indeed, Eliot has said that the method in this story—'to make a place real not descriptively but by something happening there'—was what stimulated him to try to compress so many memories of past moments of Venice into his dramatic poem, superficially so different from James, 'Burbank with a Baedeker: Bleistein with a Cigar.' [5] And what is even more significant, Eliot has perceived that James's 'real progenitor' was Hawthorne, that he cannot be understood without Hawthorne, that the essential strain common to them both was 'their indifference to religious dogma at the same time as their exceptional awareness of spiritual reality,' their 'profound sensitiveness to good and evil,' their extraordinary power to convey horror.[6]

This brings us back to the point that no more than Henry James can Eliot be understood without reckoning with the Puritan mind. Its special mixture of passion overweighed by thought (as well as the less attractive combination of high moral idealism restrained by practical prudence that was probed by Santayana in 'The Genteel Tradition'); its absorption in the problem of belief and its trust in moments of vision; its dry, unexpected wit; its dread of vulgarity, as perplexing to the creater of 'Sweeney Erect' as to Henry James; its consciousness of the nature of evil, as acute in 'The Turn of the Screw' as in 'Ethan Brand' or 'Gerontion'; its full understanding of the dark consequences of loneliness and repression which are expressed in 'The Love Song of J. Alfred Prufrock' as well as in *The Scarlet Letter;* its severe self-discipline and sudden, poignant tenderness, to be found alike in Jonathan Edwards and in the author of *Ash Wednesday*—such attributes and preoccupations are common to the whole strain to which Eliot inextricably belongs. The natural relation of Dante to many elements in that strain is at once apparent. It need only be added that from Longfellow through Charles Eliot Norton, Santayana, and Charles Grandgent there was an unbroken line of Dante scholarship at Harvard. It may be that in the end Eliot gained a more challenging insight into the technical excellences of *The Divine Comedy* through conversations with Ezra Pound, but, at all events, in the preface to his own introduction to Dante he lists as his principal aids all the names which I have just mentioned.

To arrive not only at Eliot's debt to tradition but at an understanding of what he has himself added to it, it is essential at least to suggest more specific reasons why he has been attracted to these particular poets, and the exact use he has made of them. The need is more real in Eliot's case than it would be in most, since his own verse bears everywhere evidence of how his reading has been carried alive into his mind, and thus of his conception of poetry 'as a living whole of all the poetry that has ever been written.' [7] Holding such a conception of the integral relation of the present to an alive past, believing that it is necessary for the poet to be conscious, 'not of what is dead, but of what is already living,' he naturally also believes that one of the marks of a mature poet is that he should be 'one who not merely restores a tradition which has been in abeyance, but one who in his poetry re-twines as many straying strands of tradition as possible.' Perhaps the process would have been more compellingly described as 'fusing together' rather than 're-twining'; for only by some such process can the poet's work gain richness and density.

It is hardest to suggest in brief compass the extent of Eliot's feeling for Dante, since he has himself devoted many careful pages to defining exactly what he means by calling him the most universal poet in a modern language. That he does so regard him is of considerable significance in throwing light on what qualities Eliot most values in poetry, especially since he dwells chiefly on the power of Dante's precision of diction, and of his clear, visual images. He does not hesitate to say that he believes Dante's simple style, his great economy of words, makes him the most valuable master for any one trying to write poetry himself. That he does not believe this style simple to attain is indicated by his laconic sentence: 'In twenty years I have written about a dozen lines in that style successfully; and compared to the dullest passage of the "Divine Comedy," they are "as straw." ' It is also apparent, in view both of 'The Hollow Men' and of the direction towards which he has been moving since *Ash Wednesday,* that although he carefully avoids saying that either Shakespeare or Dante is the 'greater,' he is himself drawn more closely to the latter, who, though he did not embrace so wide an 'extent and variety of human life,' yet understood 'deeper degrees of degradation and higher degrees of exaltation.' It would be glib to say that in *The Waste Land* and 'The Hollow Men' Eliot wrote his *Inferno,* and that since then his poems represent various stages of passing through a *Purgatorio;* still such a remark may possibly illuminate both his aims and achievement.

It is easier to illustrate the impact made upon Eliot by the more restricted qualities of seventeenth-century metaphysical poetry, particularly since they have also appealed to many other readers of to-day. For it is not accidental that the same people who respond to Proust and Joyce have also found something important in Donne. The remark that we have in the work of this poet 'the fullest record in our literature of the disintegrating collision in a sensitive mind of the old tradition and the new learning' might very well have been made about *The Waste Land.*[8] For, as has been frequently observed, Donne's poetry also was born in part out of an increase of self-consciousness. His probing, analytic mind was keenly aware of the actual complexity of his feelings, their rapid alterations and sharp antitheses; and our more complete awareness of the sudden juxtapositions of experience, of, in Eliot's phrase, 'the apparent irrelevance and unrelatedness of things,' has drawn us strongly to him. The jagged brokenness of Donne's thought has struck a responsive note in our age, for we have seen a reflection of our own problem in the manner in which his passionate mind, unable to find any final truth in which it could rest, became fascinated with the process of thought itself. Eliot's earlier enthusiasm for this element in Donne's mind is now considerably qualified in view of his own growing desire for order and coherence; as is also some of his first response to the realization that we have in Donne the expression of an age that "objects to the heroic and sublime and objects to the simplification and separation of the mental faculties.' But that such qualities have been deeply felt by a whole generation of readers since 1918 is demonstrated by the fact that even a character in Hemingway's *Farewell to Arms* could quote from a metaphysical poem. It may be that in reaction against Donne's previous neglect our generation has gone to the extreme of exaggerating his importance; and yet it would be hard to overestimate the value of his discoveries as an artist. What he strove to devise was a medium of expression that would correspond to the felt intricacy of his existence, that would suggest by sudden contrasts, by harsh dissonances as well as by harmonies, the actual sensation of life as he had himself experienced it. In sharp revolt against the too superficial beauty of *The Faerie Queene* and the purely 'literary' conventions of the sonneteers, he knew that no part of life should be barred as 'unpoetic,' that nothing in mature experience was too subtly refined or too sordid, too remote or too commonplace to serve as material for poetry. His great achievement lay in his ability to convey 'his genuine whole of tangled feelings,' as in 'The Extasie,' the extraordinary range of feeling—from the lightest to the most serious, from the most spiritual to the most sensual—that can inhere in a single mood. This 'alliance of levity and seriousness' by which, as Eliot has observed, the seriousness is not weakened but intensified, 'implies a constant inspection and criticism of experience'; it involves 'a recognition, implicit in the expression of every experience, of other kinds of experience which are possible.' Such recognition demands a mind that is at once maturely seasoned, wise and discerning—and imaginative, a combination sufficiently rare to cause Eliot to maintain that 'it is hardly too much to say that Donne enlarged the possibilities of lyric verse as no other English poet has done.[9]

But Donne's technical discoveries did not belong to him alone. They were a product of a whole mode of thought and feeling which has seemed to Eliot the richest and most varied that has ever come to expression in English. He has described this mode as a development of sensibility, 'a direct sensuous apprehension of thought, or a recreation of thought into feeling,' which means that for all the most notable poets of Donne's time there was no separation between life and thought, and that their way of feeling 'was directly and freshly altered by their reading.' Such interweaving of emotions and thought exists in Chapman and Webster, and in the dense, masterful irregularity of the later plays of Shakespeare. It was as true for these poets as for Donne that 'a thought was an experience' which modified their capacity of feeling. As a result they could devour and assimilate any kind of experience, so that in their poetry passages of philosophical speculation stimulated by Montaigne or Seneca throb with as living a pulse as their own direct accounts of human passion. Indeed, one has only to turn to Montaigne and *Hamlet* and *Measure for Measure,* or to North's *Plu-*

tarch and *Antony and Cleopatra* and *Coriolanus,* for complete examples of how reading as well as thought could be absorbed as vital experience.

How entirely Eliot believes such a capacity to be the only right state for the mature poet is emphasized by his extended comment that 'when a poet's mind is perfectly equipped for its work, it is constantly amalgamating disparate experience; the ordinary man's experience is chaotic, irregular, fragmentary. The latter falls in love, or reads Spinoza, and these two experiences have nothing to do with each other, or with the noise of the typewriter or the smell of cooking; in the mind of the poet these experiences are always forming new wholes.' That such a conviction concerning the creative process has sprung from one of Eliot's most recurrent discoveries about the nature of life is revealed when we find him writing, in a very different connection: 'It is probable that men ripen best through experiences which are at once sensuous and intellectual; certainly many men will admit that their keenest ideas have come to them with the quality of a sense perception; and that their keenest sensuous experience has been "as if the body thought." ' He was led to that reflection in contrasting the qualities of Henry James and Henry Adams, a contrast that brings out once more the elements that Eliot is continually stressing as characteristic of the greatest art. It also reveals a certain similarity that he felt between James and metaphysical poetry, thus making more apparent why he has been attracted to both and indicating the relations between two strands in his tradition. Deeply impressed by the acuteness of Adams's intelligence, Eliot yet felt a lack of full ripeness in his writing when compared with that of James. He expressed his distinction between them thus: 'There is nothing to indicate that Adams's senses either flowered or fruited. . . Henry James was not, by Adams's standards, "educated," but particularly limited; it is the sensuous contributor to the intelligence that makes the difference.' [10]

In perhaps the most exciting phrase in all of his criticism, Eliot has called this rare fusion a way of feeling thought 'as immediately as the odour of a rose.' Such a capacity was possessed by later men in the seventeenth century, by Crashaw and Vaughan, and, in Eliot's account, found its last mature poetic voice in Andrew Marvell. The one thing common to the whole group, so diverse in their gifts and points of view, is, in Eliot's regard, 'that firm grasp of human experience, which is a formidable achievement of the Elizabethan and Jacobean poets.' He adds a further remark: 'This wisdom, cynical perhaps but untired (in Shakespeare, a terrifying clairvoyance), leads toward, and is only completed by, the religious comprehension'—a remark more heavily freighted with implications for his own development than would have been apparent at the time it was written, in 1921, the year before the publication of *The Waste Land*.

Similarities between Eliot's technical devices and those of Donne have been often observed: [11] the conversational tone, the vocabulary at once colloquial and surprisingly strange—both of these a product of Eliot's belief in the relation of poetry to actual speech, and paralleling his use of 'non-poetic' material; the rapid association of ideas which demands alert agility from the reader; the irregular verse and difficult sentence structure as a part of fidelity to thought and feeling; and, especially, the flash of wit which results from the shock of such unexpected contrasts. But actually the manner in which sudden transitions are made in Eliot's verse owes much more to the method of the French symbolists.[12] I. A. Richards has spoken of *The Waste Land* as 'a music of ideas,' a phrase which suggests Eliot's particular attraction to Laforgue. By both poets connecting links are left out, as they are not by Donne, in an effort to utilize our recent closer knowledge of the working of the brain, of its way of making associations. That is to say, Eliot wants to suggest in the rhythms of his verse the movement of thought in a living mind, and thus to communicate the exact pattern of his meaning not so much by logical structure as by emotional suggestion. He is aware that such a method is dangerous, that it can easily lead into the false identity, 'Poésie, musique, c'est même chose,' [13] which caused the vague obscureness of so much of Mallarmé's verse. But Eliot is equally sure that poetry can approach the condition of music without sacrificing its definite core of meaning so long as it has 'a definite emotion behind it.' [14] He has understood the many-sided problem of the poet. He knows that he must not sacrifice either sense to sound, or sound to sense: 'Words are perhaps the hardest of all material of art: for they must be used to express both visual beauty and beauty of sound, as well as communicating a grammatical statement.' [15]

In the preface to his translation of Perse's *Anabase* Eliot takes pains to point out that the French poet's suppression 'of explanatory and connecting matter' is not at all owing 'to incoherence, or to the love of cryptogram,' but to the deliberate belief that he can secure his most concentrated effect by the ordered compression of his sequence of images. Eliot is likewise convinced that 'there is a logic of the imagination as well as a logic of concepts,' and, as he states elsewhere, that the one test of whether the sudden contrasts and juxtapositions of modern poetry are successful or not 'is merely a question of whether the mind is *serré* or *delié*, whether the whole personality is involved.' For, in words that take on greater significance the more one examines Eliot's own work, 'it is the unity of a personality which gives an indissoluble unity to his variety of subject.'

The principal quality which drew Eliot to the symbolists is one they possess in common with the metaphysicals, 'the same essential quality of transmuting ideas into sensations, of transforming an observation into a state of mind.' This quality might be defined more technically as 'the presence of the idea in the image,' a definition with which I shall have more to do below. In both schools there is the demand for compression of statement, for centring on the revealing detail and eliminating all inessentials, and thus for an effect of comprehensiveness to be gained by the bringing to bear of a great deal of packed experience onto a single moment of expression. In the symbolists there is an increased allusiveness and indirection, a flexibility in their verse designed to catch every nuance of their feeling. Such technical agility fascinated Eliot, especially in Laforgue, since it was coupled there with an unusual verbal adroitness—a combination of 'recondite words and simple phrasing,' which is also to be found everyhere in Eliot's own early work; and likewise with a mocking-serious, worldly-aesthetic attitude which spoke directly to his own youthful sophistication. As a result, 'Prufrock,' in the movement of its verse, its repetitions, and echoes, and even in its choice of theme, seems of all Eliot's poems to have been written most immediately under Laforgue's stimulus (though brought to a finished perfection of form which Laforgue's more impromptu verse scarcely attained); just as the verse of 'Gerontion' reveals the fullest impression of Eliot's mastery of the Jacobean dramatists.

The condensation of form that was demanded both by Donne and the symbolists logically builds its effects upon sharp contrasts, and makes full use of the element of surprise, which Eliot, as well as Poe, considers to have been 'one of the most important means of poetic effect since Homer.' It is always one of the prime functions of poetry to break through our conventional perceptions, to startle us into a new awareness of reality. As Hulme observed, 'poetry always endeavours to arrest you, and to make you continuously see a physical thing, to prevent you gliding through an abstract process.' In the poetry that Eliot most admires, poetry which has secured a union of thought and emotion, there will inevitably be an unexpected bringing together of material from seemingly disparate experiences. The reading of Spinoza and the smell of cooking will very possibly both enter into the full expression of a state of feeling, just as the most refined speculation from the Church fathers, a vivid detail from contemporary exploration, and the most coarsely sensual flash of wit unite in a single stanza of Donne's to make the expression of his love a concrete, living thing, very different from an abstract statement. Eliot's own kind of witty surprise is created in such a line as

I have measured out my life with coffee spoons.

'I have measured out my life'—the general, platitudinous reflection is suddenly punctuated with an electric shock which flashes into the mind of the reader, in a single, concrete, ironic picture, Prufrock's whole futile way of existence.[16]

But if the details of Eliot's style show everywhere the mark of his responsive mastery of the later symbolists, as well as of the metaphysicals, the impression of Baudelaire upon his spirit has been even more profound. The reason why he seems to have been stirred more deeply by *Les Fleurs du Mal* than by any other poetry written in the nineteenth century is, I think, suggested by the words which he has italicized in the sentence that indicates the nature of this debt:

It is not merely in the use of imagery of common life, not merely in the use of imagery of the sordid life of a great metropolis, but in the elevation of such imagery to the *first intensity*—presenting it as it is, and yet making it represent something much more than itself—that Baudelaire has created a mode of release and expression for other men.

For Baudelaire's intensity is the result of his having 'a sense of his own age,' a quality not easy to analyse, but one which, as Eliot stresses it again and again in the course of discussing very different poets, is revealed to be one of his fundamental tests for great poetry. Such a sense is at an opposite pole from a familiarity with the surface details of a time, or from a sense of fashion. When Eliot finds that Blake possessed this sense as well as Villon, it is seen to consist in a condensed, bare honesty that can strike beneath the appearances of life to reality, that can grasp so strongly the intrinsic elements of life in the poet's own day that it likewise penetrates beneath the apparent variations of man from one epoch to another to his essential sameness. Eliot is quite aware that the degree of consciousness on the artist's part of such a sense has varied greatly in different ages, that whereas the great French novelists from Stendhal and Flaubert through Proust were deliberately occupied with analysing conditions of society as well as the individual, with chronicling 'the rise, the régime, and the decay of the upper bourgeoisie,' on the other hand, it is in the very lack of such consciousness of social change and decay, 'of corruptions and abuses peculiar to their own time, that the Elizabethan and Jacobean dramatists are blessed. We feel that they believed in their own age, in a way in which no nineteenth- or twentieth-century writer of the greatest seriousness has been able to believe in his age. And accepting their age, they were in a position to concentrate their attention, to their respective abilities, upon the common characteristics of humanity in all ages, rather than upon the differences.'

But in any age the thing of highest importance for the poet is to 'express with individual differences the general state of mind, not as a *duty,* but simply because'—if he possesses that rare, unyielding honesty which alone will give his work depth—'he cannot help participating in it.' In such fashion Eliot dwells repeatedly on the integral relation of any poet's work to the society of which he is a part, to the climate of thought and feeling which give rise to his expression. In line with such reflections Eliot can say: 'The great poet, in writing himself, writes his time.'[17] Thus Dante, hardly knowing it, became the voice of the thirteenth century; Shakespeare, hardly knowing it, became the representative of the end of the sixteenth century, of a turning point in history.'

In the case of Baudelaire, this ability to go beneath appearances to the most recurrently pervading elements in life was the result of the peculiar dogged strength with which he felt the torturing impact of the great modern city upon the lonely individual. For the very intensity of his suffering enabled him to see through the slogans of his age in a way that Victor Hugo, for example, could not; enabled him to cut beneath its 'bustle, programmes, platforms, scientific progress, humanitarianism, and revolutions which improved nothing' to a real perception of good and evil. Such a perception Eliot defines, in *After Strange Gods,* as 'the first requisite of spiritual life.' It is very close to Yeats's mature discovery that we begin to live only 'when we have conceived life as tragedy.' For both Yeats and Eliot recognize that there can be no significance to life, and hence no tragedy in the account of man's conflicts and his inevitable final defeat by death, unless it is fully realized that there is no such thing as good unless there is also evil, or evil unless there is good; that until this double nature of life is understood by a man, he is doomed to waver between a groundless, optimistic hopefulness and an equally chaotic, pointless despair. Eliot has learned from his own experience that the distinguishing feature of a human life consists in the occasions on which the individual most fully reveals his character, and that those are the moments of intense 'moral and spiritual struggle.' It is in such moments, rather than in the 'bewildering minutes' of passion 'in which we are all very much alike, that men and women come nearest to being real'—an affirmation which again underscores his inheritance of the central element in the Puritan tradition. And he has concluded that 'if you do away with this struggle, and maintain that by tolerance, benevolence, inoffensiveness, and a redistribution or increase of purchasing power, combined with a devotion, on the part of an élite, to Art, the world will be as good as anyone could require, then you must expect human beings to become more and more vaporous.'

It is their penetration to the heart of this struggle between the mixed good and evil in man's very being, and thus to the central factors in human nature, which forms a common element between the three strains of poetry that have affected Eliot most deeply, between such writers as Dante, Webster, and Baudelaire. And consequently, when at the end of the first section of *The Waste Land*, Eliot's lines contain allusions to all three of these poets, he is not making a pastiche of his reading, or arbitrarily associating unrelated fragments:

> *Unreal City,*
> *Under the brown fog of a winter dawn,*
> *A crowd flowed over London bridge, so many,*
> *I had not thought death had undone so many.*
> *Sighs, short and infrequent, were exhaled,*
> *And each man fixed his eyes before his feet.*
> *Flowed up the hill and down King William Street,*
> *To where Saint Mary Woolnoth kept the hours*
> *With a dead sound on the final stroke of nine.*
> *There I saw one I knew, and stopped him, crying: 'Stetson!*
> *'You who were with me in the ships at Mylae!*
> *'That corpse you planted last year in your garden,*
> *'Has it begun to sprout? Will it bloom this year?*
> *'Or has the sudden frost disturbed its bed?*
> *'Oh keep the Dog far hence, that's friend to men,*
> *'Or with his nails he'll dig it up again!*
> *'You! hypocrite lecteur!—mon semblable—mon frère!'*

He wanted to present here the intolerable burden of his 'Unreal City,' the lack of purpose and direction, the inability to believe really in anything and the resulting 'heap of broken images' that formed the excruciating contents of the post-War state of mind. But his city is Baudelaire's city as

well, 'où le spectre en plein jour raccroche le passant'; it is
the modern megalopolis dwarfing the individual. And it is
given an additional haunting dimension as a realm of death
in life by being linked with Dante's Limbo, the region of
those dead who while on earth had 'lived without praise or
blame,' who had not been strong enough in will or passion
either to do good or evil, and so were condemned for ever to
wander aimlessly, in feverish, useless motion. And as this
throng moves through the murky streets of wintry London,
as dark at nine as at dawn, on its way, presumably, to jobs in
shops and offices, the poet encounters one with whom he
has shared experiences and now shares memories of war.
The sense of the agonizing, since futile, effort to escape those
memories, to bury those dead for good, is increased by a
reminiscence of the dirge in *The White Devil,* one of the
most poignantly terrifying passages in Webster's tragedy.
And thus the three principal strains of poetry which have
spoken so intimately to Eliot merge in a moment of acutely
heightened consciousness. Eliot is not making mere literary
allusions. He is not 'imitating' these poets; nor has he mistaken literature for life. Each of these references brings with
it the weight of its special context, its authentic accent of
reality, and thus enables Eliot to condense into a single passage a concentrated expression of tragic horror. And lest the
reader think that such an awareness of the Unreal City is
something special to the reading and experience of the poet,
he, as well as Stetson, is reminded that it belongs both to
Eliot and Baudelaire, and to himself, as part of the modern
world, as well.

NOTES

(In making citations from Eliot's essays I have given the detailed reference only in the case of those not included in his

half dozen small volumes, which are mentioned in my Biographical Note, or in his one-volume collection of *Selected Essays, 1917-1932*.)

1. I have cited only the outstanding figure. Paul Elmer More expounded the same general doctrine as Babbitt, with greater distinction as a stylist, but with less challenging vigour. Also following the lead of Arnold, More learned much from French criticism, especially from Sainte-Beuve, who was his model in the long series of *Shelburne Essays*. But there is a significant distinction between them: Sainte-Beuve was a psychologist, More was primarily a moralist.

Among other works of American criticism, Van Wyck Brooks's *America's Coming of Age*, 1915, holds a position of particular importance for having awakened a fresh interest in our own past for a whole decade of readers. But Brooks has always been a social critic, preoccupied with the conditions affecting the creative life rather than with analysis of the nature of literature itself; and my generalization concerning *The Sacred Wood* still holds.

2. A complete account of the traditions which have affected Eliot's poetry would have to consider his revulsions in addition to his enthusiasms, for the very fact of reacting against a thing inevitably leaves a mark of its impact upon you. Just as Coleridge and Wordsworth still display some traces of the eighteenth-century poetic diction they had so violently rejected, and Donne cannot be fully understood without the Elizabethan sonneteers who were his foil, so the course of Eliot's development can be charted only by reckoning with such figures as Shelley and Swinburne and the Pre-Raphaelites, poets by whom he did not escape being influenced during the formative years of his adolescence. Indeed, part of the reason for writing his essay on Swinburne's poetry seems to have been to give the rationale of his own reaction from it.

For a revealing description of the various stages in the growth of Eliot's interests in poetry, from boyhood through adolescence to maturity, see the 'Note on the Development of "Taste" in Poetry' appended to the first of his Norton Lectures.

3. I have attempted to sketch that chapter in *American Renaissance* (1941), particularly in 'The Metaphysical Strain.'

4. This was published in *The Egoist*, January 1918.

5. This brief indication of the essentially dramatic quality of Eliot's poetry (no less than in James's stories) will be developed in my third chapter.

6. Eliot's observations on the basic relation between James and Hawthorne were made in an unpublished lecture on the former, given at Harvard in the spring of 1933 in a course on Contemporary Literature. (The lectures on Pound, Joyce, and Lawrence to which I refer below were also part of this course. It was a great advantage for me to have access to Eliot's notes for these lectures, for which I am indebted not only to Eliot himself but also to Theodore Spencer, who collaborated in the course.)

Eliot's estimate of Hawthorne is further revealed in a review of the second volume of *The Cambridge History of American Literature* which he wrote for *The Athenaeum,* 25 April 1919:

> Neither Emerson nor any of the others was a real observer of the moral life. Hawthorne'was, and was a realist. He had, also, what no one else in Boston had—the firmness, the true coldness, the hard coldness of the genuine artist. In consequence, the observation of moral life in *The Scarlet Letter,* in *The House of the Seven Gables,* and even in some of the tales and sketches, has solidity, has permanence, the permanence of art. It will always be of use; the essays of Emerson are already an encumbrance. The work of Hawthorne is truly a criticism—true because a fidelity of the artist and not a mere conviction of the man—of the Puritan morality, of the Transcendentalist morality, and of the world which Hawthorne knew. It is a criticism as Henry James's work is a criticism of the America of his times, and as the work of Turgenev and Flaubert is a criticism of the Russia and the France of theirs.

In speaking of James's effort to present evil in 'The Turn of the Screw,' Eliot remarked that among other novelists only Hawthorne, Dostoevsky, and the Conrad of 'Heart of Darkness' were comparable in their 'essential moral preoccupation. . . Evil is rare, bad is common. Evil cannot even be perceived but by a very few.'

For further development of Eliot's relation to his American background, see *American Renaissance:* 'From Hawthorne to James to Eliot.'

7. As relevant first comment on the important question of what is living and what is dead, on what precisely is meant by 'experience,' I want simply to present the following passages from Eliot:

There is a shallow test which holds that the original poet goes direct to life, and the derivative poet to 'literature.' When we look into the matter, we find that the poet who is really 'derivative' is the poet who *mistakes* literature for life, and very often the reason why he makes this mistake is that—he has not read enough. The ordinary life of ordinary cultivated people is a mush of literature and life. There is a right sense in which for the educated person literature *is* life, and life *is* literature; and there is also a vicious sense in which the same phrases may be true. We can at least try not to confuse the material and the use which the author makes of it. (Introduction to the Poems of Ezra Pound.)

We dwell with satisfaction upon the poet's difference from his predecessors, especially his immediate predecessors; we endeavour to find something that can be isolated in order to be enjoyed. Whereas if we approach a poet without this prejudice we shall often find that not only the best, but the most individual parts of his work may be those in which the dead poets, his ancestors, assert their immortality most vigorously. And I do not mean the impressionable period of adolescence, but the period of full maturity. ('Tradition and the Individual Talent.')

One of the surest of tests is the way in which a poet borrows. Immature poets imitate; mature poets steal; bad poets deface what they take, and good poets make it into something better, or at least something different. The good poet welds his theft into a whole of feeling which is unique, utterly different from that from which it was torn; the bad poet throws it into something which has no cohesion. A good poet will usually borrow from authors remote in time, or alien in language, or diverse in interest. ('Philip Massinger.')

I hope that the point of view outlined in these passages receives adequate justification in the course of my essay, since such a point of view is crucial to any understanding of the value of history, and of what is meant by 'tradition'—a word that has been so misused by academic worshippers of the past that it is necessary to demonstrate how it can have life. Eliot's first discovery of its vitality took the following expression (in 'Tradition and the Individual Talent'):

Yet if the only form of tradition, of handing down, consisted in following the ways of the immediate generation before us in a blind

or timid adherence to its successes, 'tradition' should positively be dis-
couraged. We have seen many such simple currents soon lost in the
sand; and novelty is better than repetition. Tradition is a matter of
much wider significance. It cannot be inherited, and if you want it
you must obtain it by great labour. It involves, in the first place, the
historical sense, which we may call nearly indispensable to anyone
who would continue to be a poet beyond his twenty-fifth year; and
the historical sense involves a perception, not only of the pastness of
the past, but of its presence; the historical sense compels a man to write
not merely with his own generation in his bones, but with a feeling
that the whole of the literature of Europe from Homer and within it
the whole of the literature of his own country has a simultaneous
existence and composes a simultaneous order. This historical sense,
which is a sense of the timeless as well as of the temporal and of the
timeless and of the temporal together, is what makes a writer traditional. And it is at the same time what makes a writer most acutely
conscious of his place in time, of his contemporaneity.

The position outlined in this passage is carried to a more comprehensive maturity in *After Strange Gods*. Consequently I return to it in my sixth chapter.

8. It was made by Professor H. J. C. Grierson in connection with
Donne's 'Second Anniversary,' in the Introduction to *Metaphysical Lyrics and Poems of the Seventeenth Century* (Oxford,
1921).

9. Eliot has written of Donne not only in his essay on 'The
Metaphysical Poets' but also in a review in *The Nation and
Athenaeum,* 9 June 1923. In addition he contributed an essay
on 'Donne in Our Time' to *A Garland for John Donne,* ed.
Theodore Spencer (Cambridge, Mass., 1931). His Clark Lectures,
delivered at Cambridge, England, in 1926, on the metaphysical
poetry of the seventeenth century in comparison and contrast
with that of the Italian thirteenth century have not yet been
published. Perhaps the most trenchant evaluation of the nature
of metaphysical poetry that he has made is in his poem, 'Whispers of Immortality.' Certainly there has never been a more suggestive discernment of Donne's quality than in the two quatrains:

> *Donne, I suppose, was such another*
> *Who found no substitute for sense;*
> *To seize and clutch and penetrate,*
> *Expert beyond experience,*

> *He knew the anguish of the marrow*
> *The ague of the skeleton;*
> *No contact possible to flesh*
> *Allayed the fever of the bone.*

10. Eliot made this contrast in a review of *The Education of Henry Adams,* in *The Athenaeum,* 23 May 1919.

In the light of the similar quality that Eliot detects in James and the seventeenth-century poets, it is not surprising to find that he refers to James elsewhere as 'un romancier métaphysique.' (See his 'Note sur Mallarmé et Poe,' *La Nouvelle Revue Française,* November 1926.)

11. Particularly by George Williamson, *The Talent of T. S. Eliot* (University of Washington Chapbooks, No. 32, Seattle, 1929). Williamson also furnishes an interesting example of the fructifying power of Eliot's criticism, since in the Preface to *The Donne Tradition, A Study in English Poetry from Donne to the Death of Cowley* (Cambridge, Mass., 1930) he tells how, having first been fascinated by Eliot's kinship to Donne, he thus 'became absorbed in the Donne tradition through a contemporary poet.' That the whole point of view for Williamson's valuable study of the seventeenth century grew organically from a few of Eliot's packed remarks indicates also the great further potential value that Eliot's criticism may have for literary scholarship. A much needed, detailed critical estimate of the whole group of Elizabethan dramatists could take its fresh line of departure from Eliot's brief essays.

12. The qualities by which Eliot was drawn especially to Laforgue and Corbière, as well as in some degree to such of their more recent followers as Jean de Bosschère and Guillaume Apollinaire, have been outlined by René Taupin, *L'Influence du symbolisme français sur la poésie américaine* (1910-20) (Paris, 1929), pp. 211-40. Although Eliot has since reacted strongly against the *fin de siècle* aestheticism with which Arthur Symons diluted his translation of Baudelaire, he nevertheless still recognizes his early indebtedness to Symons, *The Symbolist Movement in Literature* (1899):

I myself owe Mr. Symons a great debt. But for having read his book I should not, in the year 1908, have heard of Laforgue and Rimbaud: I should probably not have begun to read Verlaine, and but for reading Verlaine, I should not have heard of Corbière. So the Symons book is one of those which have affected the course of my life.

Eliot's earliest published poems, those contributed to *The Harvard Advocate* in the years 1909-10, already begin to show the mark of Laforgue.

13. The phrase is actually that of the Abbé Brémond, *La Poésie pure* (Paris, 1926), p. 23; but it compresses Mallarmé's persistent belief in the possibility of developing 'un art d'achever la transposition, au Livre, de la symphonie.'

14. The whole passage, from Eliot's early essay on 'Ezra Pound, His Metric and Poetry,' 1917, is relevant to an understanding of Eliot's own position, then in process of formulation:

Such a relation between poetry and music is very different from what is called the 'music' of Shelley or Swinburne, a music often nearer to rhetoric (or the art of the orator) than to the instrument. For poetry to approach the condition of music (Pound quotes approvingly the dictum of Pater) it is not necessary that poetry should be destitute of meaning. Instead of slightly veiled and resonant abstractions, like

> *Time with a gift of tears,*
> *Grief with a glass that ran—*

of Swinburne, or the mossiness of Mallarmé, Pound's verse is always definite and concrete, because he has always a definite emotion behind it.

That Eliot has believed Mallarmé in danger of being overrated by the English reader while more expert poets among the symbolists were being ignored, did not prevent him from writing an extremely acute note on the common attributes of 'metaphysical' poetry shared by Donne, Poe, and Mallarmé. (See *La Nouvelle Revue Française,* November 1926.)

15. From the same essay on Pound.

16. This particular line is also an example of Eliot's use of the conceit, the distinguishing device by which the metaphysical poets made both their witty and imaginative connections between things apparently unlike. Eliot himself has pointed out, in his essay on 'The Metaphysical Poets,' how this kind of unexpected linking can score its effect 'by brief words and sudden contrasts'; or again by 'a development of rapid association of

thought which requires considerable agility on the part of the reader.' Donne's most characteristic use of the conceit is perhaps not to be found in the condensed form of a single line—though many of these are as memorable as 'A bracelet of bright hair about the bone'; but rather in 'the elaboration . . . of a figure of speech to the farthest stage to which ingenuity can carry it.' Such is his famous comparison of two lovers to a pair of compasses—a comparison seemingly so grotesque, but actually, in the context of the poem, so effective. A comparable example of the elaborated conceit in Eliot is his description of the fog in terms of a cat:

> The yellow fog that rubs its back upon the window-panes,
> The yellow smoke that rubs its muzzle on the window-panes
> Licked its tongue into the corners of the evening,
> Lingered upon the pools that stand in drains,
> Let fall upon its back the soot that falls from chimneys,
> Slipped by the terrace, made a sudden leap,
> And seeing that it was a soft October night,
> Curled once about the house, and fell asleep.

There is no point in entering here into further technical analysis of the nature of the conceit—a task which has been well carried out by George Williamson on the lines adumbrated by Eliot. But it is essential to emphasize that by writing in this way neither Donne nor Eliot is engaging in intellectual stunts or decorating his verse with brilliant but pointless ingenuity. For the conceit exists not just to shock or startle, though that is one of its valuable attributes. It is an integral element of the metaphysical style since it is the most compelling means of making the desired union of emotion and thought by bringing together widely divergent material in a single image. Instead of being ornamental, it is wholly functional: only by its use does the poet feel that he can express the precise curve of his meaning. If the reader objects that the meaning would be much better conveyed in plain speech without resort to such tortuous comparisons, let him bear in mind Hulme's remark that 'Plain speech is essentially inaccurate. It is only by new metaphors . . . that it can be made precise.'

To a greater degree than the objective decorative comparison the conceit enables the reader to *feel* the mind of the poet actually working; it is an image wherein the imaginative act itself has become analytical. Consequently, as Williamson has con-

cluded (and a good deal of what I have just written is a condensation of his account): the elaborated conceit is successful
'when the idea and the figure become one'; the condensed conceit is successful 'when the image is the very body of the thought.'
In both cases the test is the very one which Hulme applies to the
question of sincerity in poetry: 'If it is sincere in the accurate
sense, when the whole of the analogy is necessary to get out the
exact curve of the feeling or thing you want to express—there
you seem to me to have the highest verse, even though the subject be trivial and the emotions of the infinite far away.' (For
other passages from Hulme which closely parallel Eliot's own
views of the nature of poetry, see Chap. III, note 1, below.)

Eliot's conceits sometimes have the look of being too studied;
that is to say, of coming into existence not because the poet's
mind has actually felt keenly an unexpected similarity between
unlikes but as though he too consciously set out to shock the
reader. Such an objection might be made against the opening
lines of 'Prufrock':

> Let us go then, you and I,
> When the evening is spread out against the sky
> Like a patient etherised upon a table.

Even though the reader can perceive wherein the comparison
holds, he may still have the sensation that it is too intellectually
manipulated, not sufficiently felt. But in the general texture of
his verse Eliot really depends very little upon elaborate conceits:
the double description of the cat and the foggy evening, whereby
both are present to the reader with a richly heightened acuteness, is by far his most conspicuous use of the device in its ex-
panded form. His usual way of surprising the reader into a new
perception of reality is by means of the nuance rather than the
conceit, by the rapid associations of his shifting thought, and
by the accompanying deft and subtle exactness of his verbal
contrasts:

> At the violet hour, the evening hour that strives
> Homeward, and brings the sailor home from sea,
> The typist home at teatime, clears her breakfast, lights
> Her stove, and lays out food in tins.
> Out of the window perilously spread
> Her drying combinations touched by the sun's last rays,
> On the divan are piled (at night her bed)

Stockings, slippers, camisoles, and stays.
I Tiresias, old man with wrinkled dugs
Perceived the scene, and foretold the rest—
I too awaited the expected guest.
He, the young man carbuncular, arrives,
A small house agent's clerk, with one bold stare,
One of the low on whom assurance sits
As a silk hat on a Bradford millionaire.

The limpid description of the evening, with its romantic associations heightened by the echo of Stevenson's 'Requiem' as well as by the emulation of some lines of Sappho (of which Eliot tells us in a note), is suddenly startled into a new aspect by the introduction of the typist. It is worth observing that this effect of surprise is made partly by the equally sudden shift in syntax, whereby 'the typist,' at first the object of 'brings,' becomes in turn the subject of 'clears.' Such breaking through the rules of conventional grammar, as the irregular lines break through conventional versification, corresponds to Eliot's remark that 'the structure of the sentences [of the metaphysical poets] is sometimes far from simple, but this is not a vice; it is a fidelity to thought and feeling.'

Throughout the passage there is a similar weaving back and forth from phrases embodying traditional loveliness to phrases rising from sharp, realistic perceptions of the actual city. 'Out of the window perilously spread'—the adverb quickens anticipation, which is quickly disappointed by 'her drying combinations'; but at once another association of beauty is brought by the phrase 'touched by the sun's last rays.' So, too, the word 'divan' raises all its glamorous connotations from the Orient, which are instantly broken into by the realization that this is the kind of perfected folding divan that can be bought at a bargain at Selfridge's or Macy's, and which is designed to do double work. So, too, with the expression 'expected guest': the classic connotations of the ceremonious relation between host and guest and the anticipation of the arrival are immediately jolted by the appearance of 'the young man carbuncular.' And here, possibly, should be noted another kind of contrast: the full, deep vowel-sounds of the adjective corresponding to the natural beauty of the thing, so unfortunately altered by its human analogy.

His 'one bold stare' is an example of how great a range of meaning can be packed into a phrase when it has a double relation in the syntax, when, in this case, it modifies both 'arrives' and 'clerk.' For it thereby not only describes him at the moment of his arrival but also suggests the whole contour of his character: that this stare is perhaps his one distinguishing trait. And thus we are prepared for the summation of him in one of Eliot's most brilliantly effective condensed conceits:

> One of the low on whom assurance sits
> As a silk hat on a Bradford millionaire.

His arrogance and cheapness, his brash vulgarity, his strutting show of confidence which gives itself away at every move and betrays an inner ignorance and insecurity—all these reflections are suggested to the reader by the unexpected comparison to the awkward angle at which the crass new-rich man wears his hat.

The final effect of the whole passage, it should be noted, is not to weaken the force of either half of the contrasting terms. The beauty of the evening is not destroyed by the city. The situation of the girl is not being caricatured or mocked: its pathos is underlined by the contrast between her surroundings and those of traditional 'romantic love.' The juxtaposition and union of opposites (according to Grierson the distinguishing feature of metaphysical poetry) produces likewise here the result of intensifying both. The whole scene is presented with an extraordinary fullness of actuality.

Such manner of minute analysis is not meant to imply that Eliot's verse is a kind of special art. Indeed, equally careful reading—as Richards has demonstrated in *Practical Criticism*—is demanded of any poem in which a mature author has utilized all the resources of language and feeling at his command. This would be true of the Odes of Keats as well as of the later plays of Shakespeare.

17. As Eliot notes, an expression very close to this was used by Rémy de Gourmont in speaking of Flaubert: 'Il n'y a de livres que ceux où un écrivain s'est raconté lui-même en racontant les mœurs de ses contemporains—leurs rêves, leurs vanités, leurs amours, et leurs folies.' In any full account of the development of Eliot's critical theory it would be essential to dwell on his early obligations to de Gourmont, of whom he remarked in his essay on 'The Perfect Critic': 'Of all modern critics, perhaps Rémy de Gourmont had most of the general intelligence of

Aristotle. An amateur, though an excessively able amateur, in physiology, he combined to a remarkable degree sensitiveness, erudition, sense of fact and sense of history, and generalizing power.'

What Eliot gained from reading such books as *Le Problème du style* and *La Culture des idées* is best shown in his further remark that de Gourmont was 'the critical consciousness of a generation,' who could 'supply the conscious formulas of a sensibility in process of formation.' It is worth noting, however, that in recent years Eliot has referred to de Gourmont much less frequently; and certainly Eliot's matured critical ideas are more complex and resilient than de Gourmont's, precisely as his mind is of tougher fibre.

Eliot's more demonstrably enduring debts are to such thinkers as Irving Babbitt, Charles Maurras, and T. E. Hulme. Ants Oras has dealt with some of these relations of Eliot's thought in his informative if somewhat pedestrian study of *The Critical Ideas of T. S. Eliot* (Tartu, Esthonia, 1932).

But behind any tangible debts and obscured by their sharp divergence of approach, there is to be discovered everywhere in Eliot's work his kinship to Matthew Arnold, a kinship to be noted in their views of the relation of the individual to society, as well as on such matters as the importance of wholeness of structure in a work of art.

II

THE PROBLEM FOR THE CONTEMPORARY ARTIST

After such knowledge, what forgiveness?

IN such a passage as the conclusion of 'The Burial of the Dead' Eliot reveals the way in which he himself possesses 'a sense of his own age,' that 'peculiar honesty, which, in a world too frightened to be honest, is peculiarly terrifying. It is an honesty against which the whole world conspires because it is unpleasant.' Eliot used those words in describing Blake, and a further extension of the passage is likewise relevant to his own aims in *The Waste Land* (which he was to publish two years after this essay): 'Nothing that can be called morbid or abnormal or perverse, none of the things which exemplify the sickness of an epoch or a fashion, have this quality; only those things which, by some extraordinary labour of simplification, exhibit the essential sickness or strength of the human soul.'

In Eliot's earlier work, in such a poem as 'Sweeney among the Nightingales,' or, more particularly, 'A Cooking Egg,' it at first looked as though he was so absorbed in the splendours of the past that he was capable of expressing only the violent contrast between its remembered beauty and the actual dreary ugliness of contemporary existence, that he was merely prolonging one mood inherited from Flaubert in viewing human life crushed into something mean and sordid by bourgeois 'civilization.' But on closer examination it appears that his contrasts are not so clear-cut, that he is not confining himself to voicing anything so essentially limited and shallow as the inferiority of the present to the past. He is keenly aware of our contemporary historical consciousness, and of the problems which it creates. The modern educated man possesses a knowledge of the past to a degree hardly glimpsed a century ago, not only of one segment of the past, but, increasingly, of all pasts. If he is sensitive to what he knows, he can feel, in Eliot's words, 'that the whole of the literature of Europe from Homer . . . has a simultaneous existence.' But also, owing to the self-consciousness which results from so much knowledge (scientific and psychological as well as historical and literary), he will have a sense in any given moment, as Eliot has remarked of Joyce, 'of everything happening at once.'

Such a realization can lead either to chaos or to a sense of the potential unity of life. The difficulty with our knowledge to-day consists in the fact that instead of giving the individual's mind release and freedom, the piling up of so many disparate and seemingly unrelated details can merely oppress him with their bewildering variety, with 'being too conscious and conscious of too much,' [1] with the futility of any certainty, or, as Eliot has reflected, with the feeling that 'everybody is conscious of every question, and no one knows any answers.' The problem for the artist is to discover some unified pattern in this variety; and yet, if he believes as Eliot does that poetry should embody a man's reaction to his whole experience, also to present the full sense of its complexity. He can accomplish this double task of accurately recording what he has felt and perceived, and at the same time interpreting it, only if he grasps the similarity that often lies beneath contrasting appearances, and can thus emphasize the essential equivalence of seemingly different experiences. Such understanding and resultant emphasis constitute Eliot's chief reason for introducing so many reminiscences of other poets into the texture of his own verse. In this way he can at once suggest the extensive consciousness of the past that is inevitably possessed by any cultivated reader of to-day, and, more importantly, can greatly increase the implications of his lines by this tacit revelation of the sameness (as well as the contrasts) between the life of the present and that of other ages.[2]

This emphasis is a leading element in the method of *The Waste Land,* whose city, as we have seen, is many cities, or rather certain qualities resulting from the pervasive state of mind bred by mass civilization. But the structure of the poem embraces more than that. In his desire to make available for poetry the multiplicity of the modern world in the only way that the artist can, by giving it order and form, Eliot had discovered a clue in anthropology, in its exploration of ancient myths. It was not accidental or owing to any idiosyncrasy that he was affected profoundly by his reading of such a work as *The Golden Bough,* since the investigations of anthropology along with those of psychology have produced the most fundamental revolutions in contemporary thought and belief. It is noteworthy that Jessie Weston's *From Ritual to Romance* appeared in 1920, at the very time when Eliot was seeking a coherent shape for the mass of intricate material that enters into his poem. For reading that book gave to his mind the very fillip which it needed in order to crystallize.[3] What he learned especially from it was the recurring pattern in various myths, the basic resemblance, for example, between the vegetation myths of the rebirth of the year, the fertility myths of the rebirth of the potency of man, the Christian story of the Resurrection, and the Grail legend of purification. The common source of all these myths lay in the fundamental rhythm of nature—that of the death and rebirth of the year; and their varying symbolism was an effort to explain the origin of life. Such knowledge, along with the researches of psychology, pointed to the close union in all these myths of the physical and spiritual, to the fact that their symbolism was basically sexual— in the Cup and Lance of the Grail legend as well as in the Orpheus cults; pointed, in brief, to the fundamental relation between the well-springs of sex and religion.

The consequence of so much knowledge presents a condensed example of the general problem of the modern consciousness outlined above. When the investigations of anthropology reveal that surface differences between the customs and beliefs of mankind tend to mask profound resemblances, the result is both a freeing and a destruction. Taboos are removed, but sanctions wither. The purity of the Grail legend seems lost in symbols of generative significance; and yet at the same time it takes on a rich depth of primitive force that was wholly lost by Tennyson's denatured picture-book version. In such a perception of the nature of myths, of 'a common principle underlying all manifestations of life,' [4] Eliot found a scaffold for his poem, a background of reference that made possible something in the nature of a musical organization. He found the specific clue to the dramatic shaping of his material when he read in Miss Weston of the frequent representation of the mystery of death and rebirth by the story of a kingdom where, the forces of the ruler having been weakened or destroyed by sickness, old age, or the ravages of war, 'the land becomes Waste, and the task of the hero is that of restoration,' [5] not by pursuing advantages for himself, but by giving himself to the quest of seeking the health and salvation of the land.

The poem thus embodies simultaneously several different planes of experience, for it suggests the likenesses between various waste lands. Its quest for salvation in contemporary London is given greater volume and urgency by the additional presence of the haunted realm of medieval legend. The name of the battle where Stetson fought is that of one in which the Carthaginians were defeated, pointing the essential sameness of all wars. The opening of the final section in particular furnishes an example of the way Eliot is portraying the equivalence of different experiences by linking together various myths:

THE ACHIEVEMENT OF T. S. ELIOT

After the torchlight red on sweaty faces
After the frosty silence in the gardens
After the agony in stony places
The shouting and the crying
Prison and palace and reverberation
Of thunder of spring over distant mountains
He who was living is now dead
We who were living are now dying
With a little patience.

Reminiscence here is not only of the final scenes in the life of Christ and of the gnawing bafflement of his disciples before his appearance at Emmaus. The vigil of silence and the agony of spiritual struggle are not limited to one garden; they belong to the perilous quest of Parsival or Galahad as well. The 'shouting and the crying' re-echo not only from the mob that thronged Jerusalem at the time of the Crucifixion, but also, as is made clearer in ensuing lines, from the 'hordes swarming over endless plains' in revolt in contemporary Russia. In the 'thunder of spring over distant mountains' there is likewise a hint of the vegetation myths, of the approaching rebirth of the parched dead land through the life-giving rain. Thus he who 'is now dead' is not Christ alone, but the slain Vegetation God; he is Adonis and Osiris and Orpheus.[6] And with the line, 'We who were living are now dying,' the link is made back to the realm of death in life of the opening section, the realm which focuses all the elements of the poem and resounds through all its lines, the waste land of contemporary existence, likewise waiting for salvation, salvation that can come only through sacrifice, as is revealed in the final apocalyptic command reverberating through 'What the Thunder Said': 'Give, Sympathize, Control.'

As a result of this method of compressing into a single moment both the memory and the sameness of other moments, it becomes apparent that in 'The Fire Sermon,' the section of the poem which deals in particular with the present and the past of London, no sharply separating contrast is made between them. Squalor pollutes the modern river as it did not in Spenser's 'Prothalamion'; but there are also glimpses of beauty where

> The river sweats
> Oil and tar
> The barges drift
> With the turning tide
> Red sails
> Wide
> To leeward, swing on the heavy spar.

And, conversely, although mention of Elizabeth and Leicester brings an illusion of glamour, closer thought reveals that the stale pretence of their relationship left it essentially as empty as that between the typist and the clerk.

Use of such widely divergent details in a single poem indicates the special problem of the contemporary artist. Faced with so great a range of knowledge as a part of the modern consciousness, he can bring it to satisfactory expression in one of two ways, either by expansion or compression. It can hardly be a coincidence that each of these ways was carried to its full development at almost the same time, in the years directly following the War. Joyce chose the first alternative for *Ulysses* and devoted more than a quarter of a million words to revealing the complexity involved in the passage of a single ordinary day. In the following year Eliot concentrated an interpretation of a whole condition of society into slightly over four hundred lines. That Eliot was aware of similarities in their aims is indicated in a brief essay which he published during the year after the appearance of *The Waste Land* on 'Ulysses, Order, and Myth.' [7] He recognized how important it had been for Joyce to find a scaffold for his work in the structure of the *Odyssey* when he remarked that:

In using the myth, in manipulating a continuous parallel between contemporaneity and antiquity, Mr. Joyce is pursuing a
method which others must pursue after him. They will not be
imitators, any more than the scientist who uses the discoveries
of an Einstein in pursuing his own, independent, further investigations. It is simply a way of controlling, of ordering, of giving
a shape and a significance to the immense panorama of futility
and anarchy which is contemporary history. It is a method already adumbrated by Mr. Yeats, and of the need for which I
believe Mr. Yeats to have been the first contemporary to be conscious. It is, I seriously believe, a step toward making the modern world possible in art.

The utilization of such a discovery would clearly differ for
the novelist and the poet. With the example of the nineteenth century behind him, Eliot naturally felt that, if the
long poem was to continue to exist, there must be more to
distinguish it than length, that its energy must be increased
by the elimination of everything superfluous. To convey in
poetry the feeling of the actual passage of life, to bring to
expression the varied range and volume of awareness which
exists in a moment of consciousness, demanded, in Eliot's
view, the strictest condensation. Above all, the impression
of a fully packed content should not be weakened through
the relaxed connectives of the usual narrative structure.
Whatever may have been right at the time of the composition of *The Ring and the Book,* it was apparent to Eliot
that to-day 'anything that can be said as well in prose can
be said better in prose.' Poetry alone, through its resources
of rhythm and sound, can articulate the concentrated essence
of experience, and thus come closest to the universal and
permanent; but it can do so only through the mastery of a
concentrated form. Though he approaches the question with
a much broader understanding of all the factors involved
than was possessed by the author of 'The Poetic Principle,'
Eliot is at one with Poe in his insistence on the necessary
economy of a work of art, in his belief that a poem should

be constructed deliberately with the aim of producing a unified effect. Consequently, after composing the first draft of
The Waste Land, his revisions shortened it to less than
two-thirds of its original length, in order that he might best
create a dramatic structure that would possess at the same
time a lyrical intensity.

That Eliot does not hold up such a method of construction as an ideal necessarily to be followed is indicated by
an extended comment at the very close of *The Use of Poetry:*

To return to the question of obscurity: when all exceptions
have been made, and after admitting the possible existence of
minor 'difficult' poets whose public must always be small, I
believe that the poet naturally prefers to write for as large and
miscellaneous an audience as possible, and that it is the half-
educated and ill-educated, rather than the uneducated, who stand
in his way: I myself should like an audience which could neither
read nor write. The most useful poetry, socially, would be one
which could cut across all the present stratifications of public
taste—stratifications which are perhaps a sign of social disintegration. The ideal medium for poetry, to my mind, and the most
direct means of social 'usefulness' for poetry, is the theatre. In a
play of Shakespeare you get several levels of significance. For the
simplest auditors there is the plot, for the more thoughtful the
character and conflict of character, for the more literary the words
and phrasing, for the more musically sensitive the rhythm, and
for auditors of greater sensitiveness and understanding a meaning which reveals itself gradually. And I do not believe that the
classification of audience is so clear-cut as this; but rather that
the sensitiveness of every auditor is acted upon by all these
elements at once, though in different degrees of consciousness.

This is the kind of passage which tantalizes and infuriates
pragmatic critics of the sort who believe that a good author
should simply decide what he wants to do and should then go
ahead and do it. They would declare such reflections either
to be disingenuous or to damn out of hand the validity of
Eliot's own work. But one of the fundamental secrets of art
as of life is that the mature artist finds his strength partly by

coming to recognize and reckon with his limitations. Just
as an individual starts by accepting certain technical conventions of a given art as a means of facilitating his search for a
form that will enable him to embody what he wants to express, so, as he grows in the practice of that art and as he
comes to closer grips with his own character, he will know
that there are only certain things that he is best fitted to do,
and that he can do those adequately only through selection
and long perseverance.

Eliot's extreme awareness of the boundaries of his own
work is very similar to Hawthorne's detached perception of
the contrast between the bustling everyday Salem which surrounded him, and the realm of dim lights and dark shadows
which he was meanwhile creating in *The Scarlet Letter.*
Eliot's preference for a very different kind of poetry from
that which he is capable of writing likewise recalls Hawthorne's repeated statement that the novels he really liked
were not his own tenuous explorations of the soul, but the
solid beef-and-ale stories of Trollope. This unusual degree
of detachment which reverberates with loneliness, but which
brings with it in compensation a special development of
spiritual understanding, has grown organically out of the
conditions of American life, out of the isolation of the individual from the centre of European culture. Kindred isolation
enabled Thoreau and Emily Dickinson to study themselves
with such rare mastery. It has also enabled Poe and Henry
James and Eliot, all of them possessing the excessive provin-
cial consciousness of elements in literary tradition which
Europeans would have taken for granted—and ignored—by
that very consciousness to lead their European contemporaries into a more penetrating comprehension of the nature of art.

When he wrote that passage on the different levels of ap-
peal, Eliot had experimented with drama only in his un

finished *Sweeney Agonistes*. He knew that poems like *The Waste Land* and *Ash Wednesday,* richly significant as they may be on all the higher levels, virtually ignore the level of the pit. But the fact remains that the sincere artist writes not the way he would, but the way he must. And the most important value of the artist to society, and the one element that lends his work enduring significance, is to give expression to the most pervading qualities of life *as he has actually known it.* That Landor and Donne have appealed to restricted audiences defines but does not destroy their excellence. And no one would think of quarrelling with Lucretius for not reaching a 'popular' level.

If, in severest analysis, the kind of poetry Eliot writes gives evidence of social disintegration, he has expressed that fact as the poet should, not by rhetorical proclamation, but by the very feeling of contemporary life which he has presented to the sensitive reader of his lines. And he has presented this not merely as something which the reader is to know through his mind, but is to know primarily as an actual physical experience, as a part of his whole being, through the humming pulsating evidence of his senses.

But when a poet is as conscious of his aims and effects as Eliot has revealed himself to be in his remarks on *Ulysses* as well as in *The Use of Poetry,* there is always the suspicion lingering in the minds of some readers that his way of giving order to the content of his work is too intellectually controlled and manipulated, that what he says cannot be wholly sincere because it is not sufficiently spontaneous. It may be that the large task which Eliot set himself in *The Waste Land* 'of giving a shape and a significance to the immense panorama of futility and anarchy' of contemporary history, caused some of the experiments which he made to gain that end to appear too deliberate. Certainly some of his analogies with musical structure, in particular the summa-

theme
"Waste
Land"

[43]

tion of the themes in the broken ending of the final part, have always seemed to me somewhat forced and over-theoretical. But this is very different from saying that he is a too conscious artist. Indeed, such a charge would overlook the fact that some of the poetry of the past which across the remove of time seems most 'spontaneous,' that of Chaucer, for example, was actually a product of long experimentation in poetic theory fully as calculated as Eliot's. The greatest narrative poem in the language, *Troilus and Criseyde,* beats with equally genuine emotion in the passages where Chaucer is translating Boccaccio directly and in those where he is manipulating the structure of the Italian's poem to suit his own ends.

Despite some of the protests of the nineteenth century on behalf of the untutored genius, it still appears that the more conscious the artist the better, if that consciousness implies the degree to which he has mastered the unending subtleties of his craft. But I have mentioned Chaucer also to point a difference in modern art. As my paragraphs on our highly developed historical sense tried to indicate, Eliot as a poet is not only inevitably acquainted with a great range of possible techniques, as all expert poets since the Renaissance have increasingly been; he is, in addition, highly aware of the processes of the mind itself. This particular kind of consciousness is in part what led him to feel the necessity of grounding the structure of his longest poem in something outside himself, in an objective pattern of myths.

Ulysses, to be sure, furnishes an even fuller example of how a contemporary artist has mastered the problem of consciousness in a similar way. When one contemplates the overwhelming elaborateness of Joyce's construction, the almost unbelievable degree to which he worked out the parallel of even the smallest details in his narrative with those in the *Odyssey* (to say nothing of his intricate scheme of correspondences between the sections of his work and various

colours, arts, bodily organs, and so on), one begins by wondering why his huge creative power was not stultified by this
fantastic heaping up of seemingly pointless erudition, of
practically none of which is it necessary for the reader to be
aware in order to follow with full understanding the progress of Bloom's and Stephen's day. But finally one realizes
that the very *completeness* of this arbitrary external structure may have been the one thing that gave to Joyce's scho-
lastic mind, deprived of faith but still possessing the ingrained habits of logical formal thought, the greatest creative
release possible to him, by providing him with an entire
scaffold—and one which has the advantage of being one of
the best stories in Western civilization—on which to build
his work.

And in case there should be some feeling that either Joyce
or Eliot has revealed a kind of bookish weakness in turning
for his structure to literature rather than to life, it should be
recollected that Shakespeare himself created hardly any of
his plots, and that by the very fact of taking ready-made the
pattern of his characters' actions, he could devote his undi-
vided attention to endowing them with life. It is only an un-
informed prejudice which holds that literature must start
from actual personal experience. It certainly must end with
giving a sense of life; but it is not at all necessary that the poet
should have undergone in his own person what he describes.
Indeed, the more catholic the range of the artist, the more
obviously impossible that would be. The poet's imagination
can work as well on his reading as on the raw material
of his senses. It is a mark of human maturity, as Eliot noted
in his discussion of the metaphysical poets, that there should
not be a separation in an individual's sensibility between
reading and experience any more than between emotion and
thought.[8]

NOTES

1. F. R. Leavis, *New Bearings in English Poetry* (London, 1932), uses a similar phrase on p. 94. Mr. Leavis's interpretation of Eliot, though acutely perceptive of certain details to which I have been indebted particularly in this chapter, suffers from a certain over-intensity. He seems to be writing continually on the defensive as though he were the apostle of modern art to an unappreciative world. As a result his criticism, though eager, is somewhat wanting in balance and perspective.

2. This matter of Eliot's use of his reading (a hint of which he picked up from the symbolists, but which he has carried to far greater lengths) has been a stumbling-block to so many readers of his poetry that it requires further comment. On the one hand are those who believe that it is impossible to understand him without possessing the ability to recognize all his varied allusions, and who, therefore, indifferent to the seemingly hopeless and unrewarding task of tracing down both the wide and specialized range of his particular equipment of knowledge, have given him up as 'a poet for the learned.' On the other hand are the smaller body of readers who have done the greatest disservice to his reputation—I mean those who regard his poetry as a kind of hidden mystery for the cognoscenti. They cast the snob-vote for him. 'What?' they ask, 'you haven't read *The Golden Bough*? You don't own a Tarot pack? You haven't studied the Upanishads? You didn't even recognize that allusion to Verlaine? Why, my dear, how can you expect to understand Mr. Eliot?'

The shortest answer (which, I hope, is given full confirmation during the course of my essay) is that you begin to understand Eliot precisely as you begin to understand any other poet: by listening to the lines, by regarding their pattern as a self-enclosed whole, by listening to what is being communicated instead of looking for something that isn't. On the particular matter of what is accomplished by Eliot's literary allusions, and what equipment is necessary to comprehend them, consider the opening passage of 'The Fire Sermon':

[46]

The river's tent is broken: the last fingers of leaf
Clutch and sink into the wet bank. The wind
Crosses the brown land, unheard. The nymphs are departed.
Sweet Thames, run softly, till I end my song.
The river bears no empty bottles, sandwich papers,
Silk handkerchiefs, cardboard boxes, cigarette ends
Or other testimony of summer nights. The nymphs are departed.
And their friends, the loitering heirs of city directors;
Departed, have left no addresses.
By the waters of Leman I sat down and wept. . .
Sweet Thames, run softly till I end my song,
Sweet Thames, run softly, for I speak not loud or long.
But at my back in a cold blast I hear
The rattle of the bones, and chuckle spread from ear to ear.

If one reads these lines with an attentive ear and is sensitive to their sudden shifts in movement, the contrast between the actual Thames and the idealized vision of it during an age before it flowed through a megalopolis is conveyed by that movement itself, whether or not one recognizes the refrain to be from Spenser. If one does have the lovely pictures of his 'Prothalamion' in mind, there is then added to the contrast a greater volume and poignancy. In like manner with the startling quickening of pace in the final two lines and the terrifying shudder they induce: it is not necessary to refer this effect to Marvell's 'Coy Mistress,' although if the effect of the sudden shift in cadence in that poem is also in the reader's ear, there is again a heightening.

In neither of these cases is anything demanded of the reader different in kind from what is demanded by Milton's 'Lycidas.' A single careful reading of that poem can fascinate the reader with its extraordinary melodic richness and make him want to press on to a full comprehension of its intricate form, of the way its structure builds up through a series of climaxes. But this can be understood only through some knowledge of the whole elaborate convention that Milton inherited from the classical and Renaissance pastoral. In particular, there are many passages, the fullest relish of which depends upon the reader's bringing with him the memory of the way a similar situation has been handled by Virgil and Theocritus. In addition, certain well-known lines require for the grasp of their sense at least as much literary annotation as any passage in Eliot. For instance,

[47]

Next Camus, reverend sire, went footing slow,
His mantle hairy, and his bonnet sedge,
Inwrought with figures dim, and on the edge
Like to that sanguine flower inscribed with woe.

The wealth of mythology compressed into those lines would require a long paragraph if it were to be elucidated in prose.

The point with any poem is that if the reader starts by being enchanted by the movement of the lines, then gradually his mind can furnish itself with the information necessary to understand what they are telling him. In the case of the modern reader of a poem in a Renaissance tradition, this means reminding himself of certain mythological details once common property among educated readers, but now increasingly forgotten. In the case of reading a contemporary poet, it is more a question of accustoming yourself to an unfamiliar procedure that breaks through your preconceptions of what poetry should be (as Wordsworth broke through preconceptions inherited from the eighteenth century). As Eliot remarked in the Conclusion to *The Use of Poetry:*

The uses of poetry certainly vary as society alters, as the public to be addressed changes. . . The difficulty of poetry (and modern poetry is supposed to be difficult) . . . may be due just to novelty: we know the ridicule accorded in turn to Wordsworth, Shelley and Keats, Tennyson and Browning—but must remark that Browning was the first to be *called* difficult; hostile critics of the earlier poets found them difficult, but called them silly. Or difficulty may be caused by the reader's having been told, or having suggested to himself, that the poem is going to prove difficult. The ordinary reader, when warned against the obscurity of a poem, is apt to be thrown into a state of consternation very unfavourable to poetic receptivity. Instead of beginning, as he should, in a state of sensitivity, he obfuscates his senses by the desire to be clever and to look very hard for something, he doesn't know what—or else by the desire not to be taken in. There is such a thing as stage fright, but what such readers have is pit or gallery fright. The more seasoned reader, he who has reached, in these matters, a state of greater *purity,* does not bother about understanding; not, at least, at first. I know that some of the poetry to which I am most devoted is poetry which I did not understand at first reading; some is poetry which I am not sure I understand yet: for instance, Shakespeare's. And finally, there is the difficulty caused by the author's having left out something which the reader is used to finding; so that the reader, bewildered, gropes about for what is absent, and puzzles his head for a kind of 'meaning' which is not there, and is not meant to be there.

It is also relevant to note how the passage from 'The Fire Sermon' is an example of Eliot's way of suggesting sameness at the heart of contrast. 'The nymphs are departed': the first use of that statement, followed as it is by the line from Spenser, serves to build up the pastoral atmosphere: 'The river nymphs are departed with the oncoming of winter.' But as the ensuing lines present the picture of the present Thames in summer, the statement takes on another meaning: 'The age of romantic loveliness is gone.'

Then, when the statement is repeated a few lines later, the nymphs themselves have altered; they have now become decidedly flesh and blood. But the feeling expressed is not that the past was wholly noble and the present base. Instead, it is being suggested, if only in a minor undertone, that this glimpse of present life along the river, depressingly sordid as it is, being human cannot be wholly different from human life in the past. And, concurrently, the idealized Elizabethan young men and women who appear as attendants in Spenser's marriage songs begin to be seen with new eyes. They cannot be wholly unlike the present idle young men about town and their nymphs; and this touch of humanity removes them from the realm of the abstract and endows them with actuality. In such a manner the undertones of this 'resembling contrast' have grown directly from the depth of Eliot's psychological perception into the nature of life, of the way, for example, in which nobility and baseness are inextricably mingled in even the finest individual.

3. A point necessary to mention is that an appreciation of Eliot's poem is not dependent upon reading Miss Weston's study. I had been enjoying *The Waste Land* for several years before an interest in exploring the effect of Eliot's reading upon his development brought me to *From Ritual to Romance*. As a result of having read that book I can now follow more distinctly the logical steps by which Eliot was led to compose his structure, and can also perceive in detail the kind of stimulus and release that the book gave to his mind. I am also enabled to understand more fully how some of the widely disparate details fall into the completed pattern. For example, I had previously taken the presence of the 'wicked pack of cards' in the opening section to

[49]

be simply a sharp dramatic device by which Eliot introduced his
characters and at the same time stressed the point of their shifting identity: that, observed under varying and contrasting
appearances, human beings remain essentially the same throughout different ages. I have never seen a Tarot pack (and, if I had
to bet, my money would say that neither had Eliot himself). But
Miss Weston mentions that its four suits are Cup, Lance, Sword,
and Dish, which thus correspond to the sexual symbolism of the
Grail; and that the original use of these cards was 'not to fore-
tell the Future in general, but to predict the rise and fall of
the waters which brought fertility to the land' (p. 76). Through
such knowledge the emotional relevance to the poem of this
'wicked pack' is obviously increased.

But with the exception of a few such illuminating details, I
question whether Miss Weston's valuable study has enabled me
to feel the poem more intensely. For nearly everything of importance from her book that is apposite to an appreciation of
The Waste Land, particularly her central emphasis on the
analogous ways by which various myths express the mysteries
of sex and religion, has been incorporated into the structure of
the poem itself, or into Eliot's Notes. Unlike many sections of
Pound's *Cantos, The Waste Land* does not require recourse
to the poet's reading in order to become comprehensible. Its
structure is pre-eminently self-contained.

The very presence of the Notes may seem to give a denial to
that assertion. They are certainly an extremely artificial device,
though not without precedent in English poetry, as *The Shep-
herds' Calendar* could illustrate. But Spenser's desire to have
his poems rival the works of classical antiquity even to their
appearance in a volume with annotations by the anonymous
E. K. (who was most probably Spenser himself or at least a close
collaborator), does not play any part in Eliot's intention. His
Notes are simply a consequence of his desire to strip the form
of his poem to its barest essentials in order to secure his concentrated effect. Such elimination, particularly when added to
his method of using his reading as an integral part of his experience, demanded certain signposts of elucidation if the reader
was to follow the exact course. And, as I have already indicated
in my discussion of the closing lines of 'The Burial of the Dead,'
it is obviously necessary, for *full* understanding of some of his
passages, to be aware of the special context of his allusions to

other poets. In all cases when Eliot thinks that context essential to the reader of *The Waste Land* he has given the reference, as in this instance to the *Inferno, The White Devil,* and *Les Fleurs du Mal.* In the case of some of his less familiar allusions where the actual phrasing of the original constitutes part of his effect, he has also quoted the relevant passage. For example:

> But at my back from time to time I hear
> The sound of horns and motors, which shall bring
> *Sweeney* to Mrs. Porter in the spring.

These lines, by themselves, without the need of any reference, etch a sharp description of the surroundings of 'the dull canal . . . round behind the gashouse.' Most present-day readers of poetry would be able to supply the surprising contrast:

> But at my back I always hear
> Time's wingèd chariot hurrying near,

so that Eliot simply mentions 'To His Coy Mistress' in a note. But to enable the reader also to hear this 'sound of horns' in a double way, it is necessary for Eliot to add the lines from the little-known Elizabethan poet, John Day:

> When of the sudden, listening, you shall hear
> A noise of horns and hunting, which shall bring
> Actaeon to Diana in the spring,
> Where all shall see her naked skin. . .

And no matter how much one may object to the existence of the Notes in general, it would be hard to deny the flash of tightly packed wit that is struck by the incongruous contrast between the 'naked skin' of Diana and that of Mrs. Porter.

Some of the more general references in the Notes help to sharpen the outlines of Eliot's structure. The self-consuming burning of sterile passion which is the theme of 'The Fire Sermon' receives added emphasis from the pertinent reminder of the expression of that theme by Buddha and St. Augustine, though no reading of their work is required for understanding the poem. I have not yet read the Upanishad from which Eliot borrowed the onomatopoeic representation of 'what the thunder said'; but it is perfectly clear from his own lines what an excellent 'objective correlative' he found in that legend.

My own chief objection to the Notes is the occasional tone of what Eliot himself, in relation to passages in *The Sacred Wood*, described as 'pontifical solemnity.' But that impression should be qualified by the admission that some of the notes which struck me at first as useless pedantry or deliberate mystification of the reader, particularly the one on Tiresias, I now recognize as very useful to the interpretation of the poem. The objection to stiffness in phrasing still remains, but this quality was perhaps due in part to Eliot's desire to state the necessary details as briefly as he could; and owing to the largeness of his undertaking in this poem and the inevitable limitations of his own temperament, this was possibly the price he had to pay in order to avoid what he would have considered muffling the energy of his poem by extended connecting links in the text itself.

The stiffness may also be due to Eliot's shyness at speaking in his own person, a quality which has likewise taken itself out in the occasional ponderous over- and under-statements in his Prefaces, and in his *Criterion* Commentaries. In these Notes it crops up in a curious double-edged irony, where he appears to be mocking himself for writing the note at the same time that he wants to convey something by it. Certainly the note on the hermit-thrush which tells us that it is *turdus aonalaschkae pallasii* and quotes a description from Chapman's *Handbook of Birds of Eastern North America*, would seem as though it were the desperate effort of J. Alfred Prufrock himself to say something important, but ending only in irrelevance. But actually the note ends with a telling sentence: 'Its "water-dripping song" is justly celebrated.' By that sentence Eliot has given a suggestion of the very sound from which his lines took rise (as remarked at the close of my chapter on the auditory imagination); and for ornithologists even the passage from Chapman would have the advantage of exact description.

Comparable to Eliot's use of Notes in *The Waste Land* is the frequent presence, throughout his work, of epigraphs for individual poems—though this device is not at all open to the objection of not being sufficiently structural. Again the intention is to enable the poet to secure a condensed expression in the poem itself, as well as to induce the reader to realize, even from the moment before the poem begins, that in reading poetry every word should be paid full attention. In each case the epigraph is designed to form an integral part of the effect of the poem; and in the most successful instances a subtle aura of association is added. 'Mistah Kurtz—he dead'—the harrowing climax of Conrad's 'Heart of Darkness,' his expression of utter horror, epitomizes in a sentence the very tone of blasphemous hopelessness which issues from 'The Hollow Men.' And certainly the closed circle of Prufrock's frightened isolation is sharply underlined by inscribing this speech from the *Inferno:* 'If I thought my answer were to one who ever could return to the world, this flame should shake no more; but since, if what I hear be true, none ever did return alive from this depth, without fear of infamy I answer thee.' Prufrock can give utterance in soliloquy to his debate with himself only because he knows that no one will overhear him. The point of calling this poem a 'Love Song' lies in the irony that it will never be sung; that Prufrock will never dare to voice what he feels.

And as a final detail to this note on Notes, it is worth observing that Eliot uses his titles as well as his epigraphs as integral elements in his effect, to reiterate his belief that in writing poetry every word on the page should be designed to count. Often, in the earlier poems, the aim of the title was to surprise the reader out of all complacency. Thus 'Sweeney among the Nightingales,' which is in itself a condensed metaphysical conceit; thus also the double meaning of 'Sweeney Erect.' 'Burbank with a Baedeker: Bleistein with a Cigar' dramatically sets a stage; but in this case the ensuing epigraph which is largely composed of phrases from other writers referring to events in Venice—for example, from *Othello, The Aspern Papers,* and Browning's 'A Toccata of Galuppi's,' though calculated to call up the reader's usual wide range of associations with that city, is too much of a pastiche to be very effective. And lastly, the startling 'A Cooking Egg' requires for its comprehension the occult knowledge that an egg which is no longer fresh enough to be eaten by itself, but must be used in cooking, is so described with the accent on the participle. Thus the title relates to the epigraph from Villon, which also tells the age and condition of the hero of the poem:

En l'an trentiesme de mon aage
Que toutes mes hontes j'ay beues. . .

4. Weston, p. 36.

5. Ibid., p. 21.

6. This point was noted by Hugh Ross Williamson, *The Poetry of T. S. Eliot* (London, 1933), p. 135. Mr. Williamson's book, though not wholly decisive in its critical observations, is a useful manual of relevant explanation, to which I have been frequently indebted.

7. *The Dial*, November 1923, pp. 480-3.

8. Since writing this paragraph I have re-read the passage in Henry James's essay 'The Art of Fiction' which expresses so exactly the relation between literature and experience which I have attempted to elucidate that I reproduce it here. In addition, it indicates once again a fundamental sameness in point of view between James and Eliot. James's rejoinder to the statement that 'the novelist must write from experience' runs as follows:

It is equally excellent and inconclusive to say that one must write from experience. . . What kind of experience is intended, and where does it begin and end? Experience is never limited, and it is never complete; it is an immense sensibility, a kind of huge spiderweb, of the finest silken threads, suspended in the chamber of consciousness and catching every air-borne particle in its tissue. It is the very atmosphere of the mind; and when the mind is imaginative—much more when it happens to be that of a man of genius—it takes to itself the faintest hints of life, it converts the very pulses of the air into revelations. The young lady living in a village has only to be a damsel upon whom nothing is lost to make it quite unfair (as it seems to me) to declare to her that she shall have nothing to say about the military. Greater miracles have been seen than that, imagination assisting, she should speak the truth about some of these gentlemen. I remember an English novelist, a woman of genius, telling me that she was much commended for the impression she had managed to give in one of her tales of the nature and way of life of the French Protestant youth. She had been asked where she learned so much about this recondite being, she had been congratulated on her peculiar opportunities. These opportunities consisted in her having once, in Paris, as she ascended a staircase, passed an open door where, in the household of a *pasteur,* some of the young Protestants were seated at table round a finished meal. The glimpse made a picture; it lasted only a moment, but that moment was experience. She had got her impression, and she evolved her type. She knew what youth was, and what Protestantism; she also had the advantage of having seen what it was to be French; so that she converted these ideas into a concrete image and produced a reality. Above all, however, she was blessed with the faculty which when you give it an inch takes an ell, and which for the artist is a much greater source of strength than any accident of residence or of place in the social scale. The power to guess the unseen from the seen, to trace the implication of things, to judge the whole piece by the pattern, the condition of feeling life, in general, so completely that you are well on your way to knowing any particular corner of it—this cluster of gifts may almost be said to constitute experience, and they occur in country and in town, and in the most differing stages of education. If experience consists of impressions, it may be said that impressions *are* experience, just as (have we not seen it?) they are the very air we breathe. Therefore, if I should certainly say to a novice, 'Write from experience, and experience only,' I should feel that this was rather a tantalizing monition if I were not careful immediately to add, 'Try to be one of the people on whom nothing is lost!'

III

THE 'OBJECTIVE CORRELATIVE'

What is *not* interesting, is that which does not add to our knowledge of any kind; that which is vaguely conceived and loosely drawn; a representation which is general, indeterminate, and faint, instead of being particular, precise, and firm. . . What are the eternal objects of poetry, among all nations and at all times? They are actions; human actions.—Matthew Arnold, Preface to *Poems*, 1853.

IF the natural demands of their mediums took Joyce and Eliot to the opposite poles of expansion and compression, the qualities of experience they were endeavouring to present were enough alike to lead to marked parallels in certain of their qualities of expression. As Eliot observed in an unpublished lecture on the method of *Ulysses* (1933): 'In some minds certain memories, both from reading and life, become charged with emotional significance. All these are used, so that intensity is gained at the expense of clarity.' There could not be a closer annotation of Eliot's own method, and I therefore want to consider some of its implications. It is no longer necessary, as it would have been, before the lyrical impulse of his poetry had been generally perceived, to spend much time defending Eliot's work against the charge of being over-intellectualized. He has himself taken pains on many occasions to point out that the concern of the poet is never with thought so much as with finding 'the emotional equivalent of thought'; that the essential function of poetry is not intellectual but emotional; that the business of Dante or Shakespeare was 'to express the greatest emotional intensity of his time, based on whatever his time happened to think.' All that he insists is that the more intelligent the poet is the better, since he is thus likely to be wider in his interests and more mature in his expression of them. He believes also that 'fundamental brain-work' can be justly demanded of the reader, particularly since 'our civilization, as it exists at present . . . comprehends great variety and complexity, and this variety and complexity, playing upon a refined sensibility, must produce various and complex results.' But purely in terms of the elements of tradition which Eliot has attempted to bring to fresh expression in his own poetry, it is by now apparent that his principal desire is not for intellectual density but for richness and subtlety of emotional impression.

But in his effort to convey the full intricacy of the moment, in his own partial sacrifice of clarity for range of implication, it is perhaps still necessary to show that he is not making obscure or arbitrary associations which are too personal to be followed by the reader. Actually Eliot was not being in the least paradoxical when he stressed the importance to the poet of Dante's power to create 'clear, visual images.' For he has repeatedly insisted that 'the poet does not aim to excite—that is not even a test of his success—but to set something down.' What he means by that is the prime importance of concrete presentation of carefully observed details. (It should not be forgotten that the title of his first book was *Prufrock and Other Observations*.) He is therein close to Hulme's conviction that 'the great aim is accurate, precise, and definite description,'[1] close to Ezra Pound's preoccupation in finding the exact fresh word, related also to the sharp visual discoveries of modern painting from Cézanne to Picasso. Eliot compresses his descriptions so tightly that you have to give them time to unfold in your mind:

> *The river's tent is broken: the last fingers of leaf*
> *Clutch and sink into the wet bank. The wind*
> *Crosses the brown land, unheard.*

It takes many readings of 'The Fire Sermon' before you see how complete a picture of the river's desolation is revealed to you from the moment of those opening three lines: the tearing away of the lovely ampleness with which summer trees form a canopy over the stream, leaving the bleak bareness of autumn; the sinister undertone that is started by seeing the leaves as drowning fingers clutching at the bank; the utter desertion conveyed by the fact that the wind is unheard. It is as true of these lines as Eliot found it of Coleridge's imagery stored-up from the voyagers that 'it is usually the accurate images, the fidelity of which may still be recognized, that are the most telling.'

To be sure, Eliot's observations are not primarily of physical objects; his most sustained analysis is applied to states of mind and emotion. But he holds none the less that permanent poetry is always a presentation of thought and feeling 'by a statement of events in human action or objects in the external world.' In his view the poet's emotions are not *in themselves* important; as he remarked in elucidation of Valéry, 'not our feelings, but the pattern which we make of our feelings is the centre of value.' The lasting poem is not the result of pouring out personal emotion, for 'the only way of expressing emotion in the form of art is by finding an "objective correlative"; in other words, a set of objects, a situation, a chain of events which shall be the formula of that *particular* emotion; such that when the external facts, which must terminate in sensory experience are given, the emotion is immediately evoked.' This passage will not yield its full significance without careful reading; but it is already a *locus classicus* of criticism.[2] It furnishes, for example, the exact clue to the triumph of *Samson Agonistes,* to Milton's complete success there in finding a dramatic situation that would externalize his own emotions and thus give them universal stature. On the other hand, failure to find an adequate 'chain of events,' and a consequent confusion of purely personal feelings with those of the hero is what leaves Shelley's *Prometheus Unbound* so vague and vaporous. And the reason why 'Gerontion' is the most mature, balanced work of art among Eliot's earlier poems is that he hit upon a situation in the sombre brooding of the old man that enabled him to set down a particular statement of life in concrete objectified form.

He is not writing in his own person: [3] the situation of Gerontion is even farther from his own than that of the middle-aged Prufrock had been when Eliot created him while still in his early twenties. I do not mean that elements of Eliot's own experience, of his own thought and feeling, do not enter into these characters; in fact, the source of some of the wittiest irony in 'Prufrock' would seem to spring from Eliot's detached ability to mock also the supercultivated fastidious young man from Harvard. But the point is that the hero of the poem is not such a figure; and that, as a result, Eliot's rapier thrusts have full play with no risk of becoming clumsily involved in purely personal associations. By choosing a character apart from his immediate experience he has been able to concentrate entirely, not on his own feelings, but on the creation of his poem. Thus everything important which he had to say about a certain kind of frustration and longing also found its articulation in this objectified transmuted form; just as the double feeling of his repulsion from vulgarity, and yet his shy attraction to the coarse earthiness of common life have found their complete symbol in Sweeney. And so, in like fashion, Eliot can project into the thoughts of Gerontion an expression of one of his most moving, recurrent themes: the horror of a life without faith, its disillusioned weariness of knowledge, its agonized slow drying up of the springs of emotion.

It should now also be clear that his understanding of the value of the 'objective correlative' was what caused Eliot to base the dramatic lyric intensity of *The Waste Land* in the externalized structure of parallel myths. It also led him to give the poem even further focus by sifting it through the eyes of a central observer, Tiresias—a device which Eliot may have learned in part from Henry James's similar use of Strether in *The Ambassadors*. As Eliot states in a note, 'What Tiresias *sees,* in fact, is the substance of the poem.' And Tiresias is the exact symbol for such haunting inclusive consciousness: only Tiresias, who had experienced life both as a man and a woman, who, though blind, possessed the torturing faculty of being able to foresee the future, could contain in his vision the ranges of life in a great metropolis. Only his infinitely sensitive power to 'foresuffer all' could embrace the violent contrasts (and samenesses) that are now packed into the compass of a few square blocks: the dead luxury of the upper class, the vast uninspired bourgeois existence, the broken fragments of the talk of the poor overheard in a bar. Incidentally, the clearest perception of Eliot's range in ability to fit his style to his subject is furnished by the remarkably different manners in which he presents these three classes of society. Perhaps the sharpest dramatic effect in the whole poem lies in the contrasting halves of 'The Game of Chess,' the abrupt shift from an elaborately sensuous style that can build up an atmosphere of cloying richness to one which catches the very cadences of Cockney speech in a pub. And then, in the next section, in order to suggest the huge commercialized world that lies between these two extremes, Eliot portrays the characteristic scene between the typist and the clerk, and suggests the denatured quality of their life by a deliberate mechanization of his rhythm, as well as by the first continuous use of rhyme in the poem, which, being unexpected, contributes to heighten his effect. At the same time, beneath all these contrasts in appearance, are being stressed the similar human situations in which all these different people are found: they are all playing the same stale game, burning alike with sterile desire. They stand in common need of regeneration.

Eliot's steady emphasis on the importance of wholeness of construction perhaps explains best why it is fair to separate Pound and Eliot by saying that 'Pound avait étudié la diction poétique, Eliot étudie le style.' [4] This distinction is not intended in the least to minimize Eliot's very great obligations to Pound, or the stimulus which he received from the slightly elder poet's first enunciation of his poetic theory in the years when Eliot was just out of college. Pound dwelt on the necessity of distinct presentation of something concrete; on accuracy and economy of language—'to use absolutely no word that does not contribute to the presentation'; and, regarding rhythm, on the necessity of composing 'in the sequence of the musical phrase, not in the sequence of the metronome.' [5] That Eliot has followed all three of these technical principles is to be seen everywhere in his work.

Pound also defined the nature of an image in such a way as to stress the union of sense and thought, the presence of the idea *in* the image: 'An "Image" is that which presents an intellectual and emotional complex in an instant of time.' That definition would seem to be in the direction of the 'objective correlative,' and would certainly apply directly to what Eliot was trying to do, for instance, in such a line as

I have measured out my life with coffee spoons.

But the trouble is that Pound virtually stopped short with the definition of details; and it remained for Eliot to bring such technical discoveries to their full fruition by building them into an architectural whole. This limitation of Pound's may help to explain why his greatest success has been in his translations, where he had an external structure to rely upon and could give his entire care to his extraordinary verbal and rhythmical expertness; as well as why his *Cantos,* though they have already proved a school of versification for younger poets, are comparatively formless; and why his most living original poems are the *Hugh Selwyn Mauberley* series of 1920, which show how Pound, in his turn, had begun to feel the influence of the method of Eliot.

A passage from 'Gerontion' will furnish perhaps the best example of the kind of hard precision with which Eliot's reliance upon 'a set of objects' enables him to thread together the range of his associations:

> *I an old man,*
> *A dull head among windy spaces.*
>
> *Signs are taken for wonders. 'We would see a sign!'*
> *The word within a word, unable to speak a word,*
> *Swaddled with darkness. In the juvescence of the year*
> *Came Christ the tiger*
>
> *In depraved May, dogwood and chestnut, flowering judas,*
> *To be eaten, to be divided, to be drunk*
> *Among whispers; by Mr. Silvero*
> *With caressing hands, at Limoges*
> *Who walked all night in the next room;*
>
> *By Hakagawa, bowing among the Titians;*
> *By Madame de Tornquist, in the dark room*
> *Shifting the candles; Fraülein von Kulp*
> *Who turned in the hall, one hand on the door.*
> > *Vacant shuttles*
> *Weave the wind. I have no ghosts,*
> *An old man in a draughty house*
> *Under a windy knob.*

The transitions are sudden, but, in terms of the context, unmistakable. There could hardly be a more effective way of stressing the intimate connection between the mysteries of religion and sex than by linking together the Christian story with the upsurging energies of spring. Yet it is also 'depraved' May, and suddenly we are aware that it is not just the Holy Communion that is being eaten and drunk 'among whispers': that last phrase also relates to the empty, slightly sinister cosmopolitan world in which Gerontion's life has been betrayed, his passion and ardour have been divided and lost.[6] The series of glimpses of various figures in this world illustrates what Eliot tries to convey by his use of images. His design is to give the *exact* perceived detail, without comment, and let that picture carry its own connotations. As he said once in conversation, the images here are 'consciously concrete'; they correspond as closely as possible to something he has actually seen and remembered. But he also believes that if they are clearly rendered, they will stand for something larger than themselves; they will not depend for their apprehension upon any private reference, but will become 'unconsciously general.'

A similar example of his use of imagery is provided by a passage in the final poem of *Ash Wednesday,* which is also notable in revealing the direction in which Eliot had travelled in the ten years intervening since 'Gerontion.' His technique is greatly simplified: the quick contrasts of Donne and Laforgue have been replaced by something nearer to the limpidity of Dante. He wants to embody the reflection that although he desires to focus his mind upon God, although his spirit, in its ascent of the purgatorial mount, does not want to be distracted any longer by sensuous beauty, still,

> though I do not wish to wish these things,
> From the wide window towards the granite shore
> The white sails still fly seaward, seaward flying
> Unbroken wings
>
> And the lost heart stiffens and rejoices
> In the lost lilac and the lost sea voices
> And the weak spirit quickens to rebel
> For the bent golden-rod and the lost sea smell
> Quickens to recover
> The cry of quail and the whirling plover
> And the blind eye creates
> The empty forms between the ivory gates
> And smell renews the salt savor of the sandy earth

It is impossible to divorce the reflection from the imagery. Exact description of memories of the varied loveliness of the New England coast expresses the very sensation of his distraction, of his turning, in spite of his will, away from the contemplation of God. He is momentarily forgetful of the penance of humility appointed for Ash Wednesday; for he has been lured back to the human realm of desire and loss by the enchantment of the senses.

I do not want to give the impression of trying to make Eliot's poetry seem easy, or of trying to demonstrate that his lines possess just one restricted meaning. Indeed, by his own account of the 'consciously concrete' and 'unconsciously general,' it is apparent that he believes that poetry should suggest much more than it can state directly to the mind. However, recognition of this impalpable element in poetry, of the fact that its range of meaning inevitably varies for different readers, does not diminish in the least the poet's responsibility to centre on the specific and distinct. Eliot notes that speaking of 'the incommunicable' in literature may often mean merely 'the vague and unformed.' His understanding of the fact that 'suggestion' is of doubtful worth unless radiating from a solid core of meaning, lies behind his analysis of why a confessedly slight poem like Marvell's 'The Nymph and the Fawn' is so much more satisfactory than William Morris's comparable effort in 'The Nymph's Song to Hylas':

The effect of Morris's charming poem depends upon the mistiness of the feeling and the vagueness of its object; the effect of Marvell's poem upon its bright, hard precision. . . The verses of Morris, which are nothing if not an attempt to suggest, really suggest nothing; and we are inclined to infer that the suggestiveness is the aura around a bright clear centre, that you cannot have the aura alone.

This necessity to concentrate on something definite is exactly what Eliot means by his repeated statement that the evoca-

tion of emotion by means of complete, concrete objectification is the only right way of expressing emotion in art.

The way in which Eliot secures both definiteness of statement and indefiniteness of suggestion by building his imagery upon an objective structure can be seen in the third
poem in *Ash Wednesday*:

> *At the first turning of the second stair*
> *I turned and saw below*
> *The same shape twisted on the banister*
> *Under the vapour in the fetid air*
> *Struggling with the devil of the stairs who wears*
> *The deceitful face of hope and of despair.*
>
> *At the second turning of the second stair*
> *I left them twisting, turning below;*
> *There were no more faces and the stair was dark,*
> *Damp, jaggèd, like an old man's mouth drivelling,*
> > *beyond repair,*
> *Or the toothed gullet of an agèd shark.*
>
> *At the first turning of the third stair*
> *Was a slotted window bellied like the fig's fruit*
> *And beyond the hawthorn blossom and a pasture scene*
> *The broadbacked figure drest in blue and green*
> *Enchanted the maytime with an antique flute.*
> *Blown hair is sweet, brown hair over the mouth blown,*
> *Lilac and brown hair;*
> *Distraction, music of the flute, stops and steps of the mind*
> > *over the third stair,*
> *Fading, fading; strength beyond hope and despair*
> *Climbing the third stair.*
>
> *Lord, I am not worthy*
> *Lord, I am not worthy*
>
> > *but speak the word only.*

The symbol of the stair is perfectly concrete whether or not
we identify it with Dante's purgatorial mount. For, in either
case, the rhythms give us the feeling of difficult climbing
movement; and each turning of the stair presents a distinct

stage of spiritual struggle. The sinister horror of what he saw below him at the first turning is heightened by the very ambiguousness of the expression, 'the same shape.' Does it mean a spectre that he has been fleeing from and has felt to be pursuing him up the stair? Or, more terrifying still, does it mean his own very likeness, thus stressing the obsession with self, the inability of the individual to escape from the bonds of his own identity? Such thoughts constituted one of the principal torments for the poet of *The Waste Land,* who had

> *heard the key*
> *Turn in the door once and turn once only,*

who was unable to break through the circle of his own loneliness by giving himself up to any belief, and so, with nothing external or absolute to base his life upon, felt himself mocked equally by hope and despair, since both were equally groundless. In keeping with such reflections, the damp blackness of the second turning could represent the state of mind voiced in 'The Hollow Men,' although, speaking strictly, the utter emptiness which pervades that poem would seem to belong more entirely to an *Inferno.* But with the next turning, the poet has moved on to a third state, forgetting his despair in a glimpse of the loveliness possible in this world, and yet looking now to something 'beyond hope and despair,' to faith which shall sustain him, to his salvation through divine grace.

In such a manner Eliot's images are at the same time both exact and suggestive in their portrayal of these three spiritual stages. It is more than likely that he meant the turnings of his stair to represent something even more definite, to remind the reader that they correspond in general to the three main divisions of Dante's hill of Purgatory.[7] At the foot of the hill were those whose sin had been the greatest, who had been guilty of love distorted, those who had loved evil things instead of God, those whose self-absorbed pride had shut them off from Him. Higher up were those whose love of God had been defective; higher still, the least gravely sinful, those who had loved excessively things which should take only a secondary place in the affections, among them the sensual and lustful. (A hint of the correspondence between these particular qualities of excess and Eliot's third stair is underscored by the image describing the window itself 'bellied like the fig's fruit.') Such a reminder that the stages of the soul which Eliot is depicting correspond also to a completely developed pattern of philosophic and religious thought, would remove the experience from anything purely personal, and would thus enable it to possess a more universal significance.

Perhaps the most important thing that is revealed by applying Eliot's conception of the 'objective correlative' to his own work is the essentially dramatic nature of all his poetry. What is said by one of the speakers in his 'Dialogue on Dramatic Poetry' certainly seems expressive of one of his own most sustained beliefs:

What great poetry is not dramatic? Even the minor writers of the Greek Anthology, even Martial, are dramatic. Who is more dramatic than Homer or Dante? We are human beings, and in what are we more interested than in human action and human attitudes? Even when he assaults, and with supreme mastery, the divine mystery, does not Dante engage us in the question of the human attitude towards this mystery—which is dramatic?

In the terms of this description the dramatic element in poetry lies in its power to communicate a sense of real life, a sense of *the immediate present*—that is, of the full quality of a moment as it is actually felt to consist. It was Ezra Pound's great service to modern poetry to rescue the lyric from musical prettiness by his reaffirmation of the importance of such direct presentation of actuality, by his determination, as he declared in his manifesto 'Against the Crepuscular Spirit in Modern Poetry,' to substitute 'for dreams

[67]

—men.' [8] This ability to portray the very character of life is rare since it depends upon a firm grasp of experience, and thus demands from the poet a unified sensibility, a capacity of feeling that can closely interweave emotion and thought. It likewise demands a mature realization of the existence of both good and evil, an understanding that life takes on dramatic significance only when perceived as a struggle between these forces. Thus, despite Pound's emphasis on 'human action,' his failure to distinguish between individual responsibility for evil and social circumstance has the result of making his journalistic conception of Hell in the *Cantos* utterly lacking in tragic dignity—a Hell, as Eliot has remarked, 'for the *other people,* the people we read about in the newspapers, not for oneself and one's friends.' Such a Hell not only robs any implied Heaven of all authenticity, but also inevitably renders much of Pound's observation of human beings 'trivial and accidental.'

In the light of these reflections it becomes apparent that the ability to convey a sense of human reality is also destroyed by any facile idealization, or by any effort to escape into a dream world through the hypnosis of sound. The dramatic quality is also wholly lost by the merely reflective poet who, instead of making a union of emotion and thought, instead of thinking in images and thus bringing a living body to his ideas, tends to put his images aside and to fall back on abstract rhetoric when he comes to deliver his statements:

> *We look before and after*
> *And pine for what is not:*
> *Our sincerest laughter*
> *With some pain is fraught;*
> *Our sweetest songs are those that tell of saddest thought.* [9]

These reflections perhaps also make clear why it is accurate to say that Donne is a dramatic poet but not Spenser; that the songs of Campion and Shakespeare are dramatic but not those of Swinburne,[10] or why Keats at the time of his death was increasingly absorbed with the desire to write plays; [11] or why, among poets of seemingly equal stature like Wyatt and Surrey, the ability to cut through graceful Renaissance decoration of sentiment to a bare statement of immediate emotion is what gives a few poems of the former their heightened vitality.[12]

In defining Eliot's particular dramatic quality it is relevant to quote Rémy de Gourmont's brief characterization of symbolism, in his *Book of Masks:* 'a tendency to take only the characteristic detail out of life, to pay attention only to the act by which a man distinguishes himself from another man, and to desire only to realize essentials, results.' There could hardly be a better account of the way in which Eliot endeavours to portray 'human action and human attitudes.' He sets out to make his characters actual by confining his description of them to a perceived significant detail or characteristic gesture. This is the method by which he lets us conceive the nature of Princess Volupine by means of a glimpse of her outstretched 'meagre, blue-nailed, phthisic hand.' Or again, he creates the dramatic relevance of the figures who throng Gerontion's memory by the way he shows each of them in action. He wants to intermingle description and event in the manner in which they actually associate in a person's impressions; this is the intention emphasized by his statement that he was stimulated by Henry James' example in *The Aspern Papers* to try 'to make a place real not descriptively but by something happening there.' What 'happens' in Eliot's shorter poems is frequently no more than a single observed impression: a girl standing at the top of a stairway 'with a fugitive resentment' in her eyes; a young man handing his cousin the evening paper. Yet, as also in James, there is something both pictorial and dramatic in this single impression, something acutely revelatory of the people described. As James remarked in 'The Art of Fiction':

What is a picture or a novel that is *not* of character? What else do we seek in it and find in it? It is an incident for a woman to stand up with her hand resting on a table and look out at you in a certain way; or if it be not an incident, I think it will be hard to say what it is. At the same time it is an expression of character.

These sentences might describe the effect of Eliot's 'La Figlia che Piange' equally as well as that of one of James's own stories. The more one thinks of Eliot in relation to James, the more one realizes the extent of the similarities between them. They are similarities of content as well as of method. Both James and Eliot, no less than Hawthorne, are mainly concerned with what lies behind action and beneath appearance. In their effort to find the exact situation that will evoke an impression of the inner life, they are occupied too in expressing like states of mind and feeling. Prufrock's rankling inability to give himself to life and the kind of frustration embodied in Eliot's 'Portrait of a Lady' find their parallels many times in James. But even more significant is the realization that the qualities of spirit that rise above frustration in Eliot's later poems, as well as in James's *Portrait of a Lady* or *The Wings of the Dove,* are those which affirm the value of renunciation, sympathy, and tenderness. These qualities have long been dominant in the American strain. All three are to be found in Emily Dickinson, if with a somewhat different effect than in Hawthorne; and the two last are Whitman's most enduring tones in 'When lilacs last in the dooryard bloomed.'

NOTES

1. Hulme was killed in action in 1917, and his essays on "Humanism and the Religious Attitude,' 'Modern Art and Philosophy,' and 'Romanticism and Classicism,' written just before the First World War, were not published until 1924, under the

general title of *Speculations*. Eliot had not known Hulme personally, though he had heard much about him from Pound; and he had not read any of Hulme's essays before they were published, by which time Eliot's own theory of poetry had already matured. Nevertheless certain sentences, from 'Romanticism and Classicism' in particular, foreshadow so exactly a number of the principles which Eliot has also believed in that it is interesting to marshal them here. Especially interesting since a parallel development of thought to many of the same ends helps to make clearer why Eliot felt the urgent necessity of fresh poetic experiment, and indicates that his reaction against the loosely prevailing standards of taste and value was not idiosyncratic but part of an emerging general state of mind.

I prophesy that a period of dry, hard, classical verse is coming.
The period of exhaustion seems to me to have been reached in romanticism. We shall not get any new efflorescence of verse until we get a new technique, a new convention. . .
Exactly why this dry classical spirit should have a positive and legitimate necessity to express itself in poetry is utterly inconceivable to them [i.e. to those who 'think that verse means little else than the expression of unsatisfied emotion.'] . . . It [the necessity] follows from the fact that there is another quality, not the emotion produced, which is at the root of excellence in verse.
There are then two things to distinguish, first the particular faculty of mind to see things as they really are, and apart from the conventional ways in which you have been trained to see them. This is itself rare enough in all consciousness. Second, the concentrated state of mind, the grip over oneself which is necessary in the actual expression of what one sees. To prevent one falling into the conventional curves of ingrained technique, to hold on through infinite detail and trouble to the exact curve you want. Wherever you get this sincerity, you get the fundamental quality of good art without dragging in infinite or serious.

Hulme also formulated the contrasting views of 'romanticism' and 'classicism' which Eliot has likewise followed:

Put shortly, these are the two views, then. One, that man is intrinsically good, spoilt by circumstance; and the other that he is intrinsically limited, but disciplined by order and tradition to something fairly decent. To the one party man's nature is like a well, to the other like a bucket. The view which regards man as a well, a reservoir full of possibilities, I call the romantic; the one which regards him as a very finite and fixed creature, I call the classical.

[71]

For further ramifications of this aspect of Eliot's thought, see below, Chap. IV, note 2.

2. Eliot formulated this passage in the course of his discussion of 'Hamlet and His Problems,' as a result of his dissatisfaction with the obscurities of that play, with Shakespeare's partial inability there to handle his 'intractable' emotional material by finding an adequate objectification for it.

3. Sufficient warning to critics against the direct reading of a poet's life (or the critic's own prepossessions) into a poet's work is furnished by Eliot himself in the course of his discussion of 'the fatigued Shakespeare, a retired Anglo-Indian, presented by Mr. Lytton Strachey,' and of 'the messianic Shakespeare, bringing a new philosophy and a new system of yoga, presented by Mr. Middleton Murry.' I trust that Eliot's comment may be of use to such critics as Granville Hicks, whose whole treatment of Eliot in his history of recent American literature consists in identifying the poet's own life with some of the lines which express Gerontion's despair, and thereupon summarily dismissing him as of little value since he has no message of hope for contemporary America.

I admit that my own experience, as a minor poet, may have jaundiced my outlook; that I am used to having cosmic significances, which I never suspected, extracted from my work (such as it is) by enthusiastic persons at a distance; and to being informed that something which I meant seriously is *vers de société;* and to having my personal biography reconstructed from passages which I got out of books, or which I invented out of nothing because they sounded well; and to having my biography invariably ignored in what I *did* write from personal experience; so that in consequence I am inclined to believe that people are mistaken about Shakespeare just in proportion to the relative superiority of Shakespeare to myself.

This passage might also be pondered by C. Day Lewis, who tried to argue seriously, in *A Hope for Poetry,* that 'Prufrock' should be read as an allegory of Eliot's own life, not only up to the time of the composition of that poem, but also since.

4. René Taupin, work cited, p. 215.

5. These three propositions, along with Pound's other principal observations on the art of poetry, are to be found in the section called 'A Retrospect' in the volume of essays, *Pavannes and Divi-*

sions, 1918. They had, however, appeared previously, from 1912 onward, especially in 'A Few Don'ts by an Imagiste,' in *Poetry,* March 1913.

Eliot has written in detail about Pound not only in the Introduction to his selection from Pound's poems published in 1928, but also in the earlier, little-known pamphlet, *Ezra Pound, His Metric and Poetry,* 1917, in which he suggests what he himself had learned from Pound's craftsmanship. It is worth recalling that Eliot not only dedicated *The Waste Land* to 'il miglior fabbro,' but that in *After Strange Gods* he still believes that Pound 'is probably the most important living poet in our language.'

Any detailed study of Eliot's background and development would find a fertile field in determining how many of his tastes and opinions first crystallized as a result of his early close association with the author of *Personae.*

6. The way in which Eliot combined fragments from many lives into the character of the old man may be observed in his borrowings from *The Education of Henry Adams* and from A. C. Benson's biography of Edward Fitzgerald. The passage in Adams (which was pointed out to me by Robert G. Davis) comes at the beginning of the chapter describing his settling in Washington, and the richness of its spring so foreign to a New Englander:

The Potomac and its tributaries squandered beauty. . . Here and there a Negro log cabin alone disturbed the dogwood and the judas-tree. . . The tulip and the chestnut tree gave no sense of struggle against a stingy nature. . . The brooding heat of the profligate vegetation; the cool charm of the running water; the terrific splendor of the June thundergust in the deep and solitary woods, were all sensual, animal, elemental. No European spring had shown him the same intermixture of delicate grace and passionate depravity that marked the Maryland May. He loved it too much as if it were Greek and half human.

Eliot's theme is, of course, the loss of such ecstasy when cut off from the roots of faith.

The passage in Benson (which was noted by Morton Zabel) occurs where he is weaving together some excerpts from Fitzgerald's letters, and making interpolations of his own: 'Here he sits, in a dry month, old and blind, being read to by a country boy, longing for rain:—"Last night . . . we heard a Splash of

Rain, and I had the book shut up, and sat listening to the Shower by myself—till it blew over, I am sorry to say, and no more of the sort all night. But we are thankful for that small mercy." ' Benson's words virtually form the opening lines of Gerontion's soliloquy; and as Zabel added, in a letter to me, Benson's 'whole book, with its picture of Fitzgerald in his pathetic, charming, and impotent old age, pondering on the pessimism of Omar, and beating out the futility of his final years, may have crystallized in Eliot's mind the situation . . . of "Gerontion." ' It is notable that both the Adams and Fitzgerald passages contain allusions to water, the absence of which life-giving source was to be one of the chief symbols of *The Waste Land*.

7. This interpretation was first suggested to me by Mr. Robert Lehman, of Cincinnati, Ohio.

8. In this aim Pound was enthusiastically indebted to Browning, as his poem 'Mesmerism' declares. This enthusiasm of Pound's Eliot does not seem ever especially to have shared, though he has remarked, in an unpublished lecture on the late nineteenth-century background for modern poetry, that Browning was the only poet of that period 'to devise a way of speech which might be useful for others,' that what he had to teach lay in his 'use of non-poetic material,' in his reassertion of 'the relation of poetry to speech.' And for the eventual writer of the literary history of the twentieth century, Eliot's handling of the dramatic soliloquy, a form that has been called 'the most flexible and characteristic genre of English verse,' cannot be divorced from the impetus furnished by *Men and Women* to *Personae*.

9. The distinctions that I am trying to establish concerning the nature of the dramatic quality in poetry are sufficiently complex to demand several illustrations as the conclusion of the notes to this chapter.

Eliot himself, in his essay on 'The Metaphysical Poets,' made a similar use of the term 'reflective poet' in his contrast between the writer who can turn his varied interests and speculations into poetry, and the writer who 'merely meditates upon them poetically':

The difference is not a simple difference of degree between poets. It is something which had happened to the mind of England between the time of Donne or Lord Herbert of Cherbury and the time of Tennyson and Browning; it is the difference between the intellectual poet and the reflective poet. Tennyson and Browning are poets, and they think; but they do not feel their thought as immediately as the odour of a rose. A thought to Donne was an experience; it modified his sensibility. . . The sentimental age began early in the eighteenth century, and continued. The poets revolted against the ratiocinative, the descriptive; they thought and felt by fits, unbalanced; they reflected. In one or two passages of Shelley's 'Triumph of Life,' in the second 'Hyperion,' there are traces of a struggle toward unification of sensibility. But Keats and Shelley died, and Tennyson and Browning ruminated.

By way of contrast with the passage of rhetorical reflective poetry that I have quoted, an example of thinking in images which sustains a full dramatic quality would be the passage on Time in *Troilus and Cressida:*

> *Time hath, my lord, a wallet at his back,*
> *Wherein he puts alms for oblivion,*
> *A great-sized monster of ingratitudes:*
> *Those scraps are good deeds past; which are devour'd*
> *As fast as they are made, forgot as soon*
> *As done: perseverance, dear my lord,*
> *Keeps honour bright: to have done, is to hang*
> *Quite out of fashion, like a rusty mail*
> *In monumental mockery. Take the instant way;*
> *For honour travels in a strait so narrow*
> *Where one but goes abreast: keep then the path;*
> *For emulation hath a thousand sons*
> *That one by one pursue: if you give way,*
> *Or hedge aside from the direct forthright,*
> *Like to an entered tide they all rush by*
> *And leave you hindmost;*
> *Or, like a gallant horse fall'n in first rank,*
> *Lie there for pavement to the abject rear,*
> *O'errun and trampled on: then what they do in present,*
> *Though less than yours in past, must o'ertop yours;*
> *For time is like a fashionable host,*
> *That slightly shakes his parting guest by the hand,*
> *And with his arms outstretch'd, as he would fly,*
> *Grasps in the comer: welcome ever smiles,*
> *And farewell goes out sighing. O! let not virtue seek*
> *Remuneration for the thing it was;*
> *For beauty, wit,*
> *High birth, vigour of bone, desert in service,*
> *Love, friendship, charity, are subjects all*
> *To envious and calumniating time.*

And Dante, even in his passages of intricate philosophical speculation, still uses the most concrete imagery as a 'means of making the spiritual visible.' For example, consider the prolonged simile that enables him to put his discourse on the Freedom of the Will, and on the Soul (in the sixteenth canto of the *Purgatorio*), into the simplest, sensuous terms:

From the hands of Him who loves her before she is, there issues like a little child that plays, with weeping and laughter, the simple soul, that knows nothing except that, come from the hands of a glad creator, she turns willingly to everything that delights her. First she tastes the flavour of a trifling good; then is beguiled, and pursues it, if neither guide nor check withhold her. Therefore laws were needed as a curb; a ruler was needed, who should at least see afar the tower of the true City.

This passage is of further interest in that Eliot was indebted to it in his 'Animula,' in the opening lines which constitute the one full expression he has made of the nature of childhood:

> *'Issues from the hand of God, the simple soul'*
> *To a flat world of changing lights and noise,*
> *To light, dark, dry or damp, chilly or warm,*
> *Moving between the legs of tables and of chairs,*
> *Rising or falling, grasping at kisses and toys,*
> *Advancing boldly, sudden to take alarm,*
> *Retreating to the corner of arm and knee,*
> *Eager to be reassured, taking pleasure*
> *In the fragrant brilliance of the Christmas tree,*
> *Pleasure in the wind, the sunlight and the sea;*
> *Studies the sunlit pattern on the floor*
> *And running stags around a silver tray;*
> *Confounds the actual and the fanciful,*
> *Content with playing-cards and kings and queens,*
> *What the fairies do and what the servants say.*

10. Campion's verse owes its peculiarly exquisite music not only to the fact that it was meant to be sung, but primarily to the circumstance that it was written during the one period in English history when the art of poetry was closely allied to the art of music. Nevertheless, as Eliot himself has noted, there is never a confusion between Campion's poetic and his musical effects. His images are fresh and clear and convey a distinct meaning at the same time that his rhythm creates a pure beauty of sound. His verse is an excellent example of Eliot's rather

understated dictum that 'for poetry to approach the condition of music . . . it is not necessary that poetry should be destitute of meaning.' Sense in Campion is not sacrificed to sound; his most musical lines still present a sharp dramatic picture:

> When thou must home to shades of underground,
> And there arrivèd, a new admirèd guest,
> The beauteous spirits do engirt thee round,
> White Iope, blithe Helen, and the rest,
> To hear the stories of thy finish'd love
> From that smooth tongue whose music hell can move;
>
> Then wilt thou speak of banqueting delights,
> Of masques and revels which sweet youth did make,
> Of tourneys and great challenges of knights,
> And all these triumphs for thy beauty's sake:
> When thou hast told these honours done to thee,
> Then tell, O tell, how thou didst murder me!

Swinburne's aberration was that he tended to blur together sense and sound, to use language merely as musical incantation. As a result he seldom gives us 'clear, visual images'; he uses the most general words more for their association than for any precise denotation; and he rarely conveys the feeling that he has observed any immediate object. For example,

> I shall never be friends again with roses;
> I shall loathe sweet tunes, where a note grown strong
> Relents and recoils and climbs and closes,
> As a wave of the sea turned back by song.
> There are sounds where the soul's delight takes fire,
> Face to face with its own desire;
> A delight that rebels, a desire that reposes;
> I shall hate sweet music my whole life long.

This may seem an unfairly extravagant choice of lines, though they are from 'The Triumph of Time,' and if you don't pay much attention to what they say, their movement can produce upon you the full effect of Swinburne's peculiar hypnotic jag. And even in his most celebrated work, as in the opening chorus from 'Atalanta,' there is the same tendency to lose any clarity of outline in the intoxication with sound:

> For winter's rains and ruins are over,
> And all the season of snows and sins. . .

It is not surprising that Eliot concluded in 1920:

Language in a healthy state presents the object, is so close to the object that the two are identified. They are identified in the verse of Swinburne solely because the object has ceased to exist, because the meaning is merely the hallucination of meaning, because language, uprooted, has adapted itself to an independent life of atmospheric nourishment. . . Only a man of genius could dwell so exclusively and consistently among words as Swinburne. His language is not, like the language of bad poetry, dead. It is very much alive, with this singular life of its own. But the language which is more important to us is that which is struggling to digest and express new objects, new groups of objects, new feelings, new aspects, as, for instance, the prose of Mr. James Joyce or the earlier Conrad.

11. It is debatable whether Keats would have been able to realize this ambition. Certainly his attempt in 'Otho' revealed very little grasp of dramatic structure or of the exact nature of a scene; and, though the fragment of 'King Stephen' showed a marked advance in such respects, the fact that, unlike Shakespeare, he had no living traditions of the stage to rely upon, would have remained a heavy liability. Nevertheless the peculiar kinship between the quality of his imagination and that of the younger Shakespeare—a kinship that has been recognized by such diverse critics as Matthew Arnold and Middleton Murry—lies in Keats's ability to present with such fullness the impressions of all his senses that they embody a whole way of viewing life. For example, he can convey in three lines in a letter to his friend Reynolds a completely experienced perception (aural and kinaesthetic as well as visual):

> *A white sail shows above the green-head cliff,*
> *Moves round the point, and throws her anchor stiff;*
> *The mariners join hymn with those on land.*

Such lines are essentially dramatic; they give you the feeling of sharing immediately in an event. They possess the very quality which Eliot values most highly in both the metaphysicals and symbolists, the quality of 'transforming an observation into a state of mind.'

'Endymion' and even 'Hyperion' may seem somewhat vaporous owing to an inadequate conception of the struggle between good and evil. But the suffering out of which the final Odes sprang endowed Keats with a deep knowledge of that struggle,

[78]

and made them dramatic lyrics of the highest order, in a way
in which 'Epipsychidion' is not. (Though, as Eliot also has noted,
Shelley's last poem, the unfinished 'Triumph of Life,' revealed
him on the verge of a more adequate understanding of human
nature, and, concurrently, with a growing ability to escape from
rhetorical abstraction and to clothe his thought in more accurate
images.)

The one passage that shows what Keats might have accomplished in writing plays is the fragment, apparently addressed
to Fanny Brawne, which he left on the margin of the manuscript
of 'The Cap and Bells':

> *This living hand, now warm and capable*
> *Of earnest grasping, would, if it were cold*
> *And in the icy silence of the tomb,*
> *So haunt thy days and chill thy dreaming nights*
> *That thou would [st] wish thine own heart dry of blood*
> *So in my veins red life might stream again,*
> *And thou be conscience-calmed—see here it is—*
> *I hold it towards you.*

These lines might have been spoken by a character in an Elizabethan play.

12. Surrey did a great service to the development of English
poetry by his pioneer experiments in blank verse, and by his
naturalization of the conventions, and some of the melody, of
the Italian love lyric. But Wyatt, though less technically facile,
was able on a few occasions to break through these highly restricted 'literary' conventions, which prescribed for the lover
simply the Petrarchan tones of adoration and complaint, and
to give voice to feelings much closer to emotional reality. His
best poem deserves to be better known. It is contained in *The
Oxford Book of English Verse*, but given there in the 'edited'
form in which it was published, after Wyatt's death, by Richard
Tottel in his famous *Miscellany*. Tottel devoted his efforts to
smoothing away irregularities of accent in order to make the
lines conform to a more conventionally musical pattern. This
was unfortunate, since a good deal of the poem's peculiar vigour,
its note of directness, and its dramatic expression of passionate
scorn depend upon the very halting irregularity of the rhythm,
its sudden starts and heavily weighted pauses:

They flee from me that sometime did me seek,
With naked foot stalking in my chamber.
I have seen them gentle, tame and meek,
That now are wild and do not remember
That sometime they put themselves in danger
To take bread at my hand; and now they range
Busily seeking with a continual change.

Thankt be fortune, it hath been otherwise
Twenty times better; but once, in special,
In thin array, after a pleasant guise,
When her loose gown from her shoulders did fall,
And she me caught in her arms long and small,
Therewith all sweetly did me kiss,
And softly said: 'Dear heart, how like you this?'

It was no dream; I lay broad waking:
But all is turned thorough my gentleness
Into a strange fashion of forsaking;
And I have leave to go of her goodness;
And she also to use new-fangleness.
But since that I so kindely am served,
I fain would know what she hath deserved.

Surrey can be considered the forerunner of Daniel and the
general run of Elizabethan sonneteers; Wyatt, at his best, fore-
shadows Donne's kind of love lyric as well as Shakespeare's son-
nets. Thus Wyatt and Surrey can provide another example of
my attempted distinction between dramatic and reflective poetry
(developed in note 10 above), between poetry that communicates
emotion and poetry that merely talks about communicating it,
a contrast that could be carried through other periods of English
poetry, between such various poems as *The Rape of the Lock*
and *The Castle of Indolence;* Blake's 'Echoing Green' and *The
Deserted Village;* the 'Ode to a Nightingale' and *In Memoriam;*
The Waste Land and *The Testament of Beauty.*

IV

THE WAY A POET COMMUNICATES HIS MEANING:
THE AUDITORY IMAGINATION

The sense of musical delight with the power of producing it is a gift of the imagination.—Coleridge.

THE foregoing account of Eliot's use of images and of the method by which he fuses them into an organic structure leads directly to the way in which he believes that a poet communicates his meaning. Though the images in the lines quoted from 'Gerontion' are predominantly visual, the passages from *Ash Wednesday* underscore the fact that Eliot's observation is not simply with his eyes. What bothers him most in Arnold's poetry is the thinness of the musical quality; and in pointing out that Arnold never emphasizes such quality as one of the fundamental virtues of poetic style, he develops the most searching passage that I know on what he calls the 'auditory imagination': *Imp*

the feeling for syllable and rhythm, penetrating far below the conscious levels of thought and feeling, invigorating every word; sinking to the most primitive and forgotten, returning to the origin and bringing something back, seeking the beginning and the end. It works through meanings, certainly, or not without meanings in the ordinary sense, and fuses the old and obliterated and the trite, the current, and the new and surprising, the most ancient and the most civilized mentality. Arnold's notion of 'life,' in his account of poetry, does not perhaps go deep enough.[1]

Eliot's realization that the feeling for rhythm is 'far below the conscious levels of thought' elucidates what he meant when remarking, in connection with *The Divine Comedy*, that 'poetry can communicate before it is understood.' That is to say, it can work upon the ear the depth of its incantation; it can begin to stir us by its movement before our minds can say what it is that we feel. And Eliot's enumeration of so many qualities inhering in the pattern of the syllables reveals how much he implies when asserting that the primary means of testing a new poet is by whether or not he possesses an individual rhythm. For as he remarked, as a result of his study of Donne, 'a style, a rhythm, to be significant, must also embody a significant mind, must be produced by the necessity of a new form for a new content.' In the additional light of the above detailed description, a poet's rhythm will also indicate his particular union of past and present, his double possession of 'the most ancient and the most civilized mentality' in his awareness of the primitive magic of sound joined with his quickening sense of the new manifestations of life in his own day. His rhythm, therefore, must embody an acute feeling both for the music of words, and for their richly varied connotations.

Eliot has said that his own poems have often taken their inception from some cadence running through his head. One minor but revelatory instance is how his feeling for syllable and rhythm, encountering a striking passage even in prose, seems to have started the movement of his 'Triumphal March.' It gives us thereby a glimpse of his own auditory imagination in action. I began reading Charles Maurras's *L'Avenir de l'Intelligence* largely because Eliot had recommended it as one of the standard expositions of the classical point of view.[2] It opens with an ironic account of how each new tawdry journalistic triumph is now greeted in the streets with procession and applause. A mediocre writer is represented as talking excitedly:

—Y avez-vous pris garde? dit-il, les yeux serrés, le chef de l'État s'était fait représenter. Nous avions la moitié du Conseil des ministres et les deux préfets. Tant de généraux! Des régiments avec drapeau, des musiciens et leur bannière. Sans compter beaucoup de magistrats en hermine et de professeurs, ces derniers

sans leur toge, ce qui est malheureux.—Et les soldats faisaient
la haie?—Ils la faisaient.—En armes?—Vous l'avez dit.—Mais que
disait le peuple?—Il n'en croyait pas ses cent yeux!

I have given a whole paragraph in order that the reader can
also sense the possible way in which Eliot's ear quickened at
'Tant de généraux'; and can perceive not only the source
from which he took his final marching line: 'Et les soldats
faisaient la haie? ILS LA FAISAIENT'; but, more importantly,
the source from which he incorporated something of the
sensation of movement that he transformed into the rhythms
of his verse. In calculating what elements a poet's ear takes
from the sources of his inspiration, it should also be observed that Eliot transformed the context here into quite
a new pattern of his own, utilising, however, a suggestion
of the futile bustle of the crowd to contrast with the momen-
tary vision of the serenity of his hero.[3]

Still in the light of his account of the auditory imagination, we are now enabled to understand more completely
what he meant when, in outlining Swinburne's defects, he
declared that 'language in a healthy state presents the object,
is so close to the object that the two are identified.' That remark emphasizes again the union of sense and thought which
struck him as the chief virtue of the metaphysicals. It takes
on greater significance if placed beside another observation
on language from an uncollected essay:

Whatever words a writer employs, he benefits by knowing as
much as possible of the history of those words, of the uses to
which they have already been applied. Such knowledge facili-
tates his task of giving to the word a new life and to the language a new idiom. The essential of tradition is this: in getting
as much as possible of the whole weight of the history of the
language behind his word.[4]

Such feeling for words on Eliot's part is what endows him
with the quality singled out by Clive Bell, his unfailing distinction in 'phrasing.' He knows that a word is not a fixed

counter, that it brings with it varying colours from all its previous usages, that precisely what colour and energy flash forth
from it in his poem depends on what stress he gives it, and
on its exact position in the context. He was aware, before
Richards and Empson began their exploration of ambigui-
ties, that a word can carry different shades of meaning at
once, that its connotation is extended or shifted according to
its relation to the moving procession of other words which
precede and come after. Thus, in the passage quoted from
'Gerontion,' the utter shift in the implication of the phrase
'among whispers,' when it is seen in the light, not only of
what went before, but of the lines which follow. With the
figurative expression, 'the word . . . swaddled with darkness,' the picture of the Christ child is also present to the
imagination; and so with 'judas'—in this context it cannot
stand merely as the name of a flowering tree—it too is caught
up in the whole tone of betrayal and in turn reinforces it.
It will do the reader no good to protest that he wants his
words to behave themselves and have simply one meaning
at a time; for no more than people can words be brought
into close relationship without effect upon each other. And
one test of a poet's skill lies in the degree of his awareness
of what effects he has caused in his lines, of what forces the
flow of his rhythm has made his words release. One of the
most characteristic examples in Eliot's poetry of the power
of his auditory imagination, both for beauty of sound and
for imbedded richness of connotation, is the opening passage
of 'A Game of Chess':

> The Chair she sat in, like a burnished throne,
> Glowed on the marble, where the glass
> Held up by standards wrought with fruited vines
> From which a golden Cupidon peeped out
> (Another hid his eyes behind his wing)
> Doubled the flames of sevenbranched candelabra
> Reflecting light upon the table as

The glitter of her jewels rose to meet it,
From satin cases poured in rich profusion;
In vials of ivory and coloured glass
Unstoppered, lurked her strange synthetic perfumes,
Unguent, powdered, or liquid—troubled, confused
And drowned the sense in odours; stirred by the air
That freshened from the window, these ascended
In fattening the prolonged candle-flames,
Flung their smoke into the laquearia,
Stirring the pattern on the coffered ceiling.
Huge sea-wood fed with copper
Burned green and orange, framed by the coloured stone,
In which sad light a carvèd dolphin swam.

It is not accidental that he starts with an allusion to Shake-speare's Cleopatra, since his intention is to heap up an impression of Renaissance splendour and luxuriance. Little by little all the senses are bathed 'in rich profusion'; in fact, a comparison of the sensuous fullness of this passage with Keats's description of perfumes in 'Lamia' would not make Eliot's lines seem thin.[5] Apparently we are being given an entire sensation of magnificence; we might still be in the Renaissance; nothing intrudes to break the spell until the word 'synthetic'—in this context neutral, denatured, 'modern.' From that point (as the section goes on beyond the part quoted), the actual situation is gradually revealed. This is not Cleopatra, but a cosmopolitan society woman at her dressing table. All this opulence merely surrounds a weak meaningless existence. Gradually also the atmosphere itself is revealed as heavy and overpowering. There may be a reminiscence of the barge on the Nile; the senses may be *'drowned* in odours,' the 'carvèd dolphin' may *swim* in the 'sad light'; but all these references serve finally to remind you that there is no freshening water in this parched waste land.

This intricately sensitive awareness of words is not merely a subtle refinement. Distinction in phrasing cannot exist unless it has been created by distinction of sensibility. The principal reason why Eliot believes that it is important for the poet to know as much about language as possible is because he also believes that 'every vital development in language is a development of feeling as well'; that words and thought cannot be separated; that it follows necessarily that, since Racine and Baudelaire are the two greatest French 'masters of diction,' they 'are also the greatest two psychologists, the most curious explorers of the soul.' For only by releasing the magical possibilities in words can the poet impart the feeling that he has sunk 'to the most primitive and forgotten,' that his thought and emotions have returned 'to the origin' and have brought back a deeper sense of life.[6]

Observations like these, as well as the poetry they illustrate, extend the import of the poet's 'sense of his own age,' and the way in which he makes it articulate. Eliot knows that no experiment in art is valuable unless it is psychologically necessary, that no great innovator has cared for novelty for its own sake but, like Shakespeare, 'has been driven on, step by step, in his innovations, by an inner necessity, and that the novelty of form has been rather forced upon him by his material than deliberately sought.' This intimate inner necessity is bound up with the history of the age in which the poet lives, with its main movements of thought and of feeling. For, as Eliot has noted of Wordsworth's revolution in poetry, 'Any radical change in poetic form is likely to be the symptom of some very much deeper change in society and in the individual.'

Such an approach leads to the reason for Eliot's own irregular verse. He knows that the main point about new poetry is always 'how disturbing it is to the conventional consciousness,' that the shock tends to be 'by its syntax more than by its sentiments,' and that, speaking strictly, versification 'is essentially a disturbance of the conventional language.' What fascinated his ear in the early seventeenth-

on verse forms

century poets was the 'constant evasion and recognition of regularity,' the reliance on the iambic pentameter line and yet the continual skilful withdrawing from it. What strikes him as an essential quality in the most interesting verse is this very hesitation between regularity and irregularity, in correspondence to a psychological perception of the precarious balance that constitutes life itself: 'It is this contrast between fixity and flux, this unperceived evasion of monotony, which is the very life of verse.' The clamour for 'free verse' which was rising from some of the Imagists at the time when Eliot was beginning to write found in him its most penetrating critic.[7] For he has believed from the start that 'there is no freedom in art,' that 'freedom is only truly freedom when it appears against the background of an artificial limitation.'

Yet he has also recognized a debt to the theorists of *vers libre:* their good effect was not to free verse, but to quicken the realization that there were other ways of writing it than in the prevailing conventional Georgian modes. They demonstrated that the constant expectation of rhyme had 'thickened the modern ear,' and no doubt helped to carry Eliot forward in his perception that 'rhyme removed, much ethereal music leaps up from the word.' But whereas they stopped in that discovery, Eliot went farther and observed that 'this liberation from rhyme might be as well a liberation of rhyme'; that once rhyme was no longer dully expected, it could then be used 'for a sudden tightening-up, for a cumulative insistence, or for an abrupt change of mood'—an observation that was doubtless reinforced later by his reading of Hopkins, whose technique of sprung-rhythm has been one of the principal 'discoveries' for poets since the First World War. What Eliot learned from the 'new poetry' was that reaction against 'the erudite complexities' of Swinburne's versification should lead to more

[87]

form and not less. This was one of the reasons why he was stimulated to write several of the poems in his 1920 volume in the tight quatrains of Gautier as a corrective to the flowing excesses of *vers libre,* to write compact verse in which the mind of the poet should be actually felt to be moving.

Thus Eliot's technical experiments are seen never to be merely imitations of other poets. As a craftsman he believes that the most satisfactory verse ever written in English, in the later plays of Shakespeare or the tragedies of Webster, broke through the conventional pattern of blank verse, often 'at the moments of highest intensity,' in order to encompass a necessary shade of the poet's meaning. And with this perception goes his knowledge that 'a man who devises new rhythms is a man who extends and refines our sensibility; and that is not merely a matter of "technique." ' [8] Eliot is aware that there are unexplored, probably not wholly explorable, connections between a poet's rhythm and what can loosely be called the rhythm of his age. In the light of history, it is not just a coincidence that the melodious extravagant opulence of the Spenserian stanza was devised as a reflection of the age of Elizabeth; nor that another whole age responded to the sensible balance of the *Essay on Man.* No poet is wholly conscious of attempting to make these connections; he only knows that his inner ear responds to a certain pattern of sound as being right for what he has to express. Eliot has pointed out the folly of trying to be modern by copying the journalistic details which separate the present from the past; he knows that 'one is not modern by writing about chimney-pots, or archaic by writing about oriflammes.' Far deeper perceptions are required; their nature is adumbrated in Eliot's account of the auditory imagination. A further suggestion is added in his remark that 'perhaps the conditions of modern life (think how large a part is now played in our sensory life by the internal-combustion en-

gine!) have altered our perception of rhythms.' [9] These conditions lie behind the cadences of his occasional effective
machine-images:

> *At the violet hour, when the eyes and back*
> *Turn upward from the desk, when the human engine waits*
> *Like a taxi, throbbing waiting,*

as well as behind the deliberate mechanization of:

> *When lovely woman stoops to folly and*
> *Paces about her room again, alone,*
> *She smoothes her hair with automatic hand,*
> *And puts a record on the gramophone.*

For this is part of the idiom, the stimulus for which came
from Baudelaire, to express moments of fragile beauty in
the city, but more often the overwhelming oppression of
its weight. The conditions of modern life not only affect
machine-imagery; they lie equally behind the syncopated
rhythms of *Sweeney Agonistes* and the rich and broken music of *Ash Wednesday*.

And finally, Eliot's conception of the auditory imagination, his understanding of the fact that poetic rhythm by
means of its power of incantation is able to renew one of the
most primitive elements of man's experience at the same time
that it gives expression to the last subtle nuances of civilized
feeling, is of particular interest in throwing light on one of
the most profoundly suggestive statements that he has yet
made of his own aims as an artist. He was stimulated to this
statement by a reflection in one of Lawrence's letters that
'the essence of poetry with us in this age of stark and un-
lovely actualities is a stark directness, without a shadow of
a lie, or a shadow of deflection anywhere. Everything can
go, but this stark, bare, rocky directness of statement, this
alone makes poetry, to-day.' Upon these sentences Eliot has
remarked:

This speaks to me of that at which I have long aimed, in writing poetry; to write poetry which should be essentially poetry, with nothing poetic about it, poetry standing naked in its bare bones, or poetry so transparent that we should not see the poetry, but that which we are meant to see through the poetry, poetry so transparent that in reading it we are intent on what the poem *points at,* and not on the poetry, this seems to me the thing to try for. To get *beyond poetry,* as Beethoven, in his later works, strove to get *beyond music.* We never succeed, perhaps, but Lawrence's words mean this to me, that they express to me what I think that the forty or fifty original lines that I have written strive towards.[10]

One passage that Eliot must have had in mind when making those remarks is that of the bare but musical lines in the final section of *The Waste Land,* the creation of which seems to have taken rise from his memory of the sound of the 'water-dripping song' of the hermit-thrush, thus giving another glimpse into the way in which his own auditory imagination works:

> If there were the sound of water only
> Not the cicada
> And dry grass singing
> But sound of water over a rock
> Where the hermit-thrush sings in the pine trees
> Drip drop drip drop drop drop drop drop
> But there is no water

NOTES

1. Yeats's reaction against Arnold's conception of poetry seems to have been on similar, though less defined grounds: 'I believe that all men will more and more reject the opinion that poetry is a "criticism of life," and be more convinced that it is a revelation of a hidden life.'

2. The first indication of the direction in which Eliot's thought was going as it moved away from the region of 'The Hollow

Men,' 1925, was given in 'The Idea of a Literary Review,' the leader in *The New Criterion,* for January 1926. Eliot stated there what he meant by 'classicism,' a word which has been rendered so nearly meaningless by the variety of connotations it has picked up since the Renaissance that it requires a fresh definition at every use. I have therefore deliberately excluded it from my text, particularly since Eliot himself has recognized, in *After Strange Gods,* how much confusion both this word and its equally protean opposite, 'romanticism,' are capable of causing. The following passage, however, reveals what Eliot implies in his use of the term, and how much more resilient his conception is than that of the new Humanists:

I believe that the modern tendency is toward something which, for want of a better name, we may call classicism. I use the term with hesitation, for it is hardly more than analogical: we must scrupulously guard ourselves against measuring living art and mind by dead laws of order. Art reflects the transitory as well as the permanent condition of the soul; we cannot wholly measure the present by what the past has been, or by what we think the future ought to be. Yet there is a tendency—discernible even in art—toward a higher and clearer conception of Reason, and a more severe and serene control of the emotions by Reason. If this approaches or even suggests the Greek ideal, so much the better: but it must inevitably be very different. I will mention a few books, not all very recent, which to my mind exemplify this tendency:

Réflexions sur la violence, by Georges Sorel; *L'Avenir de l'Intelligence,* by Charles Maurras; *Belphégor,* by Julien Benda; *Speculations,* by T. E. Hulme; *Réflexions sur l'Intelligence,* by Jacques Maritain; *Democracy and Leadership,* by Irving Babbitt. Anyone who is acquainted with two or more of these books will understand my use of the word 'tendency,' for the theories and points of view are extremely different.

Nevertheless, each of the books cited would have definite importance for anyone setting out to trace the development of Eliot's thought.

3. To suggest to those unfamiliar with the poem the way in which its rhythm was started moving by Maurras's prose, the opening and closing lines will serve. It begins:

Stone, bronze, stone, steel, stone, oakleaves, horses' heels
Over the paving.

And the flags. And the trumpets. And so many eagles.
How many? Count them. And such a press of people.
We hardly knew ourselves that day, or knew the City.
This is the way to the temple, and we so many crowding the way.
So many waiting, how many waiting? what did it matter, on such a day?

The concluding lines are quoted in the course of my analysis of the poem on pp. 139-40. The mocking tone in Maurras's paragraph is also suggested in the lines that follow immediately after the prolonged recital of the innumerable machines of war:

> *What a time that took. Will it be he now? No,*
> *Those are the golf club Captains, these the Scouts,*
> *And now the société gymnastique de Poissy. . .*

There are several other instances when prose passages seem to have started cadences in Eliot's mind that were ultimately transformed into new patterns. The opening lines of 'The Journey of the Magi,' which establish the rhythm of that poem, are taken, with comparatively slight alterations, from one of the Sermons of Lancelot Andrewes. Another passage from Andrewes contains the first hint of the movement of the lines on 'The Word' which begin the fifth section of *Ash Wednesday*. (Both these selections from the Sermons are quoted by Eliot in his essay on Andrewes.)

One of Ruskin's letters to Susan Beever about Rose La Touche, the little girl with whom he fell in love when himself in middle life, seems very suggestive of some of the material that enters into 'A Cooking Egg': 'But, Susie, *you* expect to see your Margaret again, and you will be happy with her in heaven. I wanted my Rosie *here*. In heaven I mean to go and talk to Pythagoras and Socrates and Valerius Publicola. I shan't care a bit for Rosie there, she needn't think it.'

My friend John Finley, Jr., pointed out to me a certain similarity between the following sentences from Rupert Brooke's description of the first shocked impression made upon one of his friends by the announcement, 'We're at war with Germany,' and 'the heap of broken images' that set the tone of the opening of *The Waste Land*:

My friend ate and drank, and then climbed a hill of gorse, and sat alone, looking at the sea. His mind was full of confused images, and the sense of strain. In answer to the word 'Germany,' a train of vague thoughts dragged across his brain. The pompous middle-class vulgar-

ity of the buildings of Berlin; the wide and restful beauty of Munich;
the taste of beer; innumerable quiet, glittering cafés; the *Ring;* the
swish of evening air in the face, as one skis down past the pines; a
certain angle of the eyes in the face; long nights of drinking and singing and laughter . . . certain friends; some tunes; the quiet length of
evening over the Starnbergersee.

In these last two cases, however, it is wholly a question of the
possible suggestion of some of the material which Eliot's imagination seized upon, and transmuted into a new context; not
of any effect on the actual movement of his lines.

It seems apparent that, to an even greater extent than most
poets, Eliot has been sensitively responsive to the rhythms of
other writers. This can be observed not only in the lines from
other poets that he has woven into the texture of his own verse,
but also in more generalized debts. Frequently, in reading an
Elizabethan play, one can come across passages that must have
echoed in his ear, and have formed a deeply buried substratum
for his own different effort. Read, for example, this passage from
The Changeling which Eliot quoted in the essay on Middleton
that he wrote eight years after 'Gerontion':

> *O come not near me, sir, I shall defile you!*
> *I that am of your blood was taken from you*
> *For your better health; look no more upon't,*
> *But cast it to the ground regardlessly,*
> *Let the common sewer take it from distinction.*

And then read these lines from Eliot's poem:

> *I that was near your heart was removed therefrom*
> *To lose beauty in terror, terror in inquisition.*
> *I have lost my passion: why should I need to keep it*
> *Since what is kept must be adulterated?*

The content of the two passages is not at all the same; but the
contexts they rise from both express a horror of lust, and thus
adumbrate the possible reason why Middleton's cadences stirred
in Eliot's memory at the moment that he was shaping his lines.

In like fashion, a passage from Chapman's *Bussy D'Ambois*
has asserted itself near the conclusion of 'Gerontion':

> *fly where men feel*
> *The burning axletree, and those that suffer*
> *Beneath the chariot of the snowy Bear . . .*

> De Bailhache, Fresca, Mrs. Cammel, whirled
> Beyond the circuit of the shuddering Bear
> In fractured atoms.

C. L. Barber has suggested this possible connection: 'chariot' has been transformed into 'circuit' quite naturally in the modern poet's more scientific, less mythological image, while 'the sense of suffering turns "snowy" into "shuddering"; and Eliot's whole conception of a catastrophe comes out in the description of the breaking apart of Chapman's concentrated suffering "beneath the chariot"—maybe.'

4. In *The Tyro*, No. 3, 1922.

5. This comparison was suggested by Laura Riding and Robert Graves in *A Survey of Modernist Poetry* (London, 1927), pp. 170-71. The passage from Keats reads:

> Of wealthy lustre was the banquet-room
> Fill'd with pervading brilliance and perfume:
> Before each lucid pannel fuming stood
> A censer fed with myrrh and spiced wood,
> Each by a sacred tripod held aloft,
> Whose slender feet wide-swerved upon the soft
> Wool-woofèd carpets: fifty wreaths of smoke
> From fifty censers their light voyage took
> To the high roof, still mimick'd as they rose
> Along the mirror'd walls by twin-clouds odourous.

6. That Eliot has long pondered this conception that the mature artist must combine 'the most ancient and the most civilized mentality' is shown by an observation which he made fifteen years before writing the passage on 'the auditory imagination,' in a review of Wyndham Lewis's *Tarr* (in *The Egoist*, September 1918): 'The artist, I believe, is more *primitive,* as well as more civilized, than his contemporaries, his experience is deeper than civilization, and he only uses the phenomena of civilization in expressing it.'

7. The most detailed statement of his views is contained in his 'Reflections on Vers Libre,' *The New Statesman*, 3 March 1917. I have also quoted a few phrases from an unpublished lecture on Ezra Pound.

8. This sentence is from 'Isolated Superiority,' a review of Pound's *Personae* in *The Dial,* January 1928. Such a remark reveals the principal quality on which Eliot bases his claims for the value of Pound. He knows that Pound's translations are not merely technical exercises, since 'if one can really penetrate the life of another age, one is penetrating the life of his own.' Indeed, 'one of Pound's most indubitable claims to genuine originality' is the way in which he brings to life the Provençal and early Italian poets. He sees them 'as contemporary with himself, that is to say, he has grasped certain things in Provence and Italy which are permanent in human nature. He is much more modern, in my opinion, when he deals with Italy and Provence, than when he deals with modern life.'

This last passage, from Eliot's Introduction to Pound, rounds from another angle onto the question of a poet's 'sense of his own age' as well as onto the relation between literature and life. Therefore I want to quote it even further:

. . . When he deals with antiquities, he extracts the essentially living; when he deals with contemporaries, he sometimes notes only the accidental. But this does not mean that he is antiquarian or parasitical on literature. Any scholar can see Arnaut Daniel or Guido Cavalcanti as literary figures; only Pound can see them as living beings. Time, in such connections, does not matter; it is irrelevant whether what you see, really see, as a human being, is Arnaut Daniel or your greengrocer. It is merely a question of the means suited to the particular poet, and we are more concerned with the end than with the means.

These reflections have immediate bearing on one of the perennial fallacies of American criticism. Only the narrowest conception of realism can hold that an author necessarily acquires any sovereign virtue by recording the surface details of a middle-western city instead of those of eighteenth-century Peru. Shakespeare's Roman generals are no less 'timeless Englishmen' than his inhabitants of the forest of Arden. The characters in Cooper's historical novels are not as wooden as those in his satires of contemporary life: his one living figure, the Leatherstocking, owes whatever vitality he possesses to the fact that he is the imaginative symbol for a whole stage of American life and aspiration, a stage which Cooper knew only in memory. Goethe's Faust is as entirely a nineteenth-century German as Marlowe's is an Elizabethan.

To be sure, the author of a poem or novel dealing with another period or place than that in which he lives runs greater danger of tripping over properties, of mistaking costumes for people, of producing a *tour de force* or a mere museum piece. It is probably more rewarding as a rule for a writer to try to strike to the heart of life by the gradual difficult mastery of his own immediate surroundings. But it is an entire misconception of the way that the shaping imagination works to assume that a man's observation is limited to what is before his eyes; or that, once having observed, he cannot cast his findings into a transmuted guise with an enhancement rather than a loss of their energy; or that he cannot discover his symbols of living reality in memory and myth as well as in the headlines.

9. Eliot made this observation in 1926 in the course of his brief introduction to *Savonarola,* a dramatic poem written by his mother, Charlotte Eliot. As Eliot remarked, in elucidation of his belief that 'a work of historical fiction is much more a document on its own time than on the time portrayed': 'This Savonarola is a disciple of Schleiermacher, Emerson, Channing, and Herbert Spencer'—a remark which describes some of the intellectual background of the world into which Eliot was born.

10. These remarks were included in an unpublished lecture on 'English Letter Writers'—primarily on Keats and Lawrence—which was delivered in New Haven, Conn., during the winter of 1933.

V

THE INTEGRITY OF A WORK OF ART

Flaubert incorporait toute sa sensibilité à ses œuvres. . . Hors de ses livres, où il se transvasait goutte à goutte, jusqu'à la lie, Flaubert est fort peu intéressant.—de Gourmont.

Of Shakespeare notably, of Jonson less, of Marlowe (and of Keats to the term of life allowed him), one can say that they *se transvasaient goutte à goutte;* and in England, which has produced a prodigious number of men of genius and comparatively few works of art, there are not many writers of whom one can say it.—Eliot.

ELIOT'S particular sense of his age is revealed with growing clarity as you read connectedly through his work. You are left with the impression of his pre-eminent quality as one of integrity, of an extraordinary wholeness within his limits. What gives authority to the interpretation of life emerging from both his poetry and his prose is the fact that it is authentic, that it corresponds not to any preconceived standard of what he *ought* to think or believe, but to what he has actually felt and understood by listening to himself, by studying the deepest elements in his nature. It cannot be affirmed too often that one of the greatest values of poetry consists in this very authenticity. By giving an exact expression to the thing he has perceived and felt, whether it be the glimpse of a ship coming to anchor or a complex meditation on the fear of death, the poet fulfils one of his most primitive functions. Among the earliest uses of verbal art was the charm, where, by means of his skill in finding just the right words, the gifted savage was able to exorcise an evil spirit or to propitiate a good one. This power of words to enchant remains only as a metaphor. But it is still true that the most moving poetry performs a kindred service by the fullness with which it wins for us a vision of loveliness, or with which, in describing ugliness and horror, it thereby lifts from us their burden. And the secret of this power remains the same: it lies in the accuracy by which the poet, utilizing every resource lurking in word and rhythm, manages to convey a heightened sensation of the object itself.

As his epigraph for the opening essay in *The Sacred Wood* Eliot used this sentence from de Gourmont: 'Eriger en lois ses impressions personnelles, c'est le grand effort d'un homme s'il est sincère.' That Eliot recognizes this particular kind of sincerity to be among the rarest of human attainments is manifested by his praise of an author with whose view of life he would have little sympathy: 'Mr. Hemingway is a writer for whom I have considerable respect; he seems to me to tell the truth about his own feelings at the moment when they exist.' [1] But for Eliot it is not enough to tell the truth about one's own feelings, great gift though that is, and possible only to a man who is fully alive, who has cut through all conventionality and abstraction, who is endowed both with sensitiveness and with unusual technical expertness. For if such a gift is to result in valuable expression, it is necessary that the feelings themselves should be part of a balanced pattern of life; or, to put it in the terms of the epigraph from Maurras which Eliot used at the opening of his introduction to Dante: 'La sensibilité, sauvée d'elle-même et conduite dans l'ordre, est devenue un principe de perfection.'

In view of my lasting impression both of Eliot's sincerity and coherence, I am increasingly puzzled by the two most prevalent false approaches to him, by those critics who welcomed the poet of *The Waste Land* as a modern prophet for having voiced our disillusion, and now damn him because he moves towards faith; as well as by those more traditionally faithful souls, largely academic, who deplored his earlier work as dangerously radical, and now welcome him with hosannas. I am also unable to understand those who, like Paul Elmer More,[2] find an inconsistent cleavage between the

qualities of his verse and criticism. Not only does the quiet
assurance of his work in both mediums give you the sense
throughout, as Edmund Wilson observed, that Eliot has
thought connectedly and persistently 'about the relations
between the different phases of human experience'; [3] but, in
addition, his criticism steadily illuminates the aims of his
verse, while his verse illustrates many aspects of his critical
theory. The only relevant distinction that can be made between them is one he himself has suggested: 'In one's prose
reflexions one may be legitimately occupied with ideals,
whereas in the writing of verse one can only deal with actuality.'

It is certainly apparent that the same preoccupations have
pervaded his work from the beginning. What renders the
character of Prufrock not just grotesque or absurd but poignantly real is that as a result of a gradual accumulation of
undertones and especially of the final dramatic lines, one
can glimpse, beneath the banal surfaces and futile indeci-
sions of his life, his perception of beauty, his understanding
of the meaning of love and sympathy, if an utter inability to
gain them. From that early poem onward, through the much
deeper accents of 'Gerontion' and *The Waste Land,* the prevailing theme of Eliot's poems is the emptiness of life without belief, an emptiness that finally resounds with sickening
fear and desperation in 'The Hollow Men.' Though they
could hardly have been forecast before their appearance, the
religious poems follow in natural sequence from such persistent absorption in the nature of spiritual reality. They are
scarcely poems of easy faith; they mark rather the direction
in which the poet's experience is leading him, that he has
ascended step by step from the pit of his Inferno. They voice
the desire for belief, the understanding of its importance to
the human spirit, the impalpable movements of the poet's
mind from doubt towards acceptance, his gradual compre-

hension of what, encountering it in Baudelaire, he has called 'the greatest, the most difficult of the Christian virtues, the virtue of humility.' This desire and understanding re-echo through *Ash Wednesday*, and suggest one reason why so many references in that series of poems are to the structure of the Catholic Mass. For the more Eliot has reflected on life, the more he has understood that 'every man who thinks and lives by thought must have his own scepticism, that which stops at the question, that which ends in denial, or that which leads to faith and which is somehow integrated into the faith which transcends it.' And the words with which he ended his introduction to the *Pensées* of Pascal are seen to have great bearing on himself: 'I can think of no Christian writer, not Newman even, more to be commended . . . to those who doubt, but who have the mind to conceive, and the sensibility to feel, the disorder, the futility, the meaninglessness, the mystery of life and suffering, and who can only find peace through a satisfaction of the whole being.' [4] Such satisfaction for Eliot could not lie in Hawthorne's or Henry James's 'awareness of spiritual reality' with an indifference to dogma. He needed to find something in which his mind as well as his emotions could rest.[5]

But not only have Eliot's explorations of the soul followed a consistent, if difficult, path; he has given them further unity by the unusual degree to which he has composed his work around certain focal points. The line from Dante that appears among the fragments shored against his ruins in the broken ending of *The Waste Land*, 'Poi s'ascose nel foco che gli affina,' is not there by chance. The passage from which it comes has been returned to by Eliot many times:

> 'Ara vos prec, per aquella valor
> que vos guida al som de l'escalina,
> sovegna vos a temps de ma dolor.'
> Poi s'ascose nel foco che gli affina.

('And so I pray you, by that Virtue which leads you to
the topmost of the stair, be mindful in due time of my
pain.' Then dived he back into that fire which refines
them.)

Ara vos prec was the title that he gave to the collection of
his verse in 1919. The words, 'Sovegna vos,' appear in *Ash
Wednesday;* the section of that poem quoted above was first
published separately under the title *Som de l'Escalina;* and,
indeed, the theme of the speech sounds repeatedly through
the whole sequence. The lines were spoken by the Provençal
poet Arnaut Daniel, in the twenty-sixth canto of the *Purgatorio,* which describes the penance of the lustful. The fact
that Eliot has reminded his reader of this canto on such
widely separate occasions indicates that it has spoken deeply
to him of what he knows to be central factors in human life.
His way of indicating this knowledge also characterizes what
he considers valuable in an individual's experience. He objects to 'confessions,' to the way in which a Rousseau dwells
on an emotion, not because of any intrinsic importance but
merely because he himself has felt it. On the contrary, Dante,
Eliot believes, 'had experiences which seemed to him of
some importance; not of importance because they had happened to him and because he, Dante Alighieri, was an important person who kept press-cutting bureaux busy; but
important in themselves; and therefore they seemed to him
to have some philosophical and impersonal value.'

The mood of 'Gerontion,' which also recognizes the intimate relation of sex and religion, is not far from the tone of
these lines of Dante; but there is this distinction: in the reflections of the old man there is a full acceptance of suffering,
but not the realization embodied in Eliot's later poems that
'the souls in purgatory suffer because they *wish to suffer,* for
purgation.' (The tenacity of Eliot's preoccupations is revealed further by recalling that he made this statement just

before quoting once more, in his essay on *The Divine Comedy,* the Arnaut Daniel lines.)

These lines also connect directly with Eliot's belief that the creation of poetry itself springs out of suffering, a reiterated belief which helps define the particular nature of his poetry. He seems to hold as a self-evident psychological truth that all art is an effort 'to metamorphose private failures and disappointments,' that even Shakespeare 'was occupied with the struggle—which alone constitutes life for a poet—to transmute his personal and private agonies into something rich and strange, something universal and impersonal.' Eliot is convinced that life for the perceptive individual must be painful; in his view, the relative thinness of Arnold's lines is owing to the fact that Arnold knew the discipline of culture, but not enough of the discipline of suffering. He goes on to elucidate that the primary thing for the poet 'is not to have a beautiful world with which to deal: it is to be able to see beneath both beauty and ugliness; to see the boredom, and the horror, and the glory. The vision of the horror and the glory was denied to Arnold, but he knew something of the boredom.'

One factor to be firmly grasped in this account of the origin of poetry is that the poet's suffering has no especial value in itself; it brings him an understanding of human life, and is thus material for art; but to become poetry it must be transformed from something personal into something of wider validity. That is to say, in a sentence from 'Tradition and the Individual Talent,' which like so many statements from that compact essay has taken on deeper significance in the light of Eliot's later writing, 'The more perfect the artist, the more completely separate in him will be the man who suffers and the mind which creates.' Nor is any premium put upon the poet's suffering beyond the necessity of recognizing that, though pain is not desired by man, it is actual. What drew Eliot to Baudelaire was in part his 'strength merely to suffer. He could not escape suffering and could not transcend it, so he attracted pain to himself. But what he could do, with that immense passive strength and sensibilities which no pain could impair, was to study his suffering.'

Eliot realizes that such a view of life is a limitation, that it is very unlike the balance of Dante, but likewise that what gives it reality is its comprehension of existing evil, which implies at least by contrast the possibility of a positive state of good. Eliot has acknowledged that he arrived at a full appreciation of the *Paradiso* much later than of the *Inferno* owing to his hatred of the 'cheerfulness, optimism, and hopefulness' of the nineteenth century, which left him with 'the prejudice that poetry not only must be found only *through* suffering but can find its material only *in* suffering.' The strength of his dissatisfaction with the inadequacy of the previous generation's conception of the relation of good to evil is again paralleled by Yeats's horror at the brittle superficial optimism of such a view of life as Shaw's, who once appeared to him in a dream in the form of a sewing-machine, 'that clicked and shone, but the incredible thing was that the machine smiled, smiled perpetually.'

Eliot's conception of poetry as rising out of suffering suggests the limitations of his own. It is not easy to think of Homer or Chaucer or Dryden as considering poetry in this way (there is a conspicuous lack of comment on Chaucer in Eliot's criticism); and it is notable that both Dante and Shakespeare found their material in many other states of feeling as well. Eliot's view emphasizes the fact that the elements of tradition which have seemed most alive to him, in the symbolists as well as in the metaphysicals, and which have consequently given the most immediate stimulus for the shaping of his own verse, are relatively narrow and strained in their dramatic intensity. But recognition of his limits once more points to his wholeness within them: where

since Tourneur or Middleton has there been such bare sustained dramatic verse of the first order as in lines like these:

> *After such knowledge, what forgiveness? Think now*
> *History has many cunning passages, contrived corridors*
> *And issues, deceives with whispering ambitions,*
> *Guides us by vanities. Think now*
> *She gives when our attention is distracted*
> *And what she gives, gives with such supple confusions*
> *That the giving famishes the craving. Gives too late*
> *What's not believed in, or if still believed,*
> *In memory only, reconsidered passion. Gives too soon*
> *Into weak hands, what's thought can be dispensed with*
> *Till the refusal propagates a fear. Think*
> *Neither fear nor courage saves us. Unnatural vices*
> *Are fathered by our heroism. Virtues*
> *Are forced upon us by our impudent crimes.*
> *These tears are shaken from the wrath-bearing tree.*
>
> *The tiger springs in the new year. Us he devours.*
> *Think at last*
> *We have not reached conclusion, when I*
> *Stiffen in a rented house.*

And where in modern poetry are there characters realized
with such convincing definiteness as Prufrock and Sweeney?
The completeness with which Eliot has been able to suggest
them within the compass of extremely few lines might indicate how much shrewd perception is packed into their dramatic portrayal. Certainly both represent so widely pervasive
elements in modern city life that they can stand almost as
symbols. They are as unlike as two characters could well be;
and the very chasm between them is typical of the harsh
social disruption which characterizes the city near which
Eliot spent the years of his adolescence. On the one hand,
he could observe the timid inhibitions of Prufrock, re-
gretting situations unexplored but prevented from giving
himself to anything emotionally real by an excessive fas-
tidiousness—his only residue of the Puritan conscience. Such

a figure would belong to Eliot's description of Boston 'society' as 'quite uncivilized, but refined beyond the point of civilization.' At the other extreme there is 'apeneck Sweeney,' whose prototype Eliot has said he first saw in a bar in South Boston, and an enduring impression of whom is provided by one brief description:

> *Sweeney addressed full length to shave*
> *Broadbottomed, pink from nape to base,*
> *Knows the female temperament*
> *And wipes the suds around his face.*
>
> (*The lengthened shadow of a man*
> *Is history, said Emerson*
> *Who had not seen the silhouette*
> *Of Sweeney straddled in the sun.*)

And if it is objected that a middle-aged dilettante and a tough Irishman of the sort whose eyes are 'assured of certain certainties' are hardly widely typical of the life of greater Boston, and that they still don't become so even when you add Miss Helen Slingsby the maiden aunt, and Cousin Harriet with her *Transcript,* sporting Miss Nancy Ellicott who rides to hounds and dances 'all the modern dances,' the palace of dowager Mrs. Phlaccus and the teas of Professor and Mrs. Channing-Cheetah; not forgetting Rachel *née* Rabinovich, Doris 'towelled from the bath,' and Sweeney's other sinister companions from the international underworld—the answer is that even though they by no means do typify the whole life of the city, nevertheless they acutely suggest many of the fragments into which that whole is broken.

When Eliot was creating these figures, he doubtless had no feeling of giving them representative value beyond the fact that he was making ironic poems out of some of his most compellingly recurrent, if painful, perceptions. But partly for that very reason the complete difference between Prufrock and Sweeney is significant of the dangerously violent contrast that confronts any sensitive observer of the city: the thin upper-class 'culture'; the life of the half-educated mass, full-blooded but brutalized. This split yields eloquent evidence for the charge that Emerson himself brought against American life—that it was rich and salty on the common levels, but that it had a repeated tendency to become arid and bleached at the top. The dry intellectualized distrusting of the emotions, which Emerson recognized as the worst blight that had been left by waning Puritanism, still prevails in the vestiges of the genteel tradition, and thus produces distorted lives in which thought and feeling find no harmony. And the jagged cleavage that separates such lives from that of Sweeney and the mass of the populace is sufficient measure of our continued failure to establish anything like a balanced social order.

In drawing attention to the symbolic value of Eliot's two most striking characters there is no intention to suggest that he has created anything like a complete world. Indeed, it is questionable whether any poets in English except Chaucer and Shakespeare have succeeded in so doing. But some readers object that Eliot's view of life is peculiarly narrow; they object to his describing contemporary existence as a waste land. Most of the force of that objection is lost, I believe, when it is understood that he is not thus characterizing the present as distinct from the past, but is probing the implications of certain tragic elements inherent in the very nature of life. Eliot himself gave a warning against the misreading of his poem in a brief comment which he made in 1931: 'I dislike the word "generation," which has been a talisman for the last ten years; when I wrote a poem called *The Waste Land* some of the more approving critics said that I had expressed the "disillusionment of a generation," which is nonsense. I may have expressed for them their own illusion of being disillusioned, but that did not form part of my intention.' Eliot appears to be striking there at the cliché phrase, 'the lost generation,' which, at the moment it was coined by Gertrude Stein, had some relevance to the attitude behind the powerful but narrowly dated stories of Ernest Hemingway; but which, as it has been thoughtlessly if sentimentally repeated, has become increasingly meaningless. There is a great difference between an understanding that tragedy is at the heart of life, and an adolescent self-pitying of one's own generation as being especially unfortunate. The anarchy and futility of war inevitably heighten the sense of the horror in existence; but for this sense to have significance, it must be part of a total vision of the meaning of life.

The value of the tragic writer has always lain in the uncompromising honesty with which he has cut through appearances to face the real conditions of man's lot, in his refusal to be deceived by an easy answer, in the unflinching, if agonized, expression of what he knows to be true. The effect of such integrity is not to oppress the reader with a sense of burdens too great to be borne, but to bring him some release. For, if it is part of the function of every great artist to transform his age, the tragic writer does so not by delivering an abstract idealization of life, but by giving to the people who live in the age a full reading of its weakness and horror; yet, concurrently, by revealing some enduring potentiality of good to be embraced with courage and with an ecstatic sense of its transfiguring glory. Through the completeness of his portrayal of the almost insupportable conditions of human existence, he frees his audience from the oppression of fear; and stirring them to new heart by his presentation of an heroic struggle against odds, he also enables them to conceive anew the means of sustaining and improving their own lives. Only thus can he communicate both 'the horror' and 'the glory.' [6]

Consequently, objection to Eliot's particular limited kind of tragic vision would logically have to be brought also against such writers as Webster or Hawthorne; and could be

THE ACHIEVEMENT OF T. S. ELIOT

made only as a result of that 'systematic judgement' which Arnold found the most worthless of all critical attitudes: the judgement which falls farthest from seeing the object as it is by dismissing a poet for not meeting certain preconceived requirements, that would reject Dryden for not being like Shelley, or Eliot for not giving the same affirmation of life that you find in Keats. In contrast to this attitude, the final way of judging a poet is by the authentic value of what he has actually done; and to gauge this while remembering that, as Eliot himself knows, one of the greatest services of poetry lies in its power to 'make us from time to time a little more aware of the deeper, unnamed feelings which form the substratum of our being, to which we rarely penetrate; for our lives are mostly a constant evasion of ourselves, and an evasion of the visible and sensible world.'

But for many readers who were delighted by the satiric bite of Eliot's earlier poems, and for those who even accepted the present as a waste land in a sense that he hardly meant it,[7] there has grown up a barrier against further appreciation of his work in the fact that he has begun to write religious poetry. For an objection to religious poetry is a widely spread prejudice of to-day. It is felt that the acceptance of dogma is a retreat from facing our present problems, felt most keenly by those who have accepted the even stricter dogma of Karl Marx. In consequence, as Allen Tate phrased it in the only intelligent review of *Ash Wednesday* that I found in any of the well-known periodicals: 'The reasoning that is being brought to bear upon Mr. Eliot's recent verse is as follows: Anglo-Catholicism would not at all satisfy me; therefore, his poetry declines under its influence. Moreover, the poetry is not contemporaneous; it doesn't solve any labor problems; it is special, personal, and it can do us no good.'[8]

It is not my purpose here to attempt either to justify or disparage Eliot's entrance into the Church. My point is the same as Tate's: that for an appreciation of Eliot's poetry the question of our own acceptance or rejection of his doctrine remains irrelevant. This point is fundamental to any understanding of the nature of art, and hence is one of the cruxes of my interpretation of Eliot. It therefore requires some further elaboration. My contention is not that what a poet believes is without importance in determining his relation to the intellectual history of his day. Certainly the principal element in what Eliot means by the poet's 'sense of his own age' is, as we have seen, the way in which he is able 'to express the greatest emotional intensity of his time, based on whatever his time happened to think.' Now one test that might be used in determining the differing rank of poets is the degree to which they possess such a sense: thus Dante is a much more inclusive and catholic poet than Baudelaire in proportion to the greater extent to which he voiced the preoccupations of his contemporaries. Another application of this test would show that any one who set out to-day to write a poem based on the exact scheme of the universe which Dante followed would inevitably betray in every line his lack of any sense of his age, and so of any real understanding of human life. But there is always the danger of applying such a test too abstractly and externally. Particularly in approaching the work of a contemporary there is the risk that, unless his mind seems to be moving along the accustomed grooves of rationalistic scientific thought, and especially if, as in Eliot's case, he reasserts the mystery of life in religious terms, the modern reader will at once jump to the conclusion that he can have nothing valuable to say. But, although it is essential for the artist to observe humanity under the guise of his time, the way he interprets what he observes admits a wide margin of variance. What Blake *saw* was very different from what met the eyes of other men in the eighteenth century; and yet, at this distance, his is revealed to be the profound knowledge of human emotions.

[109]

For, paradoxically, part of what is meant by saying that a great poet gives expression to the life of his time depends on the way in which he reverses many of its popular maxims and cuts through the mass of conventional opinion and prejudice.

What must be remembered in any discussion of the relation of a poet to his age is the truth of the sentence with which Eliot followed the remark quoted in the last paragraph: 'Poetry is not a substitute for philosophy or theology or religion.' It has a function of its own, a function 'not intellectual, but emotional,' the nature of which can be apprehended only in terms of the effect produced by its combination of rhythmical movement with the sound and sense of words—elements which I have sought to analyse in my foregoing chapters. One of the surest ways to fail to understand a poem is to begin by trying to tear the thought from the context in order to approve or disapprove of what it seems to express. For the important thing, as Richards has reaffirmed, is 'not what a poem says, but what it *is*'; and the only way of knowing what it does express is by a sustained awareness of all the formal elements of which it is composed. Only in this way, by experiencing the poem as a whole, and then by evaluating it 'from the inside,' so to speak, by trusting the evidence of your senses for its effect, can you determine whether or not the poem is alive; and thus, in turn, whether or not the poet has a sense of his age, whether what he believes and imagines about human destiny springs from a direct contact with life. A continuously original rhythm cannot be faked; it can arise only from the poet's own response to physical and emotional movement. False diction, words that are not wholly felt, words whose implications are not understood by the poet, artificial metaphors, manufactured symbols—all quickly betray themselves to an eye experienced in the texture of verse. A borrowed structure which has not been fully assimilated—either of thought or of form—will give itself away as baldly as an affected gesture or a secondhand emotion.

The kind of approach to poetry for which I am contending was outlined in part by the demands that Eliot stressed in his early essay on 'The Perfect Critic.' He indicated there the false approach that is made by the reader who likes 'one poet because he reminds him of himself, or another because he expresses emotions which he admires'; who, in brief, simply uses art as an outlet for his egotism. In contrast to that attitude, it is Eliot's conviction that 'the end of the enjoyment of poetry is a pure contemplation from which all the accidents of personal emotion are removed; thus we aim to see the object as it really is and find a meaning for the words of Arnold.'

The attitude expressed in that sentence may seem somewhat stiff; it may seem to remove poetry too completely from everyday life. It is probable that Eliot had such a sentence in mind when, in a new preface to *The Sacred Wood* written in 1928, he regretted a certain tone of 'pontifical solemnity' in these earlier essays. In the intervening eight years he had come to understand more fully 'the relation of poetry to the spiritual and social life of its time and of other times'; [9] to understand likewise that the enjoyment of poetry cannot be wholly divorced from the beliefs it expresses. He had become more aware, for example, that part of the reason why he preferred the poetry of Dante to that of Shakespeare was because it seemed to him 'to illustrate a saner attitude towards the mystery of life'; and, likewise, that part of his distaste for the romantic poets was owing to the lack of correspondence between their beliefs and a mature understanding of experience. Nevertheless, in the course of his study of Dante in the following year, he reiterated his conclusion, which is similar to what Richards has reached from a very different angle,[10] that it is perfectly possible 'to have full literary or poetic appreciation without sharing the beliefs of the poet'; that, indeed, 'there is a distinct pleasure in enjoying poetry as poetry when one does *not* share the beliefs.' If this were not the case it would mean that the range of a modern reader's full appreciation would be limited to very few poets, that only Catholics could appreciate Chaucer, and that no one at all could appreciate Milton or Aeschylus.

Eliot's conclusion rests on the assumption which, in returning to *The Sacred Wood* to write his later preface, he realized as the central one of the book, as the one which gave his various essays whatever coherence they possessed. This assumption was the integrity of a work of art, and was emphasized by 'the repeated assertion that when we are considering poetry we must consider it primarily as poetry and not another thing.' Eliot knows that it is quite impossible to make an adequate definition of poetry; but he also knows that when we criticize and evaluate we are right to begin with the conception of poetry 'as excellent words in excellent arrangement and excellent metre.' Such a statement may seem unnecessarily obvious; but it is particularly necessary to be plain at a time when works of art are increasingly being confused with the doctrines which they embody. The confusion is especially great in dealing with literature since, in approaching an art whose medium is words, it is very hard to make relevant distinctions between content and form, to distinguish the idea from the expression. In painting it is clear that although the frescoes of Rivera spring directly from his belief in the communist cause and have great force as propaganda, his skill as an artist is something very different from this belief, and that what establishes his work as great art is what also established the frescoes of Giotto—of comparable value as propaganda for Christianity: the complete mastery of the demands of his form. Likewise no one would question the permanent worth to the human spirit of the work of such painters as Vermeer or Cézanne, neither of whom was using for his material the representation of any religious or political doctrines whatsoever, but, for the most part, the everyday objects and scenes which surrounded him, and which each transformed into a new realm of space, colour, and design.

It is equally true that although a poem grows organically out of the life of its time, it is not a document but a work of art; that is to say, it possesses in a very real sense a life of its own which is distinct from the biography of its creator and also from any idea or belief that it expresses. Crashaw's poetry has been enjoyed by agnostics as well as by Catholics; it is not read as a statement of doctrine, but because of the burning imagery and ecstatic music with which the poet could invest his feelings. Professor Lowes's demonstration of the extraordinary range of associations from reading and life which fused to form 'The Ancient Mariner' certainly enables us to understand more fully the relation of that poem to the tangled web of newly stirring interests which culminated in the romantic movement, as well as giving us a glimpse into the creative process itself. But the finished poem remains distinct both from those interests and from that process. It is certainly not read for the metaphysical speculation which fascinated Coleridge, or primarily for any other reason than that it is 'an excellent arrangement' of fresh words and haunting rhythm. In the case of Wordsworth, it is true that one cannot read him without at least some sympathy for his transcendental approach to nature. But sympathetic understanding is very different from acceptance; and, the fact that 'Tintern Abbey' is a great poem does not depend on the question of whether or not we agree with Wordsworth's views, but on the realization that these lines beat with the convincing note which only a rarely sincere and original rhythm can communicate, and thus persuade of the genuineness of their vision as they make us share it.

If it is maintained that the preoccupations and beliefs from which Wordsworth's and Coleridge's poetry issued were more central to the emotional and intellectual life of their day than Eliot's preoccupations and beliefs are to ours, I find that extremely hard to demonstrate except in the light of further history. It is too often forgotten that the first rather narrow circulation of the *Lyrical Ballads* of 1798 did not make that date appear to be the beginning of a new epoch that it has since become. In fact the publishers gave away the copyright of the volume because it did not seem valuable enough to keep. But even granting that the current of thought in which Eliot is moving is not the major current of the day, that would not alter my contention, which is also his, that the centre of value in a work of art is in the work produced and not in the emotions or thoughts of the poet, that 'it is not the "greatness," the intensity, of the emotions, the components, but the intensity of the artistic process, the pressure, so to speak, under which the fusion takes place, that counts.' Although they do not embrace any important volume of thought and cannot stand as the major expression of an age, the poems of Marvell are quite as alive still as those of Milton. For Marvell's particular essence, his mature 'alliance of levity and seriousness,' the wise urbanity beneath his 'slight lyric grace,' has been fused into a perfection of form, the only means of creating anything that will endure beyond the irrelevances of change. And such mastery is a rare enough human accomplishment to make us want to understand as much of its secret as we can.

Of all Eliot's poems *Ash Wednesday* would have the best chance of appealing to an audience that could neither read nor write. Even though the feelings which he is expressing are extremely complex, and the sequence of his thought is by no means easy to follow, it nevertheless remains true that on its first hearing the poem is capable of making an instantaneous impression purely through the beauty of its sound. For here Eliot has been able to summon up all the resources

of his auditory imagination in such a way that the listener
can begin to feel the rare force of what is being communicated and to accept the poem as a kind of ritualistic chant,
long before his mind is able to give any statement of its
'meaning.'

As we turn to reading the poem rather than listening to it
aloud, we are increasingly struck by the fresh clarity of the
words and are led to a reflection similar to Eliot's on Dante,
that the style 'has a peculiar lucidity—a *poetic* as distinguished
from an *intellectual* lucidity. The thought may be obscure,
but the word is lucid, or rather translucent.' This is especially true in the second section—for the structure consists
of a series of six progressive developments of a theme rather
than a single whole—where an extraordinarily pure impression of whiteness is created by the imagery which presents
'three white leopards,' the 'brightness' of scattered bones,
'the cool of the day, with the blessing of sand,' as well as
the Lady who

is withdrawn
In a white gown, to contemplation, in a white gown.

Noticing Eliot's resort to allegory, we are again reminded
of what he said in relation to Dante: that 'the allegorical
method makes for simplicity and intelligibility,' that 'for a
competent poet,' it 'means *clear visual images.*' And we realize that it was no accident that *Ash Wednesday* was published in the year after Eliot's essay on Dante, but that his
renewed study of *The Divine Comedy* and the *Vita Nuova*
had flowered into stimulus for his own verse. One marked
departure, however, from Dante's use of allegory is the inevitable absence in Eliot of the strict medieval interpretation of what the figures stand for. In this respect he shows
himself still close to the method of the symbolists (just as
his rhythm in some sections seems to reveal the new influence of Hopkins). For example, when he begins:

Lady, three white leopards sat under a juniper-tree
In the cool of the day, having fed to satiety
On my legs my heart my liver and that which had been contained
In the hollow round of my skull,

it is manifest that the three leopards are less definite in their signification than the three beasts from the opening canto of the *Inferno* which they naturally call to mind, the leopard, the lion, and the she-wolf—though for that matter one also recalls the jungle of commentary that has grown up around the dispute to explain exactly what Dante himself meant to symbolize. Dante possibly intended to have his beasts stand for historical figures and warring political states as well as for the worldly pleasure, ambition, and avarice which were preying on the poet's life. With Eliot we are simply presented the picture of his three beasts 'having fed to satiety'; and for their emotional significance here that picture seems adequate; it is unnecessary to translate them into abstractions such as the world, the flesh, and the devil.

Exactly what Eliot's method is in handling allegory may be seen more plainly in considering the figure of his Lady, for, as a result of the way in which she is described in distinct definite images and yet left at the same time indefinite and suggestive, she can stand at once as Beatrice or a saint or the Virgin herself, as well as being an idealized beautiful woman. Thus, under a very different aspect, we observe an intrinsic likeness here to Eliot's method of expression in *The Waste Land,* and, indeed, in such earlier poems as 'Sweeney among the Nightingales': his desire for a paradoxical precision in vagueness.[11] That is to say, he again wants to make as accurate a description of the object as he can and then let its indefinite associations unfold variously in different readers' minds. For readers of to-day who no longer believe in the elaborate hierarchies and gradations of Dante's system, the figures of Beatrice and the Virgin, though distinct, possess similar connotations. They convey like attributes of merciful intercession. And the way Eliot manages to suggest this quality of both without naming either is another instance of how he indicates the general in the particular, of how he can impart in a single passage a range of different and yet related experiences.

In such fashion are we shown concrete evidence of how a modern poet can profit from Dante, and yet not become archaic. Eliot's suggestion of the purgatorial mount in his prolonged image of the winding stair is equally alive since it does not involve the acceptance of an outmoded cosmography, for no physical existence is implied for the hill, which has been wholly transmuted into a symbol for spiritual struggle and conquest. By his use of the symbol of the Lady, Eliot reveals again what that method of presentation is designed to accomplish in Blake and Yeats as well as in the French poets. The successful symbol possesses its peculiar concentrated vitality through communicating the sense of standing for something larger than itself. Only by its embodiment of the indefinite in the definite, the impalpable in the concrete, can the symbol create the illusion that it is giving expression to the very mystery of life.

Readers of Eliot's earlier poetry, missing the electric shock of his special kind of surprise, may object that the texture of *Ash Wednesday* seems thin. But even in its most limpid passages there is gradually disclosed an unexpected density of implication. Consider the strange aura of feeling which surrounds these three leopards. The act they have done is terrifying, and yet they are so portrayed that our principal reaction is a fascination with their beauty. Just for that reason they seem to set the tone for this second section of the poem, which mounts to its conclusion:

Under a juniper-tree the bones sang, scattered and shining
We are glad to be scattered, we did little good to each other
Under a tree in the cool of the day, with the blessing of sand,

Forgetting themselves and each other, united
In the quiet of the desert. This is the land which ye
Shall divide by lot. And neither division nor unity
Matters. This is the land. We have our inheritance.

Through *The Waste Land* and 'The Hollow Men' resounded the poet's dread of death and dissolution, a shudder at the thought of bones 'rattled by the rat's foot only, year to year.' But here that terror has been transcended in a vision of death itself as the promised land. And in such a mystical vision of the serenity that will follow upon release from the body, even the very agents of dissolution themselves no longer seem terrifying, but are merged into the radiance of death itself become life.

If Eliot is no longer employing the method of sharp contrasts that voiced his poignant sense of the similarity of opposites and thus brought a wide scope of life into his condensed passages, he still can endow his words with an equally valuable potential range of meaning. The fourth section of *Ash Wednesday,* following directly after the tortuous ascent of the stair, presents a glimpse of an earthly paradise whereby the poet evokes imagery that will express the emotions he feels in contemplating the doctrines of Grace and Redemption. Its final lines may appear almost too naïvely simple, with their liquid sounds and transparent colours:

The silent sister veiled in white and blue
Between the yews, behind the garden god,
Whose flute is breathless, bent her head and signed but spoke no
*   word*

But the fountain sprang up and the bird sang down
Redeem the time, redeem the dream
The token of the word unheard, unspoken

Till the wind shake a thousand whispers from the yew

And after this our exile

[118]

But the visionary loveliness is punctuated by that short final line: 'after this glimpse, the exile once more of our life on earth.' The line itself is a phrase from the prayer, 'Salve Regina,' which follows the celebration of the Catholic Mass. The immediate context is: 'To thee do we send up our sighs mourning and weeping in this valley of tears; turn, then, most gracious advocate, thine eyes of mercy towards us; and after this our exile, show unto us the blessed fruit of thy womb, Jesus.' If the reader is also aware of that context, the line in the poem not only points away from the vision back to life, but also from life once more back to the vision, and thus re-emphasizes the turning movement upon which so much of the entire poem is built.

In fact, that movement—which is set up with the rhythm of the opening lines of the first section,

> *Because I do not hope to turn again*
> *Because I do not hope*
> *Because I do not hope to turn,*

crabbed lines that suggest turning in their very denial of its hope—more than any other element in the poem enforces the final impression that this is not an accomplished literary exercise in the traditional materials of devotional verse, but a work that corresponds to some of the deepest and most enduring feelings in the mind of its creator. So far in my analysis, by focusing on some of the most immediately appealing passages of sensuous beauty, I have probably obscured this integral element in the rhythm: the way it suggests the movement of the mind of the poet back and forth from doubt to acceptance. Perhaps the most evident measure of Eliot's technical expertness is the extraordinary alternation throughout the poem of two contrasting styles: one through its quiet clearness suggesting his moments of vision; the other through its laboured cadences expressing the returning agony of his debate with himself. Shortly after his glimpse of beatitude in the garden follows the tormented series of questions:

Will the veiled sister pray for
Those who walk in darkness, who chose thee and oppose thee . . .
Will the veiled sister pray
For children at the gate
Who will not go away and cannot pray:
Pray for those who chose and oppose . . .
Will the veiled sister between the slender
Yew trees pray for those who offend her
And are terrified and cannot surrender
And affirm before the world and deny between the rocks
In the last desert between the last blue rocks
The desert in the garden the garden in the desert
Of drouth, spitting from the mouth the withered apple-seed.

This is the same dry torturing desert of rock that haunted the poet in the final section of *The Waste Land;* and the balance that is sustained in *Ash Wednesday* between knowledge of the desert and perception of the garden gives a tone of authority to both, and thus to the range of experience which they encompass. This poem is not an escape from the problem of life into an easy dream world. Its most urgent notes are suggested by the connotations of its title. On Ash Wednesday is performed the ritual of anointing the forehead with ashes, while the priest recites: 'Remember, man, that thou art dust, and unto dust thou shalt return.'

In a few sentences in *After Strange Gods* Eliot put his finger on the usual weakness of religious poetry:

Why, I would ask, is most religious verse so bad; and why does so little religious verse reach the highest levels of poetry? Largely, I think, because of a pious insincerity. The capacity for writing poetry is rare; the capacity for religious emotion of the first intensity is rare; and it is to be expected that the existence of both capacities in the same individual should be rarer still.

People who write devotional verse are usually writing as they want to feel, rather than as they do feel.

It is apparent from all of Eliot's work that he would like to be able to feel a more compelling faith than he does, that one of the severest problems of life to-day as he has found it is the great difficulty for the individual to give himself completely to any belief. Nevertheless, he has not written as he would like to feel, or as he thinks he ought to feel, but as he does feel; and consequently, in *Ash Wednesday* as in *The Waste Land,* he has given dramatic expression to a whole complex state of mind. Failure to perceive his dramatic structure has led to the most obvious quarrel with the poem. 'I am made a little tired,' wrote Edmund Wilson, and many others have echoed him, 'at hearing Eliot, only in his early forties, present himself as an "aged eagle" who asks why he should make the effort to stretch his wings.' That question, which is asked in the halting opening lines, depends for its final significance on the way that it is seen in the light of the completed poem. In these opening lines, as in 'Prufrock,' Eliot is turning his irony upon himself; here is the dramatic portrayal of an individual as he appears to himself at one moment of soliloquy. The emptiness of the attitude disclosed in this question is thrown into sharpest relief by the way in which the final section of the poem recurs to this phrase, but with the significant shift from 'Because I do not hope to turn again' to 'Although I do not hope to turn again.'

For as a result of his acceptance of humility and his partial ascent of the purgatorial mount, the fibre of his life has been strengthened, so that even his moments of temptation and perplexity no longer take the form of the unrelieved blackness of hopelessness, but of an unexpected renewal of desire for life of the senses. And this fresh understanding of the possibilities of life is pointed by the contrast in imagery between these lines in the first section:

Because these wings are no longer wings to fly
But merely vans to beat the air
The air which is now thoroughly small and dry
Smaller and dryer than the will

and these in the last:

. . . though I do not wish to wish these things
From the wide window towards the granite shore
The white sails still fly seaward, seaward flying
Unbroken wings

And the lost heart stiffens and rejoices. . .

Once more Eliot has devoted his attention to finding the right 'objective correlative.' His lyrical poetry is still primarily dramatic—it is illuminating that he made one of the characters in his 'Dialogue on Dramatic Poetry,' written two years before *Ash Wednesday,* say that 'the consummation of the drama, the perfect and ideal drama, is to be found in the ceremony of the Mass.' And it seems to me as false to object to his utterance of a mood of world-weariness as, making all distinctions between the volume of experience brought to bear, it would be to consider it a defect that Shakespeare, still under forty, spoke his disillusion in the soliloquies of *Hamlet.* Only by means of the uncompromising sensitiveness with which Eliot has persisted in his effort to find the exact pattern for his expression, has he succeeded in communicating to the reader the shades and nuances which compose for any experience its living character. As a result, by the time we reach the last poem of the the series, we have a full sense of the wavering of an individual spirit, its desire to lose itself in the universal Will, and yet its continual distraction back to the world of desire and loss. In proportion to the human reality of this indecision, we are able to feel how his doubt is 'integrated into the faith that transcends it' in the soaring desire for union voiced in the final prayer:

[122]

Blessèd sister, holy mother, spirit of the fountain, spirit of the
  garden,
Suffer us not to mock ourselves with falsehood
Teach us to care and not to care
Teach us to sit still
Even among these rocks,
Our peace in His will
And even among these rocks
Sister, mother
And spirit of the river, spirit of the sea,
Suffer me not to be separated

And let my cry come unto Thee.

The feelings expressed in *Ash Wednesday* not only furnish grounds for the principal contemporary objection to religious poetry by denying the present goodness and progressive perfectibility of man. In addition, many of them run counter to the demand for an unqualified affirmation of optimistic confidence and a faith in the unfailing efficacy of immediate action. Nevertheless, though I do not share Eliot's belief in Anglo-Catholic dogma, by every test of word and rhythm, sense and sound, I receive a reiterated impression of the honesty with which *Ash Wednesday* has faced the nature of actual human existence, and thus of its being a wholly authentic poem.[12]

NOTES

1. Commentary in *The Criterion,* April 1933.

2. In 'The Cleft Eliot,' *The Saturday Review of Literature,* 12 November 1932.

3. Wilson's chapter on Eliot in *Axel's Castle: A Study in the Imaginative Literature of* 1870-1930 (New York, 1931), is less satisfactorily rounded than those on Joyce and Proust since he is seemingly not as sensitive to the nature of poetry as to that of prose, and at all events devotes too great a proportion of his

effort to outlining the influences and thought which enter into Eliot's poetry, not enough to analysis of the quality which welds these materials into their significance—Eliot's pre-eminent ability as an artist. As a result he states Eliot's importance, but does not enable us adequately to feel it. Nevertheless, as with everything Wilson writes, this essay has the rare quality of persevering honesty, the determination to state exactly what he has perceived, which makes him the most valuable of contemporary critics in this country.

4. Everyman Library Edition, 1931. As Eliot writes about Pascal's conversion we are given a different example of the way in which a writer can find 'an objective correlative,' of how he can tell us everything relevant to an understanding of his own state of mind by focusing his attention completely on the description of a similar state of mind in an historical figure.

5. Some of the qualities that attracted Eliot to the tradition of the Anglican Church are suggested in his essay on Lancelot Andrewes:

To the ordinary observer the English Church in history means Hooker and Jeremy Taylor—and should mean Andrewes also: it means George Herbert, and it means the churches of Christopher Wren. This is not an error: a Church is to be judged by its intellectual fruits, by its influence on the sensibility of the most sensitive and on the intellect of the most intelligent, and it must be made real to the eye by monuments of artistic merit. The English Church has no literary monument equal to that of Dante, no intellectual monument equal to that of St. Thomas, no devotional monument equal to that of St. John of the Cross, no building so beautiful as the Cathedral of Modena or the basilica of St. Zeno in Verona. But there are those for whom the City churches are as precious as any of the four hundred odd churches in Rome which are in no danger of demolition, and for whom St. Paul's, in comparison with St. Peter's, is not lacking in decency; and the English devotional verse of the seventeenth century—admitting the one difficult case of conversion, that of Crashaw—finer than that of any other country or religion at the time.

The intellectual achievement and the prose style of Hooker and Andrewes came to complete the structure of the English Church as the philosophy of the thirteenth century crowns the Catholic Church. To make this statement is not to compare the 'Laws of Ecclesiastical Polity' with the 'Summa.' The seventeenth century was not an age in which the Churches occupied themselves with metaphysics, and none of the writings of the fathers of the English Church belongs to the category of speculative philosophy. But the achievement of Hooker and Andrewes was to make the English Church more worthy of intellectual assent. No religion can survive the judgment of history unless the best minds of its time have collaborated in its construction; if the Church of Elizabeth is worthy of the age of Shakespeare and Jonson, that is because of the work of Hooker and Andrewes.

But it should not be assumed that Eliot has accepted the dogma of the Church mainly because of its fruits, or that he has been led thereto for aesthetic reasons. The passage from Hulme which he quotes against the Humanists seems akin to the chain of reasoning which led to his own conversion:

I hold the religious conception of ultimate values to be right, the humanist wrong. From the nature of things, these categories are not inevitable, like the categories of time and space, but are *equally objective*. In speaking of religion, it is to this level of abstraction that I wish to refer. I have none of the feelings of *nostalgia,* the reverence for tradition, the desire to recapture the sentiment of Fra Angelico, which seems to animate most modern defenders of religion. All that seems to me to be bosh. What is important, is what nobody seems to realize—the dogmas like that of Original Sin, which are the closest expression of the categories of the religious attitude. That man is in no sense perfect, but a wretched creature, who can yet apprehend perfection. It is not, then, that I put up with the dogma for the sake of the sentiment, but that I may possibly swallow the sentiment for the sake of the dogma.

Eliot adds this comment:

Most people suppose that some people, because they enjoy the luxury of Christian sentiments and the excitement of Christian ritual, swallow or pretend to swallow incredible dogma. For some the process is exactly opposite. Rational assent may arrive late, intellectual conviction may come slowly, but they come inevitably without violence to honesty and nature. To put the sentiments in order is a later and an immensely difficult task: intellectual freedom is earlier and easier than complete spiritual freedom.

6. John Strachey, in his plausible but summary account of contemporary literature in *The Coming Struggle for Power* (New York, 1933), though perceiving that the tragic view of life 'is the one thing which all the great writers of all ages have had in common,' nevertheless objects to what he conceives to be an inferiority in the work of present tragic writers owing to the fact

that they confuse the unavoidable tragedies of human existence in general with the entirely avoidable tragedies of the decaying capitalistic system. His principal charge against them is that 'since they do not extricate themselves from present-day society, since they are unable to stand outside of it, conceiving of a new basis for human life, they are themselves, inevitably, infected by their surroundings of decay.' That Joyce, Eliot, and Lawrence have all written as they have because of the conditions of life in the period in which they have lived, they themselves would be the last to deny. And notwithstanding their marked differences of approach, the fact of contemporary social decay has been an observation common to them all. But the assumption that the tragic writer can stand outside his age abstractly conceiving a new basis for human life, and at the same time create a vision of life as he has known it, seems to me inhuman; indeed, it seems purely verbalistic. Yet it is one of the most widespread contemporary fallacies that confuse the nature of art.

An individual sees tragedy in the life surrounding him; if he is greatly perceptive, like Dante, he may be able to endow that tragedy with universal significance. He may be appalled by the horror of life in his age like Swift or Baudelaire or the creator of Stephen Dedalus. He may fight bitterly against his age like Milton or Tolstoy or Lawrence, and reveal the evil resulting from its assumptions. But in so far as he conceives new possibilities for mankind, he can give those imaginings an illusion of reality only if he remains integrally a part of his age, only, that is to say, if the tragedy which he creates in words corresponds to potential elements in existence as he himself has experienced it. Tolstoy's pamphlets like *What is Art?* and *What is to be done?* undoubtedly owed their immediate effectiveness to their simplified distortion. But the great enduring value of *Anna Karenina* is attributable primarily to the fact that Tolstoy there did not write of life as he would like it to be, but as it was—and is.

If the writer stands outside of his age, he can envisage an ideal state like Rousseau or Marx; indeed, it is only by such *abstraction* that philosophical or political thought becomes possible. But the first requisite for the tragic poet or novelist is to comprehend and portray *concrete* experience. He may heighten and idealize it like Sophocles; but he must not thereby lessen the real existence of both evil and good. But such is at once the effect if he takes refuge in the abstraction of 'a new basis for life.'

I do not mean by these remarks to deny the value of propaganda; or to make an impossible separation between it and art. I know that it is perfectly possible for a great artist like Milton to write, in addition to his poems, important political and religious tracts as well. My point is simply once more the chief assumption of my essay: that the poet and the political theorist, the artist and the philosopher, though all relating integrally to the age which produces them, express that relation in different ways. That does not impute a necessary superiority in value to the expression of the artist over that of the others. It is clear, for instance, that the works of greatest lasting value to come out of the Russian Revolution so far are the writings of Lenin and Trotzky. But a great poet would express the fact of the Revolution in a different manner. He might convey a new awareness of multitudinous possibilities of life, its glowing promise and yet bitter realities, as Shakespeare expressed the revolution that was transforming the bases of thought and feeling in his day. Or, like Milton, he might embody in concrete form the principal tenets of the thought itself. But in any case it would no longer be the historical accuracy of his statements, nor even the quality of his thought, that gave his poems their value. Milton's pamphlets are read for the importance of their ideas in relation to the development of seventeenth-century political theory; but readers are drawn to *Samson Agonistes* by a quality that still enables it to be a moving experience whether or not one is a special student of the seventeenth century. For, although many of Milton's same ideas are voiced in *Samson Agonistes,* what gives the poem its life is its quality of emotional expression through its expert fusion of content and form.

7. Certain writers, among them Conrad Aiken and Waldo Frank, seem to regard Eliot as a new incarnation of 'the lost leader.' Frank in particular appears to consider it the duty of the modern man to accept the blackness of the waste land, to plunge into it, to refuse to turn back to any old solution, but to cross courageously to a new mysterious dawn of the Whole. Perhaps his own words will give a clearer idea of his meaning:

Only athletic souls can face a world that has become, perhaps more than any other era, an overwhelmingly open and darkened future.

The temptation to limit this world, either by rationalistically charting its future (a disguised reactionism) or by merely advocating its reform in an image of the past, is great and manifold. . . The one way of life that has no limit and affords no comfort is the way ahead—into the bitter and dark and bloody dawn of a new world, wherein mankind shall integrate without loss the stormy elements that make the chaos of our day, and its promise. ('The "Universe" of T. S. Eliot,' *The New Republic,* 26 October 1932.)

A sympathy with Frank's passionate conviction of the necessity for the reintegration of modern life cannot blind one to the loose rhetoric and wishful thought of such a passage. The basic fallacy in the kind of criticism of which Frank's work is a notable exemplar is suggested in his own statement in *The Rediscovery of America:* 'I am not discussing art: I am using art, in a purpose of research.' The assumption that you can 'use' art in this way is dangerous. For it is impossible even to understand a work of art unless you are devoted to observation and contemplation of the concrete work itself. And if, instead of keeping your eye trained on the whole object, you manipulate the content of a poem to cast light on historical tendencies, or, worse still, take lines out of their context and generalize upon them as sociological evidence, you usually end by reading into the poem the tendencies you want to reveal by it. In addition, by reducing the poem to a document, you lose all contact with the experience that a work of art exists to communicate.

8. Some further sentences are relevant here:

To accept the poetry seems to amount to accepting an invitation to join the Anglican Church. For the assumption is that the poetry and the religious position are identical. If this were so, why should not the excellence of the poetry induce them to join the Church, in the hope of writing as well, since the irrelevance of the Church to their own needs makes them reject the poetry? The answer is, of course, that both parts of this fallacy are common. There is an aesthetic Catholicism, and there is a Communist-economic rejection of art because it is involved with the tabooed mode of salvation. (*The Hound and Horn,* Winter, 1931.)

The only other useful review of *Ash Wednesday* which I saw was by W. J. Gorman in *The Inlander,* November 1930. I am indebted to Mr. Gorman's valuable enumeration of some of the allusions in the poem to the Bible and to the Catholic Mass.

9. He had also become more fully aware that appreciation of literature cannot be divorced from an understanding of history and philosophy. In commenting on the career of Edmund Gosse (in *The Criterion*, July 1931), he remarked that Gosse, unlike Sainte-Beuve, 'was interested in literature for literature's sake; and I think that people whose interests are so strictly limited, people who are not gifted with any restless curiosity and not tormented by the demon of thought, somehow miss the keener emotions which literature can give.'

10. Richards's most matured discussion of poetry and belief is contained in *Practical Criticism* (London, 1929). His earlier brief treatment of the subject in *Science and Poetry* (London, 1926) is so oversimplified as to be almost without value.

11. Eliot once remarked that all he consciously set out to create in 'Sweeney among the Nightingales' was a sense of foreboding. Yet the very exactitude with which he has built up his impression by means of the close details of his night-town scene, as well as by the way he underlines his effect through a reference both in the epigraph and in the final stanza to another scene of foreboding that ended in the murder of Agamemnon, inevitably causes his delineation to take on wider implications. The contrast that seems at first to be mocking a debased present as it juxtaposes Sweeney with the hero of antiquity, ends in establishing also an undercurrent of moving drama: for a sympathetic feeling for Sweeney is set up by the realization that he is a man as well as Agamemnon, and that his plotted death is therefore likewise a human tragedy, as the end of Agamemnon's career was also sordid.

There is always a danger in reading poetry of making interpretations which are too rigidly detailed, or of exercising a super-subtlety—the word was Irving Babbitt's—which transforms a poem into a kind of puzzle to be solved. The interpretation of 'A Cooking Egg,' which I first heard in a lecture by I. A. Richards, and which was later published in Elizabeth Drew's *Discovering Poetry* (New York, 1933), does not escape from this danger.

> *Pipit sate upright in her chair*
> *Some distance from where I was sitting;*
> 'Views of the Oxford Colleges'
> *Lay on the table, with the knitting.*

Daguerreotypes and silhouettes,
Her grandfather and great great aunts,
Supported on the mantelpiece
An 'Invitation to the Dance.'

The age of the 'I' in the poem having been established through the epigraph as thirty, the following reasoning is brought to bear on these opening stanzas to determine the identity of Pipit: 'She is sitting "upright," "some distance" away—she obviously can't be the poet's mistress. To whom does one send *Views of the Oxford Colleges* during one's first term up? And who alone would keep the volume on the table after twelve years? Who, indeed, but one's old nurse?'

Such ingenuity, although it springs from the realization that every word in a well-made poem is designed to contribute to the presentation, nevertheless overreaches itself through passing by a more obvious meaning to pursue a more recondite one. Pipit is clearly not the poet's mistress, though you are not told so except by the exact description that starts with the first line. But her name might suggest that she is a little girl, an impression that is reinforced by several other details in the poem, and made most apparent by

But where is the penny world I bought
To eat with Pipit behind the screen?

The *Views of the Oxford Colleges* are only one of the accurately observed details by which the poet depicts the room that surrounds the small existence of Pipit and separates it from that of the thirty-year-old 'cooking egg.' And the total impression of the poem is thus much simpler than if the reader goes through the uncalled-for gymnastics of first jumping the hero back twelve years to account for the *Views;* and then again back to his childhood to account for the penny world which he bought at that time to eat with his old nurse. And in the simpler account, the contrast between the sophisticated world of the hero, with its smart disillusion and social decay, and the innocent world of Pipit, becomes, if anything, more affecting.

There is an important distinction, as Richards himself has demonstrated, between a sensitive awareness to every potential shade of connotation in the words of a poem, and an over-alert kind of detective sense that is determined to ferret out hidden meanings.

12. In discussing the quality of doubt common to Montaigne, Pascal, and La Rochefoucauld, and to the French tradition generally in contrast with the English, Eliot remarked on 'the honesty with which they face the *données* of the actual world.'

VI

THE SENSE OF HIS OWN AGE

My opinion is this: that deep thinking is attainable only by a man of deep feeling, and all truth is a species of revelation. . . It is insolent to differ from the public opinion in opinion, if it be only opinion. It is sticking up little i by itself, i against the whole alphabet. But one word with meaning in it is worth the whole alphabet together. Such is a sound argument, an incontrovertible fact.—Coleridge.

EVEN sympathetic readers of *Ash Wednesday* and 'Triumphal March' may feel that they show a decline from *The Waste Land* in that they do not give expression to so fully packed a range of experience. But, unfortunately for sociological critics, an artist's career cannot be regarded as a continual 'progress,' nor plotted on a steadily rising curve. 'The Love Song of J. Alfred Prufrock' brought into union Eliot's ironic attitude with all the stimulus that he had received from his initial reading of Laforgue. As a result it possesses a finished mastery both of the material and of the form into which it is cast that puts it far beyond any of the other poems in his first volume of 1917—with the exception of 'Portrait of a Lady'—though they were written during the following five years. In like manner, 'Gerontion,' in 1919, marks a second crystallization and synthesis which lifts it entirely above the rank of the poems composed at about that time, such as 'The Hippopotamus' or 'Mr. Eliot's Sunday Morning Service' which read as though they were the work of a much younger, less mature man. Eliot himself, while commenting on Pound, has described the only way in which a poet's curve can be charted: his

work may proceed along two lines on an imaginary graph; one of the lines being his conscious and continuous effort in technical excellence, that is, in continually developing his medium

[132]

for the moment when he really has something to say. The other line is just his normal human course of development, his accumulation and digestion of experience (experience is not sought for, it is merely accepted in consequence of doing what we really want to do), and by experience I mean the results of reading and reflection, varied interests of all sorts, contacts and acquaintances, as well as passion and adventure. Now and then the two lines may converge at a high peak, so that we get a masterpiece. That is to say, an accumulation of experience has crystallized to form material of art, and years of work in technique have prepared an adequate medium; and something results in which medium and material, form and content, are indistinguishable.

The very completeness of this union may cause confusion for the first readers of a new work: it may make them find difficulties that don't exist; mistake perfection for simpleness or slightness; or underestimate the force of what is being communicated. We tend too easily to pride ourselves on our superiority to the initial stupid reviewers of Wordsworth and Keats, and to forget that new art, a fresh way of interpreting life, has always to make its own audience. When Eliot's first poems appeared during the War, they were read, if at all, as an odd kind of *vers de société;* only gradually was it discovered that this slender volume was to have the effect, as Wyndham Lewis described it, of the little musk that scents a whole room.

In similar fashion, an impression of the comparative tenuousness of Eliot's later poems may prove illusory. It was probably impossible for him to strive towards a focused clarity of expression for his developing religious and political convictions without sacrificing part of his earlier complexity. But if there is loss in quickening surprise through the lessening of his sudden contrasts, there is in compensation a pervading, if less conspicuous quality: a sureness of accent and a quiet depth of tone. The one constant element through all the stages of his work has been his exact fitting of means to end, his rarely failing ability to perfect in each case the very kind of form he wanted for the particular content. The relative slimness of his production has tended to obscure his remarkable range in style. Indeed, as you read through his poems chronologically, he seems to have become expert in one mode of presentation only to move on to something else. After the 1917 volume the re-echoing manner of Laforgue diminishes, and such loosely flowing experiments as 'Rhapsody on a Windy Night' disappear altogether. Then, having carried his study of French versification to the point of writing some poems in that language, he mastered his handling of the quatrain of Gautier and thereafter has used it no more. Likewise his meeting of the late Elizabethan dramatists so completely on their own ground has never been repeated since 'Gerontion.' Both *The Waste Land* and *Ash Wednesday* are notable for the great variety of original verse forms that they employ within a short space; but the difference between these forms in the two poems is almost total.

Such versatility in style should in no degree be mistaken for mere technical virtuosity. Eliot is an example of the type of artist—and Joyce is another—whose motivating desire is to bring his expression to the greatest excellence he can, and then not to repeat it. Certain social implications can assuredly be drawn from the fact that not only Joyce and Eliot, but such other representative artists as Stravinsky and Picasso, have all felt within the past four decades a common urgency not to rest in the development of one manner, but to press on from each discovery to another. In the case of both the novelist and the poet their unwillingness to be confined long to any given method of presentation is obviously owing in part to their extraordinary historical consciousness, to their knowledge of so many possible techniques that they cannot remain satisfied with the limitations of any one. Probing beneath considerations of technique to the reasons for such a period of widespread experimentation in all the arts, one can undoubtedly link it with our contemporary sense of chaotic change and upheaval, of disequilibrium and insecurity. At the same time it is too easily forgotten in the current generalizations about the collapse of our culture that experiment, the trial of new possibilities, is a sign of life and not of death. And the ominous feeling that the fluctuation of the arts furnishes only one of many evidences that we are witnessing the final breakdown of all tradition often fails to take into consideration similar instability in other ages. Perhaps too much has been made of the fact that Donne's experiments, when seen against the background of his day, are even more radical than Eliot's; yet his restless invention of more than forty stanzaic forms is one unmistakable mark of his unsatisfied quest for certainty. But to take a seemingly far more traditional artist: it should not be obscured by time that Milton's whole career, his unending search for truth that rejected in turn the Anglican and Presbyterian creeds to pass to more and more independent definitions, is paralleled by the remarkably different stages in his development as a poet. Approached without preconceptions 'Arcades' and *Paradise Regained* would scarcely seem to be the work of the same man any more than *Chamber Music* and *Ulysses*. This juxtaposition may seem less incongruous the more one reflects on a remark that I heard Eliot make in conversation, that Joyce is the greatest master of the English language since Milton.

To return from this excursus: the value of any experiment in art lies in the length to which it is carried, whether it is merely the by-product of erratic or undisciplined fancy, or whether it has built up into a completed masterwork. Throughout Eliot's variety persists the enduring sameness that I have already noted, a result of the unusual degree to which he has composed all his work around certain focal centres that possess for him a special symbolical value. He has revealed other long preoccupations of a significance comparable to his persistent return to the twenty-sixth canto of the *Purgatorio*. A pattern could be made of his recurring images: of how often a sudden release of the spirit is expressed through sea-imagery which, with its exact notation of gulls and granite rocks and the details of sailing, seems always to spring from his own boyhood experience off the New England coast, just as his city-imagery belongs to Boston and London; of the equally numerous times when certain spring flowers, lilacs and hyacinths, appear in passages which express the stirring of desire warring against the memory of previous failure; of the widely varied occasions when he presents a moment of beauty and its loss by a glimpse of a girl, 'her hair over her arms and her arms full of flowers'; [1] of how, in such different poems as 'Prufrock' and *Ash Wednesday*, a sudden ecstatic loveliness is caught in 'blown hair':

> . . . *brown hair over the mouth blown,*
> *Lilac and brown hair;*
> *Distraction* . . .

The drama of *The Waste Land* is built upon the contrast of repeated and varying symbols of drought and rain; much of its unified effect depends upon the frequent return of the theme of the Unreal City, with its 'trams and dusty trees,' its murky streets 'under the brown fog of a winter noon,' its dull canal made suddenly horrible by the slimy belly of a rat. In such repulsive images, in his insistent use of the sordid and disgusting to picture disintegration and decay, Eliot is again comparable to Webster. But, in considering Eliot's relatively narrow stock of repeated images, is is gradually discovered that what enables them to embrace a wider range of experience than would at first appear is the fact that they release markedly different shades of feeling according to their contexts. The desert rocks and dry bones of *The Waste Land* and the soaring gull at the close of

'Gerontion' carry very different implications from similar objects in *Ash Wednesday*. The subtly differing connotations of the chief symbols within the course of *The Waste Land* itself are one of the strongest means by which the poet conveys the complexity of the existence that confronts him. The life-giving element of water can alone restore the kingdom (water is one of the most ancient symbols of sexual fertility); but in order to break the drought the hero must give himself up to the perilous quest. The necessity of self-sacrifice and the instinctive revulsion from it, the inability to commit himself to belief and the mounting fear that makes him recoil even from the vital forces of life in his dread of defeat and failure—such elements form the situation in which the hero, as unable as Hamlet to come to a resolution, is haunted by the thought of 'death by water.' The doubt that paralyses his desire to give himself is rendered concrete by the way in which water itself so often in the poem is made to appear anything but life-giving, as the squalid Thames instead of the 'damp gust bringing rain' that is longed for. In like manner, the basic symbol of fire is employed in a double sense. In 'The Fire Sermon' it stands for the destroyer, for the sterile lusts of the city, for the desire that burns without any definite object; it is only in the closing lines of the final section that fire, seen under a different aspect, represents the purifier, the purgatorial flame. Thus, purely in terms of Eliot's dominant images, it can be discerned how both their repetition and divergence help to bind together his various observations into a unified vision.[2]

In view of the emerging contours in his most recent work, one of the most significant of Eliot's symbols is what he finds in the figure of Coriolanus. The statement in one of his earlier essays that '*Coriolanus* may not be as "interesting" as *Hamlet,* but it is, with *Antony and Cleopatra,* Shakespeare's most assured artistic success,'[3] might have prepared us for the realization that the meaning of this play is deeply implanted in Eliot's consciousness. In 'A Cooking Egg' Coriolanus is linked with Sir Philip Sidney as a type of the hero; in The Waste Land he appears in the reflections of the poet on the second of the three commands heard in the rumbling of the thunder—'Give, Sympathize, Control':

> I have heard the key
> Turn in the door once and turn once only
> We think of the key, each in his prison
> Thinking of the key, each confirms a prison
> Only at nightfall, aethereal rumours
> Revive for a moment a broken Coriolanus

The individual locked in his solitary identity can escape from this obsession only by self-surrender and by sympathy with others. Calling him 'a broken Coriolanus' at first seems only another instance of Eliot's manner of contrasting the present and the past: the historic splendour of the great individual is gone; in the modern world the aristocrat has been crushed by the mob—again we are not far from the dilemma voiced by Flaubert. But as a relevant undertone here, it must not be forgotten that, in spite of all his noble strength and his gifts of leadership, Coriolanus at least in part deserved his tragedy; pride alienated him from his people and brought him to his destruction, pride which is the worst of sins in Dante's theology (as well as in the view of life which lies behind 'Ethan Brand' and The Scarlet Letter), since, being at the opposite pole from humility, it cuts the individual off both from man and from God.

Further extension is given to such implications in 'Triumphal March.' Coriolanus is not specifically suggested as the hero there; but Eliot subsequently grouped this poem and its sequel under the title Coriolan, thus possibly reminiscent of Beethoven's overture as well. And in the second poem, 'Difficulties of a Statesman,' there is mention of the

Volscians, and words directly borrowed from Shakespeare's play. I suppose 'Triumphal March' would be described by Michael Gold as a Fascist poem; but it was written before Hitler's advent to power and none of the qualities of its hero glimpsed for a moment by the waiting crowd suggest either his or Mussolini's:

> *Look*
> *There he is now, look:*
> *There is no interrogation in those eyes*
> *Or in the hands, quiet over the horse's neck,*
> *And the eyes watchful, waiting, perceiving, indifferent.*
> *O hidden under the dove's wing, hidden in the turtle's breast,*
> *Under the palmtree at noon, under the running water*
> *At the still point of the turning world. O hidden.*

In fact the weave of this poem is so intricate, as a result of Eliot's desire to suggest the dense pattern of reality, that the isolation of any one strand into a prose statement runs the risk of oversimplifying its meaning. There is an observed beauty in the heavy processional movement:

> *Stone, bronze, stone, steel, stone, oakleaves, horses' heels*
> *Over the paving.*

But there is likewise a full recognition of both the horror and futility of war as it sweeps by in the prolonged inhuman enumeration of its millions of rifles and machine-guns. What is being portrayed is not just one procession; it takes place not only in post-War London or Paris, since there are eagles and trumpets and a sacrifice at the temple. The crowd in the streets is both a Roman crowd waiting with its stools and sausages, and a modern crowd in the final fragments of conversation:

> *And Easter Day, we didn't get to the country,*
> *So we took young Cyril to church. And they rang a bell*
> *And he said right out loud,* crumpets.

[139]

> *Don't throw away that sausage,*
> *It'll come in handy. He's artful. Please, will you*
> *Give us a light?*
> *Light*
> *Light*
> Et les soldats faisaient la haie? ILS LA FAISAIENT.[4]

What is to be the symbol for spiritual reality to a world that goes to church only when it can't get to the country, which recognizes in the sign commemorating the presence of the Host simply a bell that reminds young Cyril of the crumpet-man in the street? In the shadow of that question, the casual 'Please, will you give us a light?' suddenly reverberates. What flashes forth from the reiterated word 'light' is not merely the flicker of a match, but searching speculation as to the source from which the light for our age is to come.[5]

In such a context the central figure of the poem is seen to be neither Coriolanus nor a modern statesman alone, no more an Elizabethan than a Roman general; not even a symbol for leadership so much as the embodiment of qualities of spiritual perception and mastery that are integral to any deep apprehension of the meaning of life, and thus also to the existence of any adequate society. The hidden sources of inner life, the reserved balance, which sustain this individual and mark him off from the shallow chaotic flux of mere externalized rootless existence, make him almost a symbol for the harmonious union of emotion and thought that Eliot has so frequently stressed as characteristic of a 'firm grasp of human experience'; these qualities likewise demand a sustained equilibrium in the relations between the individual and the social structure. The ripely developed human being has gained the integrity that comes from self-knowledge, and he therefore understands that no wholeness exists in isolation, that the individual cannot find fulfilment except through also giving of himself to society—a truth none the less implied in 'Difficulties of a Statesman' by the fact that what is presented there is the breakdown of the relation between the leader and the state in the hopeless confusion of bureaucracy.

These reflections perhaps disclose some of the reasons why Shakespeare's *Coriolanus* has appealed to Eliot with a special urgency. A feeling that this play has an immediate relevance to our own age because of the particular problem of life with which it deals has not been limited to Eliot. A brilliant younger critic, Harry Levin, wrote during the winter of 1934 of his impressions of the recent performances of a new translation of *Coriolanus* at the Comédie Française, which was done with full 'grandeur and stateliness,' with 'a ghastly Breughelesque mob'; and 'the audience cheered fervently at any slightest political implication. . . Surely, if certain of Shakespeare's great tragedies have a special significance for certain periods (*Antony and Cleopatra* for the Restoration, *Hamlet* for the romantic movement), *Coriolanus* is the play that should have the richest meaning in our time.'

'Triumphal March' is not a Fascist poem any more than Shakespeare's play, but it points to the problem of the relation of the individual to the social organism, the imperfect solution of which has led directly into the ruthless brutality of the Fascist movement. It is worth calling attention to Eliot's growing interest in politics which forms the background for the appearance of this poem in 1931; especially since he articulated, in his introduction to Pound, the gradual way in which a poet gathers his material by a process 'largely unconscious, subterranean, so that we cannot gauge its progress except once in every five or ten years,' when all the amassed experience 'accumulates to form a new whole and finds its appropriate expression.' (It must be noted, if only in passing, that this description of the poetic process emphasizes once more Eliot's fundamental belief that a poem is not to be the overflowing of the mood of a moment, but the blending into a concentrated unity of the dominant thoughts and feelings of several years.) The part of Eliot's experience which was to crystallize into 'Triumphal March' and 'Difficulties of a Statesman' began to be evident in his preoccupation with political subjects in several of the essays in *For Lancelot Andrewes,* the composition of which stretched from 1925 to 1928. In addition, the Commentary in *The Criterion* for those years was increasingly taken up with contemporary politics, with the problem in the huge modern state caused by the heavy apathy of all elements in society to the responsibilities of intelligent representative government. The right to vote having been won by all men and women in democratic England and America, regard for its individual value seemed to be steadily dwindling. In the confused welter of modern society, the mass of mankind, unable to believe in anything very strongly or to understand any situation very well, was in constant danger of being led astray by any show of power in the streets, unable to distinguish between wise leadership and 'the golf club Captains,' liable to be swept away by any bread and circuses.

In line with such thought, Eliot noted in the spring of 1929: 'If, as we believe, the indifference to politics as actually conducted is growing, then we must prepare a state of mind towards something other than the facile alternative of communist or fascist dictatorship.' In the summer of that same year, in rejoinder to two essays in *The Criterion* defining the philosophic positions of those alternatives, he indicated more exactly what he meant when, in connection with the philosophy behind the Action Française, he spoke of 'the reintroduction of the idea of loyalty to a King, who incarnates the idea of the Nation. And in this idea is, I think, the *alternative* to Nationalism. Fascism seems to me rather (in the form in which it has succeeded up to date) to represent the Napoleonic idea. The latter, in contrast to the idea of Monarchy, is a familiar conventional modern idea: it is the doctrine of success.' The connection of this thought with the Action

Française will damn it instantly with many readers, to whom no political group could seem more useless for the needs of England or America.[6] I am not here concerned with the direct applicability of Eliot's political ideas; indeed, he frequently confesses himself an amateur in such matters, and yet defends the valid and valuable distinction between political ideas and actual politics, a distinction particularly necessary in a time of social disruption, when practice lags behind theory, when, indeed, the only way of clarifying the chaotic jungle of events is by subjecting them to the scrutiny of an articulated theory. But what is important to understand in the present context is that the strain of thought which characterizes Eliot's conception of the ideal state also runs throughout his conception of the nature of art.

He objects to the modern worship of success, the journalistic 'great man complex,' which sets up alike a Henry Ford or a Hitler and which, in glorifying alike the office-boy-to-millionaire or the corporal-to-dictator ideal, acclaims as necessary an unscrupulous directness of action. What seems to Eliot most false in such an ideal is that by exalting man's petty triumph it loses all view of anything more important than the individual, of the individual's inevitable limitations and his finding his completion only in something greater than himself, of the ruler's responsibility to his people, of the nation's to other parts of the world. The view of man symbolized in the comparative myths which Eliot drew upon for *The Waste Land* and the view of man lying behind *Ash Wednesday* emphasize in common the doctrine of incarnation, of the word made flesh. As Miss Weston summarized it in her chapter on 'The Secret of the Grail' (though Eliot would long since have found a more authoritative statement): 'The end of all the Mystery institutions was the revelation of the Mystery of Man. The central doctrine is that of the Man, the Heavenly Man, the Son of God who . . . though originally endowed with all power, descends into weakness and bondage, and has to win his own freedom, and regain his original state.' [7] But the heart of the story lies in the fact that he does not win salvation for himself, but only through the giving of himself in sacrifice; and thus it symbolizes the mystery which discloses also the way of Everyman's redemption from Hades. Such a view of man, in contrast to the deification of the Hero, does not exalt man at the expense of society. In recognizing man's potentiality for salvation, it does not confuse the perfection of the idea with his inescapable imperfection. In perceiving the divinity in man, it does not set up an overweening worship of individual power, but stresses the likeness of men, their common aspiration and fallibility, their one basis for brotherhood, not in a sentimental humanitarianism, but in their humility before God.

Throughout his life Eliot has been in reaction against the centrifugal individualism which characterized the America into which he was born. His deep-seated desire to link himself with a living tradition grew directly out of his revulsion against the lawless exploitation by which late nineteenth-century American individuals made any coherent society impossible. He was equally dissatisfied with the undefined spirituality of Emerson or Arnold: neither 'Self-Reliance' nor 'The Buried Life' was adequate. The tenets of the one led logically to an inhuman extreme of individualism, those of the other to a blurring of fundamental distinctions. Neither was restrained by the controlling anchor of dogma. The kind of control Eliot wanted was suggested in Hulme's condensed notes on 'the religious attitude,' a fact which reveals the fertility of that thinker's *Speculations* not only in demanding the qualities of poetry for which Pound and Eliot were to strive, but likewise in foreshadowing many of the bases of Eliot's maturing religious and political thought. What Hulme insisted on was the fundamental confusion that had been brought about 'by the failure to recognize the *gap* between the regions of vital and human thought and things, and that of the *absolute* values of ethics and religion. We introduce into human things the Perfection that properly belongs only to the divine, and thus confuse both human and divine things by not clearly separating them.' Hulme might have been thinking of either Emerson or Arnold when he wrote those sentences, although any other nineteenth-century 'prophet' would have served him as well. The religious attitude, as Hulme defines it, consists in its view of man 'as essentially limited and imperfect. He is endowed with Original Sin. While he can occasionally accomplish acts which partake of perfection, he can never himself *be* perfect. Certain secondary results in regard to ordinary human action in society follow from this. A man is essentially bad, he can only accomplish anything of value by discipline—ethical and political. Order is thus not merely negative, but creative and liberating. Institutions are necessary.' Eliot quoted this last passage in his essay on Baudelaire. One could not find a more compact expression of the gradually hardening lines of his own thought, as he has moved from and yet retained so many elements of the Puritan strain.

But as Eliot's mind has reached towards the Catholic position, he has been acutely conscious of the new violent extreme which threatens society to-day, the overwhelming of valuable impulses in the individual life by the narrow iron standardization of dictatorship. Not that he holds any brief whatsoever for the value of the expansive expression of an uncontrolled 'personality,' for the impure artist who, like Rousseau or Byron, exploits his idiosyncratic temperament at the expense of society instead of finding its fulfilment in the impersonal structure of a work of art. Nevertheless Eliot knows well that art can come into existence only through the free play of impulses; that it is worthless to try to demonstrate that 'if Milton had held more normal doctrines he would have written a better poem,' since the source of Milton's inspiration was bound up with his passionate desire to express those very doctrines. What, however, Eliot insists to be disastrous 'is that the writer should deliberately give rein to his "individuality," that he should even cultivate his differences from others; and that his readers should cherish the author of genius, not in spite of his deviations from the inherited wisdom of the race, but because of them.' For Eliot understands that the greatest art 'is impersonal, in the sense that personal emotion, personal experience is extended and completed in something impersonal, not in the sense of something divorced from personal experience and passion.' [8]

The very title 'Tradition *and* the Individual Talent' indicates the stress he has continued to put on the fact that a poem is not a turning loose of personal emotion, that 'no artist produces great art by a deliberate attempt to express his personality. He expresses his personality indirectly through concentrating upon a task which is a task in the same sense as the making of an efficient engine or the turning of a jug or a table-leg.' There is the voice of the craftsman in that remark, of the man who has admired Dryden's skill and Pound's technical expertness, who understands the self-contained quality of a finished masterpiece. But there is more than that: the realization that nothing great has ever been created by a human being without the creator's 'surrendering himself wholly to the work to be done,' without a continual self-sacrifice 'of himself as he is at the moment to something which is more valuable.'

In *The Sacred Wood* such views were restricted to observations on the writing of poetry, in the elaboration of Eliot's belief that the artist 'must be aware that the mind of Europe, the mind of his own country . . . is much more important than his own private mind.' But during the intervening years, as we have seen, Eliot has widened his quest, and become deeply concerned with both religion and politics. In *After Strange Gods* [9] he attempted a description of what he means by orthodoxy to put beside his conception of tradition, itself now extended to a wider context:

I hold—in summing up—that a *tradition* is rather a way of feeling and acting which characterizes a group throughout generations; and that it must largely be, or that many of the elements in it must be, unconscious; whereas the maintenance of *orthodoxy* is a matter which calls for the exercise of all our conscious intelligence. The two will therefore considerably complement each other.

His conception of the differences between these two elements, and his understanding of the intricate counteraction and interplay between them in a complex civilization, demonstrate his opposition to the falseness of any over-simplified pattern of the social structure. Eliot is careful to make clear that he is not using orthodoxy in the strict theological sense of the term (although, in his own experience, the significance that would now attach itself to his belief in the creative act as consisting in the individual's sacrifice 'of himself as he is at the moment to something which is more valuable' would connect integrally with his growing belief in dogma). What he stresses in his account of the importance of orthodoxy is 'the inherited wisdom of the race,' the carefully sifted central values of human experience that are always at war with extreme individualism in any form. Exactly what he means is disclosed in his remark that in examining contemporary literature he is 'not concerned with the authors' *beliefs,* but with orthodoxy of sensibility and with the sense of tradition'; and that in such light D. H. Lawrence is 'an almost perfect example of the heretic. And the most ethically orthodox of the more eminent writers of my time is Mr. Joyce.'

Eliot developed further the contrast between these two writers (in the unpublished lecture already referred to): that Lawrence is always concerned merely with the relations between two individuals and their failure, 'always looking for the perfect relationship and of course never finding it'; that Joyce, on the contrary, is 'concerned with the relation of man to God.' Joyce's scepticism may have carried him beyond the point where he could believe in anything; yet his understanding of the sense of sin is the key to Stephen Dedalus's behavior in both *The Portrait of the Artist as a Young Man* and in *Ulysses*. And throughout the sordid picture of contemporary Dublin, you still have 'the Catholic idea, the sense that society is more important than the happiness of the individual, hence none of the sentimentality you find in *Sons and Lovers*. In the latter you find only individuals, in the former you find society.' That is to say, in Joyce you have 'a sense of history'; in Lawrence only 'of the moment'—though Eliot's strictures on the inadequacy of Lawrence's interpretation of life did not blind him to the extraordinary sensibility that enabled Lawrence to describe, in a way that Joyce could not, the pain and ecstasy of individual relationships, and to communicate, in visionary flashes, the sensuous fullness of 'the moment.'

In a further reflection on Joyce, Eliot expressed as searching a comment as he has yet made on the relation of the individual to society: 'the Catholic paradox: society is for the salvation of the individual and the individual must be sacrificed to society. Communism is merely a heresy, but a heresy is better than nothing.' [10]

The reason why Eliot is a poet-critic of the first order is that, like Dryden or Arnold, he has not been content to be merely that. Like the author of *Absalom and Achitophel* and *The Hind and the Panther* his mind has wrestled increasingly with some of the main problems of his day. But unlike the author of *Literature and Dogma,* and aided in part by his mistakes, the increased sphere of Eliot's interests has not caused him to confuse their different functions. Eliot is hardly more qualified for metaphysical speculation than Arnold was—he himself has spoken of his 'incapacity for abstruse reasoning'; in spite of his long training in philosophy, his mind is too heavily concrete, his insight too purely intuitive, to qualify him for sustained flight in the realm of pure logic. Nor, in all probability, will either his political or religious thought build up into a wholly adequate system. But his consistent concern with these spheres of thought and action has yielded him a much deeper understanding of the nature of art and its value for society than was possessed by the author of 'Tradition and the Individual Talent.' For now, as he says, he conceives of tradition as being of the blood, as 'the means by which the vitality of the past enriches the life of the present.' Orthodoxy is of the brain, and is not unrelated to the quality which he previously discovered in the philosopher Bradley (the author of *Appearance and Reality* and perhaps Eliot's chief master in prose style): the quality of wisdom which 'consists largely of scepticism and uncynical disillusion.' In comparison with Bradley's thought, however, orthodoxy would probably appear as something 'older, more patient, more supple and more wise.'

In the co-operation between tradition and orthodoxy 'is the reconciliation of thought and feeling.' And that brings us once more to the very heart of Eliot's most fundamental belief as an artist: the necessary union of intellect and emotion. He finds it in 'the consummate art' of the finest philosophic prose style in our language, 'in which acute intellect and passionate feeling preserve a classic balance.' [11] Such union, in which words are 'so close to the object' that the two become identified, as surely in Eliot as in Donne or Baudelaire, is the chief attribute of great poetry as well.

THE ACHIEVEMENT OF T. S. ELIOT

NOTES

1. This line is from 'La Figlia che Piange.' Similar images occur
in the 'hyacinth girl' passage in 'The Burial of the Dead' section
of *The Waste Land* as well as in 'Portrait of a Lady.'

Eliot's penetrating remarks on the 'mixture of biography and
allegory' incorporated into the *Vita Nuova* reveal that he recognizes a vision of idealized loveliness attendant upon the first adolescent awakening of sex to be a fundamental human experience.
It is the loss of such loveliness in the failure of actual sexual
experience to measure up to it that constitutes the emotional
undercurrent of his flower-imagery, and creates its peculiar tone
of mingled frustration and longing. Similar material is presented,
in a very different sardonic form, in 'Dans le Restaurant' in the
obscene boastful reminiscences of the old waiter of his first
sexual awareness at seven years old, reminiscences which deform
the vision of loveliness into something salacious and ugly. Re-
gaining the purified vision in later life is the theme particularly
of the second and fourth poems in *Ash Wednesday,* and of
'Marina.'

2. D. S. Mirsky made some thoughtful observations on the way
in which Eliot's use of these symbols reveals the decay of contemporary civilization, in 'T. S. Eliot et la fin de la poésie
bourgeoise,' *Échanges,* numéro 5, December 1931. Despite his
keen appreciation of *The Waste Land* and his belief that Eliot
is the most accomplished of living poets, Prince Mirsky, as a
result of his conversion to communism, held, like the other, less
intelligent sociological critics, that Eliot's career reached its
dead-end with 'The Hollow Men,' that all his work since has
been mere flight and evasion.

3. It is worth remembering that Eliot had *Coriolanus* in mind
as a model when he was making his definition of the 'objective
correlative.'

4. It is perhaps just worth noting that this passage and that from
the close of 'The Burial of the Dead' (analysed above on pp. 21-
2) are the particular two which John Sparrow cites, in *Sense and
Poetry* (1934), in order to prove Eliot's obscurity and unintel-
ligibility, and 'how an established reputation and a novel man-

ner can impose upon the public and the critics.' (A third
passage from Eliot's early 'Rhapsody on a Windy Night' is
attributed by Mr. Sparrow to *The Waste Land*.) It is curious
that such total misapprehension should come from a sometime
editor of Donne's *Devotions*, except that Mr. Sparrow's mind
represents English criticism at its most hardened conventional
level. He combines considerable knowledge of the past, a certain
amount of common sense in pointing out the excesses of some
minor figures in modern art, and an almost complete lack of
taste or of ability to discriminate between Eliot and Edith Sitwell. His kind has been familiar, and unchanging, since the
Quarterly Reviewers.

A position similar to Mr. Sparrow's was developed by Max
Eastman, with greater vigour and trenchancy though with no
more discrimination or respect for accurate statement, and with
an almost wilful obtuseness, in *The Literary Mind* (1931). A
sample of Mr. Eastman's plain-man-of-sense-not-to-be-fooled critical approach is furnished by his characterization of Eliot's
meditation on the Word, at the opening of the fifth poem in
Ash Wednesday, as an 'oily puddle of emotional noises.' This is
certainly a puzzling approach from a man who had previously
written an enthusiastic book called *The Enjoyment of Poetry*,
except that one of Mr. Eastman's defects has always been a kind
of debater's zeal that will use any means to prove his point.

5. The final chorus in *The Rock* develops this theme of the
Light, as its opening stanzas can indicate:

> *O Light Invisible, we praise Thee!*
> *Too bright for mortal vision.*
> *O Greater Light, we praise Thee for the less;*
> *The eastern light our spires touch at morning,*
> *The light that slants upon our western doors at evening,*
> *The twilight over stagnant pools at batflight,*
> *Moon light and star light, owl and moth light,*
> *Glow-worm glowlight on a grassblade.*
> *O Light Invisible, we worship Thee!*

> *We thank Thee for the lights that we have kindled,*
> *The light of altar and of sanctuary;*
> *Small lights of those who meditate at midnight*
> *And lights directed through the coloured panes of windows*
> *And light reflected from the polished stone,*
> *The gilded carven wood, the coloured fresco.*

Our gaze is submarine, our eyes look upward
And see the light that fractures through unquiet water.
We see the light but see not whence it comes.
O Light Invisible, we glorify Thee!

A relevant commentary on Eliot's aim in writing this chorus
is furnished by his remarks on Dante's detailed imagery in the
final canto of the *Paradiso:*

An understanding of the rightness of such imagery is a preparation
for apprehending the last and greatest canto, the most tenuous and
most intense. Nowhere in poetry has experience so remote from
ordinary experience been expressed so concretely, by a masterly use
of that imagery of *light* which is the form of certain types of mystical
experience.

> *Nel suo profondo vidi che s'interna,*
> *legato con amore in un volume,*
> *ciò che per l'universo si squaderna;*
> *sustanzia ed accidenti, e lor costume,*
> *quasi conflati insieme per tal modo,*
> *che ciò ch'io dico è un semplice lume.*
> *La forma universal di questo nodo*
> *credo ch'io vidi, perchè più di largo,*
> *dicendo questo, mi sento ch'io godo.*
> *Un punto solo m'è maggior letargo,*
> *che venticinque secoli alla impresa,*
> *che fe' Nettuno ammirar l'ombra d'Argo.*

Within its depths I saw ingathered, bound by love in one
mass, the scattered leaves of the universe: substance and accidents and their relations, as though together fused, so that
what I speak of is one simple flame. The universal form of this
complex I think I saw, because, as I say this, more largely I
feel myself rejoice. One single moment to me is more lethargy
than twenty-five centuries upon the enterprise which made
Neptune wonder at the shadow of the Argo (passing over
him).

One can feel only awe at the power of the master who could thus
at every moment realize the inapprehensible in visual images. And I
do not know anywhere in poetry more authentic sign of greatness than
the power of association which could in the last line, when the poet
is speaking of the Divine vision, yet introduce the Argo passing over
the head of wondering Neptune. . . It is the real right thing, the
power of establishing relations between beauty of the most diverse
sorts; it is the utmost power of the poet.

In view of this passage, it may perhaps not seem too fanciful to conjecture that Eliot's attempt in the two lines beginning 'Our gaze is submarine' may have been stimulated by Dante's very different image of Neptune and the shadow of Argo; for Eliot's appreciation of Dante's method of describing light is obviously one of the sources of his own sustained employment here of the 'clear, visual images' of humble and intimate lights that enable him so successfully to give body to the impalpable.

6. At the time Eliot was writing, the pro-Fascist sympathies of Charles Maurras and his group had not yet been demonstrated.

7. Weston, work cited, pp. 145-7. I have somewhat compressed the phrasing.

8. This last statement comes from Eliot's preface to Mark Wardle's translation of Valéry's *Le Serpent*, 1924.

9. My reiterated stress on Eliot's growth during the fourteen years between *The Sacred Wood* and *After Strange Gods* requires some qualification. Certainly the Norton lectures, *The Use of Poetry and the Use of Criticism*, 1933, were a partial disappointment, owing to the fact that Eliot adopted there the historical method of a survey of principal tendencies in English poetry and critical theory since the Renaissance, a method for which he possessed little aptitude and which led him into many rather commonplace statements (for example, on Wordsworth and Coleridge), as well as into some one-sided and therefore misleading reflections on 'The Modern Mind' and particularly on I. A. Richards. But it would have been almost worth writing the whole book for the sake of the passage on the auditory imagination; and there were a great many other passages which threw penetrating light on Eliot's conception of the nature of poetry. Nevertheless, it was not until he returned to his own particular approach to art and society in *After Strange Gods* that he deepened the contours of his thought beyond *For Lancelot Andrewes*, 1928, as that volume of 'essays on Style and Order' had marked a different orientation from *Homage to John Dryden*, 1924.

10. In the light of this remark should be read his further reflection in the Commentary of *The Criterion*, April 1933: 'I would even say that, as it is the faith of the day, there are only a small

number of people living who have achieved the right not to be communists. My only objection to it is the same as my objection to the cult of the Golden Calf.'

11. This is Eliot's tribute to Bradley's style in the Commentary of *The Criterion*, October 1924. He concluded a longer essay on him in 1926 with this observation: 'Bradley, like Aristotle, is distinguished by his scrupulous respect for words, that their meaning should be neither vague not exaggerated; and the tendency of his labours is to bring British philosophy closer to the great Greek tradition.' This precision in language is what caused Eliot to rank Bradley higher as a prose writer than Arnold. Arnold, to be sure, as Eliot noted in his essay on 'Arnold and Pater,' 'produced a kind of illusion of precision and clarity; that is, maintained these qualities as ideals of style.' But the distinction is well taken that Bradley's prose actually mastered these qualities, largely owing to his 'intense addiction to an intellectual passion.'

It is interesting that Eliot makes a similar approach to the ordonnance, precision, and 'relevant intensity' of the Sermons of Lancelot Andrewes, to their balance of reason and emotion: 'Intellect and sensibility were in harmony; and hence arise the particular qualities of his style.'

Andrewes's Sermons also furnish one final example of the 'objective correlative':

When Andrewes begins his sermon, from beginning to end you are sure that he is wholly in his subject, unaware of anything else, that his emotion grows as he penetrates more deeply into his subject, that he is finally 'alone with the Alone,' with the mystery which he is seeking to grasp more and more firmly. One is reminded of the words of Arnold about the preaching of Newman. Andrewes' emotion is purely contemplative; it is not personal, it is wholly evoked by the object of contemplation, to which it is adequate; his emotion is wholly contained in and explained by its object.

VII

THE PLAYS

A verse play is not a play done into verse, but a different kind of play: in a way more realistic than 'naturalistic drama,' because, instead of clothing nature in poetry, it should remove the surface of things, expose the underneath, or the inside, of the natural surface appearance. It may allow the characters to behave inconsistently, but only with respect to a deeper consistency. It may use any device to show their real feelings and volitions, instead of just what, in actual life, they would normally profess or be conscious of; it must reveal, underneath the vacillating or infirm character, the indomitable unconscious will; and underneath the resolute purpose of the planning animal, the victim of circumstance and the doomed or sanctified being. So the poet with ambitions of the theatre, must discover the laws, both of another kind of verse and of another kind of drama.—Eliot, Introduction to S. L. Bethell's *Shakespeare and The Popular Dramatic Tradition*, 1944.

THE interplay between Eliot's created work and his criticism, so illuminating to the comprehension of his poems, is inevitably something different in the case of his dramas. His theory of poetry has been borne out by his practice, and both have been greatly influential now throughout a generation. But his conception of drama, his belief in the need for poetic drama, still remain more in the realm of theory even in his own experiments, as well as in their limited effect on the general course of the drama in our time. As he observed in his 'Dialogue on Dramatic Poetry,' which he wrote as a preface to Dryden's great discussion of the subject, 'It is one thing to discuss the rules of an art when that art is alive, and quite another when it is dead.'

At the start of Eliot's career Yeats and the Abbey Theatre were making a limited revival of plays in verse, but the prevailing relation between English poetry and drama was summed up in one of Eliot's early statements: 'Browning wrote dull plays, but invented the dramatic monologue or

[155]

character.' For several years it appeared as though Eliot would confine his strong dramatic impulses to the realm of Browning's successes, but by 1926, a year or two before he wrote his 'Dialogue,' he had already experimented with *Sweeney Agonistes*. He had always been absorbed with the great age of the English theatre, as his many essays on Elizabethan playwrights bear witness. But his earliest comprehensive formulation of what he demanded from drama and did not find on the contemporary stage remains buried in an uncollected review, 'The Beating of a Drum,' where in the course of discussing Olive Busby's *Studies in the Development of the Fool in Elizabethan Drama,* he remarked:

The essentials of the drama were, as we might expect, given by Aristotle: 'poetry, music, and dancing constitute in Aristotle a group by themselves, their common element being imitation by means of rhythm—rhythm which admits of being applied to words, events, and the movements of the body.' It is the rhythm, so utterly absent from modern drama, either verse or prose, and which interpreters of Shakespeare do their best to suppress, which makes Massine and Charlie Chaplin the great actors they are, and which makes the juggling of Rastelli more cathartic than a performance of *A Doll's House*.[1]

You do not have to agree with his final example—which was a sally in the war he shared with Yeats against the limitations of realism—in order to perceive that he has grasped the conception of poetic drama as an organic whole. He realizes, as the nineteenth-century imitators of Shakespeare did not, that verse is not something merely added to a play as an extra ornament or trimming, but that the poetic pattern and the dramatic pattern must subsist together as integral products of one act of imagination. This, incidentally, is what Granville-Barker, who knew both the stage and poetry, has demonstrated again so persuasively in relation to Shakespeare's plays.

To the extent that the nineteenth century, following in

[156]

the wake of Coleridge, divorced the poetic philosopher from the workaday playwright, it misunderstood and falsified Shakespeare. To the extent that it confined poetry to the closet, it also, in Eliot's view, impoverished the drama. In a radio broadcast in 1936, the year after the considerable success of *Murder in the Cathedral* on the stage, he made his position as explicit as possible: 'I believe . . . that poetry is the natural and complete medium for drama; that the prose play is a kind of abstraction capable of giving you only a part of what the theatre can give; and that the verse play is capable of something much more intense and exciting.' [2]

By then the drive for realism had become far less dominant in the theatre, which could so easily be beaten on this ground by the film. Consequently Eliot could hold it

reasonable that the stage should not attempt to compete with the film in illusion of scenery . . . and event. It should turn to the voice, to movement which is meant to be seen from several angles, and to things which can be done by the actor himself and which cannot be done by his pictures. And all this points to the verse play.

To work out a play in verse . . . is to see the thing as a whole musical pattern. . . The verse dramatist must operate on you on two levels at once. . . It is fatal for a poet trying to write a play, to hope to make up for defects in the movement of the play by bursts of poetry which do not help the action. But underneath the action, which should be perfectly intelligible, there should be a musical pattern which intensifies our excitement by reinforcing it with feeling from a deeper and less articulate level.

This describes what Eliot has striven for in his own plays. As usual his work is of greatest interest in its technical experiments, and in the reasons he gives for them. One of his strongest convictions about the nature of a living tradition is the unlikeliness that any verse form can be renewed for the same purpose for which it was widely current in the past. He would doubt that either the Popean couplet or the *Don Juan* stanza could serve any longer for satire, except as an occasional *tour de force*. He would be even more certain that the expectedness of blank verse for drama would keep it from being anything more than a poor imitation of Shakespeare, would prevent it from 'contributing anything to the life of our own time.'

'The problem for us, therefore,' he continued in his radio talk,

is to get away from Shakespeare. . . That is not so easy. I have found, in trying to write dramatic verse, that however different a metre from blank verse I was working with, whenever my attention has relaxed, or I have gone sleepy or stupid, I will wake up to find that I have been writing bad Shakespearean blank verse: and I have had to scrap the lot and start all over again. Hence we have to make use of suggestions from remote drama, too remote for there to be any danger of imitation, such as *Everyman,* and the late medieval morality and mystery plays, and the great Greek dramatists.

When he was writing *Sweeney Agonistes,* Eliot was already convinced that 'the recognized forms of speech-verse are not as efficient as they should be; probably a new form will be devised out of colloquial speech.' He expressed that conviction in his self-revelatory introduction to *Savonarola* (1926), his mother's closet drama, in rhymed couplets, where he also declared that after the discursive conversational pieces of Shaw, the drama needed an intensification, a tightening, that 'the next form of drama will have to be a verse drama but in new verse forms.'

Eliot subtitled his first brief scenes 'fragments of an Aristophanic melodrama,' but the source of the verse spoken by Sweeney and his friends was much nearer at hand. The poet was trying to utilize vaudeville rhythms for reasons that he had recently articulated in his appreciation of Marie Lloyd as 'the greatest music-hall artist of her time.' He felt

that she 'represented and expressed that part of the English
nation which has perhaps the greatest vitality and interest';
and that any hope for a popular drama would spring from
the robust entertainment of the lower class, and not from
the 'morally corrupt' middle class, already given over to the
lifeless mechanism of the standardized cinema. The songs in
Eliot's play, 'Under the bamboo tree' and 'My little island
girl,' found their stimulus in American jazz, as did the syn-
copation of the dialogue. As a result Eliot's verse here seemed
less novel than usual to American ears, but it became one
of the starting points for Auden's charades.

In the method of projecting his content Eliot was indebted
again to Henry James. The hero is so different a character
from the 'apeneck Sweeney' of the poems that Eliot might
better have given him a different name. And while the epigraphs from St. John of the Cross and Aeschylus' *Choephori*
may seem at first glance another of Eliot's pieces of elaborate
irony, the words quoted from Orestes' speech about the
Furies—'You don't see them, you don't—but *I* see them: they
are hunting me down'—are directly relevant to Eliot's intention. For, like James, Eliot was presenting characters of differing degrees of consciousness. Doris and Dusty and the
visitors to their flat were meant to be 'material, literal-
minded, and visionless.' Sweeney, in his meditations on
'birth, copulation, and death,' can not communicate his
feelings to them, but only to the sentient members of the
audience. This complete isolation of Sweeney from the rest
of the cast was well conveyed both in Hallie Flanagan's
production at Vassar (1933), and in Rupert Doone's for the
Group Theatre in London (1935). But such an extreme
development of James' device would hardly seem workable
for a play of much length, and it is not surprising that Eliot
left Sweeney's 'agon' a fragment.

His 'Dialogue on Dramatic Poetry' suggests—half a dozen
years before he undertook *The Rock*—where he would turn

[159]

next. He cites again the satisfying formality of the ballet, the elimination of all inessentials in its concentrated 'liturgy' of 'traditional, symbolical, and highly trained movements.' As one of the speakers in the 'Dialogue' remarks, 'Here seemed to be everything that we wanted in drama, except the poetry.' But the mention of liturgy leads on to the remark that 'the consummation of the drama . . . is to be found in the ceremony of the Mass.' Another speaker takes exception. Granted that the origin of drama is in religious liturgy, granted that 'the Mass is a small drama, having all the unities,' and that 'if you consider the ritual of the Church during the cycle of the year . . . you have represented the full drama of Creation,' nevertheless, 'even if you are a believer, you will have dramatic desires which crave fulfillment otherwise. . . Religion is no more a substitute for drama than drama is a substitute for religion.'

The consensus to which Eliot's speakers come is the same that he had voiced in his introduction to *Savonarola:* 'In genuine drama the form is determined by the point on the line at which a tension between liturgy and realism takes place.' In reaction against the photographic tendencies of realism, Eliot wanted to move again towards heightened convention. William Archer's *The Old Drama and the New* was a central point for attack, and in the position he took up against this apostle of Ibsenism, Eliot revealed a break with current standards of drama even more complete than his poetry had made with Tennyson and Swinburne. In answer to Archer's charge that the weakness of Elizabethan drama lay in its unrealistic conventions, Eliot said that on the contrary it had never been conventional enough. 'The great vice of English drama from Kyd to Galsworthy has been that its aim of realism was unlimited. In one play, *Everyman,* and perhaps in that one play only, we have a drama within the limitations of art.' We may gasp, as often in Eliot, at the astringency of his example, which seems to close more doors rather than to open the possibility of any. But he made clearer the grounds of his admiration, in a lecture on 'Religious Drama: Medieval and Modern' (1937): 'In *Everyman* the religious and dramatic are not merely combined, but wholly fused.'³ Even if that fusion is the mark of classic wholeness, Eliot can still perceive that something lay beyond the medieval drama's scope. It may be a relief to turn back to 'the austere close language' and to 'the simplicity of the mysteries,' but 'if new influences had not entered, old orders decayed,' we should not have had the less orderly magnificence of *King Lear*.

But in our time of broken standards and beliefs he wanted to see what reinvigoration for drama might lie in a return to its source in liturgy. The structure of *Ash Wednesday,* as we have observed, draws upon the drama of the Mass. In *The Rock,* performed at Sadler's Wells in 1934, Eliot set himself to write a play on behalf of the fund to preserve the old churches of London. Strictly speaking, *The Rock* is a pageant, not a drama. That is to say, its situation does not give rise to any intense struggle or conflict; its structure consists of a series of scenes of a related tone, scenes which decorate the theme of the building of the Church, the hardships it has encountered in various crises of the past as well as the present, and the firmness of its triumph. The scenario was not original with Eliot, but provided for him by Martin Browne; Eliot's task was to produce the dialogue, the bulk of which is in prose. Many of the scenes are hardly of interest beyond their original purpose of furnishing the text for a formal spectacle, which was accompanied by music and ballet. And some of them, in their very conception, do not escape from unctuousness. But the passages of verse, which run to several hundred lines, though spoken mostly by the Chorus, include also the whole of the most energetic scene, that in which the Church is confronted by Redshirts, Blackshirts, and Plutocrats. This scene shows Eliot trying his hand

THE ACHIEVEMENT OF T. S. ELIOT

at the kind of material that Auden, whose first experiments
owed so much to Eliot, had already made ambitious efforts
to handle in *The Dance of Death*.[4]

Although its choruses give voice to some of the same profound kind of meditative poetry that he was to develop in his
Quartets, *The Rock* hardly meets Eliot's test for a religious
play, 'that it should be able to hold the interest, to arouse
the excitement, of people who are not religious.' Nor,
through the very nature of its inception, could it possibly
rise to his far more exacting demand of creating an indis-
severable double pattern of poetry and drama. Such a set-
piece could not possess the wholeness of vision and movement of a *Polyeucte* or an *Athalie*. But the case was very
different with the play which Eliot wrote for the Canterbury
Festival the following year.

Murder in the Cathedral, like many of the morality plays,
is a drama of temptation, but Becket as the great archbishop
proves superior to his tempters. One of the most conspicuous
technical triumphs in all Eliot's poetry is in the choruses
that were designed to be spoken by the working women of
Canterbury. Here he carried further his experiments in
finding verse forms suitable for ritualistic drama. He had
no living stage tradition upon which to draw, but he believed that a chorus could still perform something of the
same fundamental function that it had for the Greeks. It
could 'mediate between the action and the audience'; it
could 'intensify the action by projecting its emotional consequences, so that we as audience see it doubly, by seeing
its effect on other people.'

Eliot's women are there to watch and suffer, and their
feelings are nearly all in the most sombre key. Their gamut
is from nameless dread of foreboding to horror at the fact
of Becket's murder. Their lines are generally iambic, of
greatly varying lengths, though, as in *The Rock*, Eliot usually avoided the pentameter. He explored some of the pos-

sibilities of Hopkins' sprung-rhythm, and carried it on occasion into a patterned prose, quickened by alliteration and
internal rhyme. He was very dexterous throughout in organizing his speeches according to natural breath lengths.

His actors are also characterized by the verse they speak,
so that there is a marked difference between the lilting
cadences of the First Tempter, who tries to lure Becket by
the memory of old pleasures, and the bluntness and force
in the lines of those who tempt by power, either of the
Chancellorship or of a new alliance with the barons against
the King. The Fourth and last Tempter is at the top of a
rising scale. For while the resumption of the role of Chancellor lay almost as remote from Becket's present desires as
did worldly pleasure, and while a coalition with the barons
could stir him only momentarily, the Fourth Tempter alone
is unexpected by Becket, and tempts him by his own deepest
thoughts:

> *You know and do not know, what it is to act or suffer.*
> *You know and do not know, that acting is suffering*
> *And suffering is action. Neither does the actor suffer*
> *Nor the patient act. But both are fixed*
> *In an eternal action, an eternal patience*
> *To which all must consent that it may be willed*
> *And which all must suffer that they may will it,*
> *That the pattern may subsist, for the pattern is the action*
> *And the suffering, that the wheel may turn and still*
> *Be forever still.*

This had been Becket's first speech in the play, reflecting
on the lot of the Chorus, and the Fourth Tempter flings it
back at him almost word for word. The firmness of its doctrine reveals how far Eliot has advanced in his possession
of Dante's conception of grace, 'la sua voluntade è nostra
pace.' [5] Eliot no longer dwells as he did earlier on 'the eternal burden' alone, but, in this subtle interweaving of suffering, striving, and acceptance, on the possibility of 'the perpe-

tual glory.' But by making the Fourth Tempter penetrate
to the same deep level of understanding, Eliot dramatizes
Becket's chief peril, the temptation to the proud mind to
become so confident in its wisdom that it seeks—and takes
for granted—a martyr's crown as its reward.

> *The last temptation is the greatest treason:*
> *To do the right deed for the wrong reason.*

In the meditation that closes the first act Becket wins through
to the recognition that no man can will his way to martyr-
dom. 'I shall no longer act or suffer to the sword's end,' he
concludes, and submits his will to God's.

In the sermon that serves for an interlude between the
two acts, Becket reveals himself secure in this deeper reliance,
and then, holding fast to his belief in the supremacy of God's
law above man's law, he encounters the wrath of the Knights,
who are the same as the four Tempters of the first act, and
goes to his death unflinchingly. The blasphemy of the
Knights' deed is underscored by the fact that they advance
to their bloodshed with phrases borrowed from spirituals
and revival hymns just after the Chorus has voiced a despair-
ing passage, 'Numb the hand and dry the eyelid,' in the
cadences of 'Dies Irae.' The Knights then turn to the audience and in a passage of dramatic shock (which seemed too
sudden in some performances, though highly effective in
others) they drop into the prose of modern debate, and try
to justify their act by all the rationalizations of expediency.
But the ending belongs to the Priests and the Chorus mounting to a prayer of intercession to 'blessed Thomas.'

Murder in the Cathedral was immensely successful for its
immediate purpose in the chapter house at Canterbury. It
demonstrated what Eliot meant by saying, in the final lines
of his 'Dialogue': 'A continuous hour and a half of *intense*
interest is what we need.' Despite the problem created by a
chorus on the modern stage, the play demonstrated this again

in a long run at the Mercury Theatre in London under
Ashley Dukes and Martin Browne. It was one of the great
successes of the WPA theatre in New York, where the Chorus
was handled by dividing its lines among several individual
speakers, and where Harry Ervine's interpretation brought
more vitality to the title role than the somewhat too ritualistic performance of Robert Speaight. In the spring after the
liberation of France it scored a renewed triumph at the
Vieux Colombier in a translation by Henri Fluchère.

Stimulated by his first reception on the regular stage, Eliot
attempted in *The Family Reunion* something far more difficult, a play that would use the setting and characters of
drawing-room comedy and that would still include the
Eumenides in its cast. He seems to have been thinking of
the method evolved by James for his 'ghost' stories, where
the design was to have 'the strange and sinister embroidered
on the very type of the normal and easy.' ⁶ 'Nothing is more
dramatic than a ghost,' observed one of the speakers in
Eliot's 'Dialogue,' but it is one thing to suggest an eerie
presence in fiction, quite another to present the Eumenides
in evening dress in the embrasure of a window on the modern stage, and here Eliot's inexperience in the theatre betrayed him into a device that failed badly in its effect.

He may have been thinking also of Chekhov's haunted
world of social decay, and it is significant that two other
Americans of Eliot's generation, O'Neill in *Mourning Becomes Electra* and Jeffers in *The Tower Beyond Tragedy,*
have dramatized the theme of a curse on a house by a re-
handling of the Orestes story. Eliot's device for his chorus
here is also comparable to some of O'Neill's previous experiments in having his characters withdraw momentarily from
the action to voice their inner thoughts. Eliot's choric group
consists of the hero's uncles and aunts, who are on hand for
his return, after a long absence, for his mother's birthday.

They are unlike the usual Greek chorus in that their role is not to illuminate the action, but to express their baffled inability to understand what is happening:

> *We do not know what we are doing. . .*
> *We have lost our way in the dark.*

Eliot is absorbed again, in much the same fashion as he was in *Sweeney,* in projecting different levels of consciousness, but one danger here is that his country-house social group is so inert and lifeless that we can hardly become interested in them even as a contrast with the hero, the titular head of the house, Harry, Lord Monchensey. Most of the verse that they speak has a deliberate flatness, and seems, indeed, to have been designed to sound on the stage hardly distinguishable from prose. In this kind of effort to approximate colloquial speech, Eliot seems to have forgotten his earlier and wiser principle that verse should always be used for a heightening, that whatever can now be said just as well in prose is better said in prose.

The hero is in a state of mind which he finds it almost impossible to explain to anyone else. Seven years before, after a brief and disastrous marriage, while travelling on an ocean liner, he either pushed his wife overboard or at least watched her slip and drown. He is not quite clear which, but he had wanted to kill her, and has felt himself pursued ever since, as though by the Furies. The difference from the Furies in Aeschylus is profound, and suggests that in handling his ambiguous material Eliot failed to keep to his realization that the action in a play must be 'perfectly intelligible,' that, in fact, he failed on this occasion to find an adequate 'objective correlative.'

Only in the last play of Aeschylus' trilogy are the Erinys transformed into the Eumenides. The moment is of the widest social significance. The baleful Furies who have tracked down the murderer Orestes are forced by Athena to yield and to become benevolent guardians of the state. What is dramatized thereby is the immense step that was taken by mankind in giving up primitive blood-vengeance, a life for a life, and submitting to the ordered process of courts of law. Orestes is then released as having done sufficient expiation for his terrible vengeance of his father's death upon his mother, and the curse on the house is at an end.

Eliot wanted to suggest a comparable transformation. Harry has long felt himself followed and watched, but it is only upon his return to Wishwood that he finally sees his pursuers and comes to recognize their true meaning. The two scenes in which they appear on the stage are between Harry and his cousin Mary, whom his strong-willed mother had once designed for his wife, and between Harry and his Aunt Agatha, the one deeply perceptive and sympathetic member of his family. But these scenes, though here Eliot quickened and intensified his verse, are very obscure, owing to Harry's own obsessed state, and do not begin to convey to the audience the intention that Eliot outlined in a letter to Martin Browne:

The scene with Mary is meant to bring out, as I am aware it fails to, the conflict inside him between . . . repulsion for Mary as a woman, and the attraction which the *normal* part of him that is left, feels toward her personally *for the first time*. This is the first time since his marriage ('there was no ecstasy') that he has been attracted towards any woman. The attraction glimmers for a moment in his mind, half-consciously as a possible 'way of escape,' and the Furies (for the Furies are *divine* instruments, not simple hell-hounds) come in the nick of time to warn him away from this evasion—though at that moment he misunderstands their function. Now, this attraction towards Mary has stirred him up, but, owing to his mental state, is incapable of developing; therefore he finds a refuge in an ambiguous relation—the attraction, half of a son and half of a lover, to Agatha, who reciprocates in somewhat the same way. And this gives the cue for the second appearance of the Furies, more patently in their role of divine messengers, to let him know clearly that the only way out is purgation and holiness. They become exactly 'hounds of heaven.' And Agatha understands this clearly, though Harry only understands it yet in flashes. So Harry's career needs to be completed by an *Orestes* or an *Oedipus at Colonnos*.

In the scene with Agatha, Harry comes at least to know his situation. She tells him, to relieve his mind, that his father, long since dead, had fallen in love with her and had wanted to kill Harry's mother, but that she, Agatha, had kept him from doing so. Nevertheless, the thought was there, and Harry must now expiate a repetition of the same crime. Or rather,

> *What we have written is not a story of detection,*
> *Of crime and punishment, but of sin and expiation. . .*
> *It is possible*
> *You are the consciousness of your unhappy family,*
> *Its bird sent flying through the purgatorial flame.*
> *Indeed it is possible. You may learn hereafter,*
> *Moving alone through flames of ice, chosen*
> *To resolve the enchantment under which we suffer.*

By finding an equivalent for the transformation of the Furies through the difference between Hell and Purgatory, in the acceptance of the purifying fire, Eliot has tied the Eumenides into his pattern of thought, but he has hardly been explicit enough to take an audience with him. Also, the inferiority for dramatic purposes of Harry's story to that of Orestes is manifest, since the hatred of a wife, though repeated in two generations, does not, as Eliot handles it, assume much more than private significance.

There are also some echoes of *Hamlet* in Harry's situation. As he says,

> *It is not my conscience,*
> *Not my mind, that is diseased, but, the world I have to live in.*

And when his family, still maintaining that he suffers from delusions, sets the old family doctor to spy out the cause of his neurosis, they suggest the behavior of the King and Polonius. Strangely enough, there is also a reminder of what Eliot found unsatisfactory in *Hamlet* as a play: that Shakespeare gives the sense there of struggling with some 'intractable' material that he could not bring to light, that the

supposed identity of Hamlet with his author is genuine to this point: that Hamlet's bafflement at the absence of objective equivalent to his feelings is a prolongation of the bafflement of his creator in the face of his artistic problem. Hamlet is up against the difficulty that his disgust is occasioned by his mother, but his mother is not an adequate equivalent for it; his disgust envelops and exceeds her.

Eliot has found the peculiar genius of Cyril Tourneur to consist in his expression of 'the loathing and horror of life itself.' Something of that quality is infused into Harry, Lord Monchensey, but his objective situation simply will not support it. After Agatha's revelation, Harry accepts the fact that his destiny is to suffer more, not to evade, no longer to flee from but to 'follow the Furies'—a phrase which at one time was Eliot's tentative title for the play. Yet Harry can speak of his future in only the most general terms:

> Where does one go from a world of insanity?
> Somewhere on the other side of despair.
> To the worship in the desert, the thirst and deprivation,
> A stony sanctuary and a primitive altar,
> The heat of the sun and the icy vigil,
> A care over the lives of humble people,
> The lesson of ignorance, of incurable diseases.
> Such things are possible. . .
> I must follow the bright angels.

But when, in lieu of the traditional chariot of the *deus ex machina,* we have the highpowered car in which his faithful valet, after returning to pick up his Lordship's cigarette case, is to drive him away, the break between the surface of the play and the depth it is meant to symbolize becomes ludicrous and irreparable. By no suspension of disbelief can we conceive how Harry, whose life seems to have been passed mainly in resorts and luxury hotels, can undergo the discipline of suffering in any broadly meaningful sense. And when, after his departure, Agatha closes the play by reciting a rune to end the curse while she and Mary make a stylized dance around the birthday cake and blow out the candles, so that the 'last words shall be spoken in the dark,' as in the service of *tenebrae,* the effect seems an unintentional parody of liturgy rather than a reinvigoration from it.[7]

Eliot's belief in the value of poetic drama is based on its richer resources for transcending 'the ephemeral and superficial,' and for concentrating upon 'the permanent struggles and conflicts of human beings.' Only through such struggles is character revealed. One of Eliot's greatest gifts in his earlier dramatic lyrics was the power to suggest the essence of a character in a few lines. But a play requires more than the flash of suggestion; it requires development through a significant action.[8] The most devastating aspects of *The Family Reunion* are the unexamined implications of Harry's conduct. Whether or not he pushed his wife overboard, she went to her death by drowning; but the loss of her life, other than as a phase of the hero's education, is made a ground of no remorse. It seems only a re-enactment of Sweeney's macabre statement:

> *Any man has to, needs to, wants to*
> *Once in a lifetime, do a girl in.*

Harry's heightened awareness, through his talk with Agatha, of the meaning of what has happened to him produces no access of pity for his wife, but only a renewed ruthlessness towards his mother. Unlike Orestes, he does not murder her, but he becomes none the less the instrument of her death. Warned by the doctor that his mother is at an age where she cannot stand a shock, he produces one by breaking with her and leaving Wishwood; and we learn that she is dead before the curtain falls. Hers is the character of blind pride and selfish will that brings on *nemesis,* but Harry's utter lack of compunction seems none the less unnatural. We are reminded very forcibly of the sentence from St. John of the Cross that Eliot prefixed to *Sweeney:* 'Hence the soul cannot be possessed of the divine union, until it has divested itself of the love of created beings.' Though Agatha may tell Harry that 'Love compels cruelty/To those who do not understand love,' Eliot has not succeeded in persuading us that Harry has anything of the overmastering love of God that alone could give sanction to the mystic's terrible renunciation.

The contrast with Eliot's Becket is revelatory. His presentation of the archbishop was limited but coherent. He was not writing a drama of disastrous pride like *Lear,* but a drama of pride overcome. His Becket, after resisting the tempters, is a 'sanctified being,' such as Eliot described in the epigraph to this chapter. Such an image, to be sure, greatly simplifies the actual figure concerning whom historians are still divided as to whether he fought at the last 'for an idea' or 'for the humiliation' of his opponent Henry II. In Eliot's Anglo-Catholic belief Becket is a martyr, but the poet makes him a saint even in this life. He gives none of the flare-up of the natural man who was reported to have met Reginald FitzUrse, the leader of the murderers, with the angry denunciation, 'you pander.' But if Eliot lost something of the human being in the ritualistic priest, even if his Becket, in the consciousness of his mission, barely escapes from 'the pride that apes humility,' Eliot managed to dramatize permanent issues.

He could do it since—as was not the case in *The Family Reunion*—he had grasped and interpreted a social context. He was aware that his conception of history ran contrary to that of a secular age, and one of his most striking passages is that in which Becket addresses the audience with a prophetic vision:

> *I know*
> *What yet remains to show you of my history*
> *Will seem to most of you at best futility,*
> *Senseless self-slaughter of a lunatic,*
> *Arrogant passion of a fanatic.*

The Fourth Tempter also looks ahead to the Reformation, when Becket's shrine will be pillaged, but adds:

> *later is worse, when men will not hate you*
> *Enough to defame or to execrate you,*
> *But pondering the qualities that you lacked*
> *Will only try to find the historical fact.*
> *When men shall declare that there was no mystery*
> *About this man who played a certain part in history.*

One reason why Eliot could give an urgency to these reflections is that he was not writing about the past alone. As Becket went on to denounce indifference, oppression, and exploitation, as he gave his life 'to the Law of God above the Law of Man,' Eliot was writing also against the then rising menace of Fascism, when violent men comparable to Reginald FitzUrse took power into their own hands. Eliot bore out again thereby what he asserted about Pound's translations, that in possessing the past a poet could suggest the present. When he wrote *The Waste Land,* he had also proved the converse, but he could not do so in *The Family Reunion.* Perhaps his increasing sense of the degradation and decay of the modern world had gradually numbed him against any strong feeling for such immediate issues as Becket had faced. Although he wrote an essay about 'the idea of a Christian society,' when confronted with one of the sharpest-drawn crises of our own time, he replied to a questionnaire on loyalist Spain: 'While I am naturally sympathetic, I still feel convinced that it is best that at least a few men of letters should remain isolated, and take no part in these collective activities.' One wonders whether such detachment could be possible for any dramatist who would meet the exacting standards held up by Granville-Barker: that the dramatic art in its fully developed form is the working-out . . . not of the self-realization of the individual, but of society itself.'

Whatever the reason, Eliot could not contrive to endow his Eumenides with any of the collective significance that they posessed for the Greeks. It may also be argued that a mind as saturated with St. John's 'dark night of the soul' as Eliot has revealed himself to be in his *Quartets* may produce profound contemplative poetry, but is unlikely to have sufficient closeness to human beings to present their conflicts concretely. In a recent essay on 'The Social Function of Poetry,' [9] Eliot wrote: 'We may say that the duty of the poet, as poet, is only indirectly to his people: his direct duty is to his *language,* first to preserve, and second to extend and improve.' Eliot was careful to emphasize, once again, that this is not a duty merely to form, in isolation from content, since the poet 'discovers new variations of sensibility which can be appropriated by others. And in expressing them he is developing and enriching the language which he speaks.'

In spite of the failure of *The Family Reunion,* therefore, one should not underestimate the new possibilities that Eliot has already opened for poetic drama. We have only to turn to Tennyson's *Becket* to perceive how far *Murder in the Cathedral* has gone towards revitalizing the genre. Tennyson used the loose five-act structure of a chronicle play in which the nineteenth century imitated the Elizabethans, and though he presented Becket as a spiritual man, in answer to the sceptics, he did not succeed in creating much tension. He ranged over Becket's whole career from the days of his earliest friendship with the King, he introduced an immense cast of characters, and provided a love interest through

Henry's affair with Rosamund. Only in his final scene did he come to Becket's return, after his long exile in France, to the situation out of which Eliot made his whole play. But even more remarkable than Eliot's dramatic concentration is the resonance of his verse, the variety that he gains through its stylized patterns. For one symptomatic instance of why he felt traditional blank verse to be played out, take the difference in dramatic energy between Becket's two speeches to his priests at the moment when the Knights attempt to break into the Cathedral:

Tennyson

> *Undo the doors: the church is not a castle:*
> *Knock, and it shall be open'd. Are you deaf?*
> *What, have I lost authority among you?*
> *Stand by, make way.*

Eliot

Unbar the doors! Throw open the doors!
I will not have the house of prayer, the church of Christ,
The sanctuary, turned into a fortress.
The Church shall protect her own, in her own way, not
As oak and stone; stone and oak decay,
Give no stay, but the Church shall endure.
The church shall be open, even to our enemies. Open the door!

Murder in the Cathedral, including the sombre magnificence of its choruses, is the most sustained poetic drama in English since *Samson Agonistes,* and playable as that work was not designed to be. In spite of its stiffly restricted content, Eliot's drama is particularly impressive when set off against the dead background of the commercial theatre during the past decade. With the radio, as Auden and MacLeish have also argued, we have returned to a period when an audience can again depend entirely upon the spoken word. That may have something to do with the fact that even large moving-picture audiences now respond to Shake-speare's verse as delivered by Laurence Olivier, and that stage revivals of Webster and Middleton and of Yeats's trans-lation of *Oedipus* are again being attempted. At least we are faced with a situation that might challenge the fullest resources of a dramatic poet. Despite the long interruption of the war and the isolating rigors of Eliot's thought, it may be hoped that his play-writing is not yet a finished chapter.

NOTES

1. *The Nation and Athenaeum,* 6 October 1923. The quotation within the passage is from Butcher's commentary on *The Poetics.*

2. This was printed in *The Listener,* 25 November 1936.

3. *The University of Edinburgh Journal,* Autumn 1937.

4. This interchange suggests an interesting sequence. Without Eliot's revolt against the art for art's sake of the 'nineties, his steady insistence that no part of life should be barred from poetry, and his growing example of how a poet can turn for his material both to religion and to politics, Auden's generation would not have found the ground so clear for their own han-dling of contemporary affairs. But Auden's political plays, as well as Spender's *The Trial of a Judge,* are much more im-plicated in immediate events, and owe a great deal to the theatre of Berthold Brecht.

5. Eliot's passage is also closely akin to Jonathan Edwards: 'In efficacious grace we are not merely passive, nor does God do some, and we do the rest. But God does all and we do all. God produces all, and we act all. God is the only proper author and fountain; we are the proper actors. We are, in different respects, wholly active and wholly passive.' In moving towards Catholi-cism Eliot has also preserved the rigor of his Puritan forebears, and his dramas of pride are still in the tradition from Haw-thorne.

6. That Eliot had in mind James' story, 'The Jolly Corner,' while composing his play is made apparent by one of the open-

ing speeches describing how Eliot's hero, like James' exile returning to his old home, will be confronted everywhere by the specter of his past:

> *The man who returns will have to meet*
> *The boy who left. Round by the stables,*
> *In the coach-house, in the orchard,*
> *In the plantation, down the corridor*
> *That led to the nursery, round the corner*
> *Of the new wing, he will have to face him—*
> *And it will not be a very jolly corner.*

The reference was even more pointed in the manuscript draft, which continued:

> *I am sorry, Gerald, for making an allusion*
> *To an author whom you never heard of.*

7. This seems to have been the case both in the play's limited run in London (1939), under the direction of Martin Browne, and in the amateur performance by the Harvard Dramatic Club (1940).

8. Matthew Arnold's realization of his failure to find such 'human actions' for his plays gave rise to the formulation quoted as an epigraph to my chapter on 'The Objective Correlative' (p. 56 above).

Maud Bodkin, in *The Quest for Salvation* (1941), pointed out some of Eliot's limitations when contrasted with the archetypal patterns of Aeschylus. C. L. Barber's essay, 'T. S. Eliot after Strange Gods' (*The Southern Review*, Autumn 1940), utilizing a Freudian technique, is the most extensive examination of the inadequacy of the play's symbols.

9. In *The Norseman*, November 1943, and, in a more extended form, in *The Adelphi*, July 1945.

. . . a white light still and moving.

IN the course of an artist's development certain phases may detach themselves and challenge comprehension as completed wholes. Eliot rounded out such a cycle with 'Little Gidding' (1943), and we are now able to see the full significance of the experiments with structure which he inaugurated in 'Burnt Norton' eight years previously. He speaks of the four poems which form this cycle as 'quartets,' and has evolved for them all the same kind of sequence of five parts with which he composed 'Burnt Norton.' *The Waste Land* was also composed in this fashion, but the contrast is instructive. In his earlier desire for intense concentration the poet so eliminated connectives that *The Waste Land* might be called an anthology of the high points of a drama. It was as though its author had determined to make his poem of nothing but Arnold's 'touchstones,' or had subscribed to Poe's dictum that no longer poem could exist than one to be read at a sitting. In the intervening years Eliot has given further thought to the problem, and he has recently concluded that 'in a poem of any length there must be transitions between passages of greater and lesser intensity, to give rhythm of fluctuating emotion essential to the musical structure of the whole.' He has also enunciated 'a complementary doctrine' to that of Arnold's 'touchstones': the test of a poet's greatness by 'the way he writes his less intense but structurally vital matter.'

None of the four quartets is much more than half as long as *The Waste Land,* but he has included in them all transitional passages that he would previously have dismissed as 'prosaic.' His fundamentally altered intention is at the root of the matter. The dramatic monologues of Prufrock or Gerontion or of the various *personae* of *The Waste Land* have yielded to gravely modulated meditations of the poet's own. The vivid situations of his *Inferno* have been followed by the philosophic debates of his *Purgatorio*. He has made quite explicit the factors conditioning his new structures in the essay from which I have just quoted, 'The Music of Poetry.' [1] As is always the case with Eliot, this essay throws the most relevant light upon his poetic intentions, and is thus a further piece of refutation to those who persist in the fallacy that there is no harmony between his 'revolutionary' creative work and his 'traditionalist' criticism.

Looking back now over the past generation, he finds the poetry of our period to be best characterized by its 'search for a proper modern colloquial idiom.' He develops the same theme near the close of 'Little Gidding' where he envisages the right equilibrium between 'the common word' and 'the formal word.' Only through their union of opposites do we get

> *The complete consort dancing together.*

Eliot, no less than the later Yeats, has helped to restore to poetry the conversational tones which had been muffled by the ornamental forms and diction of the end of the century. But now Eliot is thinking of the other partner to the union, and remarks that 'when we reach a point at which the poetic idiom can be stabilized, then a period of musical elaboration can follow.' Just as Donne, in his later work, returned to the formal pattern of the sonnet which he had mocked in the broken rhythms of his early lyrics, so Eliot now believes that there is such a 'tendency to return to set, and even elaborate patterns' after any period when they have been laid aside.

The present phase of his own return seems to have started

with 'New Hampshire' and 'Virginia,' the short musical evocations which grew out of his renewed impressions of America in the early nineteen-thirties. The impulse to write a series of such place-name poems led on in turn to the more ambitious 'Burnt Norton,' which borrows its title from a Gloucestershire manor near which Eliot has stayed. The titles of the other three quartets indicate more intimate relationships: East Coker, in Somerset, is where the Eliot family lived until its emigration in the mid-seventeenth century to the New England coast; the Dry Salvages, a group of rocks off Cape Ann, mark the part of that coast which the poet knew best as a boy; Little Gidding, the seat of the religious community which Nicholas Ferrar established and with which the names of George Herbert and Crashaw are associated,[2] is a shrine for the devout Anglican, but can remind the poet also that

History is now and England.

The rhythmical pattern of 'Burnt Norton' is elaborated far beyond the delicate melodies of the brief 'Landscapes.' Eliot seems to have found in the interrelation of its five parts a type of structure which satisfied him beyond his previous experiments. For he has adhered to it with such remarkably close parallels in the three succeeding quartets that a description of the structure of one of them involves that of all, and can reveal the deliberateness of his intentions. In each case the first part or movement might be thought of as a series of statements and counterstatements of a theme [3] in lines of an even greater irregularity than those of the late Jacobean dramatists. In each of these first movements a 'landscape' or presented scene gives a concrete core around which the poet's thoughts gather.

The second movement opens with a highly formal lyric: in 'The Dry Salvages' this is a variant of a sestina, rising from the clang of the bell buoy; in 'Little Gidding' each of the three eight-line stanzas ends with a refrain—and thus

[179]

does Eliot signalize his own renewal of forms that would have seemed played out to the author of 'Prufrock.' In the other two poems he has also illustrated a remark which he has been repeating in his recent essays, that 'a poem, or a passage of a poem, may tend to realize itself first as a particular rhythm before it reaches expression in words.' The lyric in 'Burnt Norton'—which is echoed perhaps too closely in 'East Coker'—is as pure musical incantation as any Eliot has written. Not only does its opening image, 'Garlic and sapphires in the mud,' take its inception from Mallarmé's line 'Tonnerre et rubis aux moyeux'; [4] but the rhythm of the poem in which that line occurs, 'M'introduire dans ton histoire,' seems also to have haunted Eliot's ear until it gave rise to a content which, with the exception of its opening line, is wholly different from Mallarmé's.

Following the lyric in the second movement, Eliot has relaxed his rhythms for a sudden contrast; and in 'The Dry Salvages,' and especially in 'East Coker,' has carried his experiment with the prosaic virtually over the border into prose:

> That was a way of putting it—not very satisfactory:
> A periphrastic study in a worn-out poetical fashion,
> Leaving one still with the intolerable wrestle
> With words and meanings. The poetry does not matter.
> It was not (to start again) what one had expected.

The sharp drop from incantation is designed to have the virtue of surprise; but it would seem here to have gone much too far, and to have risked the temporary collapse of his form into the flatness of a too personal statement. The variant in 'Little Gidding' substitutes for such a sequence a modified terza rima, where the poet uses instead of rhyme a sustained alternation of masculine and feminine endings, in a passage that makes the strongest testimony for the value of formal congruence.

What the third parts have in common is that each is an account of movement. In 'Burnt Norton' it is a descent into the London underground, which becomes also a descent into the dark night of the soul. In 'East Coker' the allusion to St. John of the Cross is even more explicit. The poet's command to his soul to

> be still and wait without hope,
> For hope would be hope of the wrong thing,

borrows its sequence of paradoxes directly from the text of the sixteenth-century Spanish mystic. In 'The Dry Salvages' where the concluding charge is

> Not fare well
> But fare forward, voyagers,

the doctrine of action beyond thought of self-seeking is, again explicitly, what Krishna urged to Arjuna on the field of battle; and we recall Eliot's remarking, in his essay on Dante, that 'the next greatest philosophical poem' to *The Divine Comedy* within his experience was the *Bhagavad-Gita*. In 'Little Gidding' the passage of movement is the terza rima passage at the close of the second part, and the deliberately prosaic lines open the third section. The movement described is the 'dead patrol' of two air-raid wardens.

The versification in these third parts is the staple for the poems as a whole, a very irregular iambic line with many substitutions, of predominantly four or five beats, but with syllables ranging from six to eighteen. The fourth movement, in every case, is a short lyric, as it was in *The Waste Land*. The fifth movement is a resumption and resolution of themes, and becomes progressively more intricate in the last two poems, since the themes are cumulative and are all brought together at the close of 'Little Gidding.'

It seems doubtful whether at the time of writing 'Burnt Norton,' just after *Murder in the Cathedral*, Eliot had already projected the series. His creative energies for the next three years were to be largely taken up with *The Family Reunion*, which, to judge from the endless revisions in the manuscript, caused him about as much trouble as anything he has done. With 'East Coker' in the spring of 1940 he made his first experiment in a part for part parallel with an earlier work of his own. Again Donne's practice is suggestive: when he had evolved a particularly intricate and irregular stanza, he invariably set himself the challenge of following it unchanged to the end of his poem. But in assigning himself a similar problem for a poem two hundred lines long, Eliot has tried something far more exacting, where failure could be caused by the parallels becoming merely mechanical, and by the themes and rhythms becoming not subtle variations but flat repetitions. 'East Coker' does indeed have something of the effect of a set piece. Just as its high proportion of prosaic lines seems to spring from partial exhaustion, so its resumption of themes from 'Burnt Norton' can occasionally sound as though the poet was merely imitating himself. But on the whole he had solved his problem. He had made a renewal of form that was to carry him successively in the next two years through 'The Dry Salvages' and 'Little Gidding.' The discrimination between repetition and variation lies primarily in the rhythm; and these last two poems reverberate with an increasing musical richness.

A double question that keeps insisting itself through any discussion of these structures is the poet's consciousness of analogies with music, and whether such analogies are a confusion of arts. One remembers that Eliot, in accepting Lawrence's definition of 'the essence of poetry' as a 'stark, bare, rocky directness of statement,' drew an analogy with the later quartets of Beethoven.[5] This does not mean that he has ever tried to copy literally the effects of a different medium. But he knows that poetry is like music in being a temporal rather than a spatial art; and he has by now

thought much about the subject, as the concluding paragraph of 'The Music of Poetry' shows:

I think that a poet may gain much from the study of music: how
much technical knowledge of musical form is desirable I do not
know, for I have not that technical knowledge myself. But I believe that the properties in which music concerns the poet most
nearly, are the sense of rhythm and the sense of structure. I think
that it might be possible for a poet to work too closely to musical
analogies: the result might be an effect of artificiality.

But he insists—and this has immediate bearing on his own
intentions—that 'the use of recurrent themes is as natural to
poetry as to music.' He has worked on that assumption
throughout his quartets, and whether he has proved that
'there are possibilities of transitions in a poem comparable
to the different movements of a symphony or a quartet,' or
that 'there are possibilities of contrapuntal arrangement of
subject-matter,' can be known only through repeated experience of the whole series. All I wish to suggest here is the
pattern made by some of the dominant themes in their interrelation and progression.

'Burnt Norton' opens as a meditation on time. Many comparable and contrasting views are introduced. The lines are
drenched with reminiscences of Heraclitus' fragments on
flux and movement. Some of the passages on duration remind us that Eliot listened to Bergson's lectures at the Sorbonne in the winter of 1911 and wrote an essay then criticiz-
ing his *durée réelle* as 'simply not final.' Other lines on the
recapture of time through consciousness suggest the aspect
of Bergson that most stimulated Proust. But the chief contrast around which Eliot constructs this poem is that between
the view of time as a mere continuum, and the difficult
paradoxical Christian view of how man lives both 'in and
out of time,' how he is immersed in the flux and yet can
penetrate to the eternal by apprehending timeless existence
within time and above it. But even for the Christian the

[183]

moments of release from the pressures of the flux are rare, though they alone redeem the sad wastage of otherwise un-illumined existence. Eliot recalls one such moment of pecul-iar poignance, a childhood moment in the rose garden—a symbol he has previously used, in many variants, for the birth of desire.[6] Its implications are intricate and even am-biguous, since they raise the whole problem of how to dis-criminate between supernatural vision and mere illusion. Other variations here on the theme of how time is conquered are more directly apprehensible. In dwelling on the exten-sion of time into movement, Eliot takes up an image he had used in 'Triumphal March': 'at the still point of the turning world.' This notion of 'a mathematically pure point' (as Philip Wheelwright has called it) seems to be Eliot's poetic equivalent in our cosmology for Dante's 'unmoved Mover,' another way of symbolising a timeless release from the 'outer compulsions' of the world. Still another variation is the passage on the Chinese jar in the final section. Here Eliot, in a conception comparable to Wallace Stevens' 'Anecdote of the Jar,' has suggested how art conquers time:

> *Only by the form, the pattern,*
> *Can words or music reach*
> *The stillness, as a Chinese jar still*
> *Moves perpetually in its stillness.*

'Burnt Norton' is the most philosophically dense of the series, and any adequate account of Eliot's development of his themes would demand detailed analysis. With the open-ing phrase of 'East Coker,' 'In my beginning is my end,' he has extended his meditation on time into history. In such a phrase, which is close to Heraclitus' 'The beginning and the end are common,' the poet has also indicated the recur-rent attraction he feels to the reconciliation of opposites which characterizes that pre-Socratic philosopher. Eliot is using these words in a double sense. He is thinking historically—as the first section goes on to make clear, he is thinking back to the conception of order and harmony as propounded by a sixteenth-century Thomas Elyot in his *Booke named the Governour*. And near the close of the poem, the overtones of history and of family are blended in the phrase, 'Home is where one starts from.' But the continuity with which he is concerned is not simply that of race. He is also thinking in religious terms—in my beginning, in my birth, is implied my end, death; yet, in the Christian reversal of terms, that death can mean rebirth, and the culminating phrase of 'East Coker' is 'In my end is my beginning.'

As his thought becomes involved with the multiple meanings of history, with how the moments of significance and illumination bisect 'the world of time,' he dwells also on the course of the individual history, and his reflections become deeply personal as he confronts the disappointments of old age. He weighs the 'limited value' of what can be learned from experience, since its accustomed pattern may restrict and blind us to what comes with the 'new and shocking' moment. When the soul is sick, it can learn only through humility, only if it accepts the paradox which is developed both by St. John of the Cross and by Marvell in his 'Dialogue Between the Soul and Body,' that 'Our only health is the disease.' Man may come to the end of his night of dark vacancy only if he learns that he 'must go by the way of dispossession.'

The three middle sections of 'East Coker' are as sombre as anything Eliot has written, and culminate in his pronouncing his career which has fallen between two wars as 'twenty years largely wasted.' The danger of such a declaration is that it risks false humility, and the inertness of these lines contrasts unsatisfactorily with the comparable passage in 'Burnt Norton' on what is gained through form. But the contrast is structurally deliberate, and with the phrase,

'Home is where one starts from,' there comes the quickening
reflection that old men should be explorers 'into another
intensity/ For a further union.' What they must pass through
is such 'empty desolation' as the sea's, and in developing
that image in the concluding lines of 'East Coker,' the poet
prepares the most thrilling transition of the whole series.
For 'The Dry Salvages' opens with a contrast between the
river and the sea, between the two forces that have most
conditioned Eliot's sense of rhythm. For nationalist critics
of the Van Wyck Brooks school who declare that Eliot has
broken away from his roots since he has not included in his
poems realistic details from the Middle West, it could be
profitable to note that the river is 'the big river,'—at first the
frontier, then the 'useful, untrustworthy' conveyor of ship-
ping, then a problem to be solved by the bridge builder, and
at last 'almost forgotten' by city dwellers. This passage gives
an insight into the sources of a poet's rhythm; and into how
he penetrates for his material beneath all surface details, in
order to repossess his essential experience. The significance
of the river for Eliot shows in what he wrote to a St. Louis
paper in 1930:

I feel that there is something in having passed one's childhood
beside the big river, which is incommunicable to those who have
not. Of course my people were Northerners and New England-
ers, and of course I have spent many years out of America altogether; but Missouri and the Mississippi have made a deeper
impression on me than any other part of the world.

The contrapuntal balance of sea and river reinforces,
throughout 'The Dry Salvages,' the themes of time and
movement. And yet the underlying changelessness of the sea
beneath its tides, with its tolling bells measuring 'time not
our time,' underscores also the contrasting theme of the
timeless. History is again dwelt on, and is now discerned as
not just the blind corridor it seemed to Gerontion, since
'Time the destroyer is time the preserver.' This perception

gives foundation for Krishna's counsel of disinterested action. Then, after the bell buoy's 'perpetual angelus' has resounded through the lyrical fourth movement, as it had in the sestina at the opening of the second, Eliot makes his most complete articulation of what can be involved in 'the intersection of the timeless with time.' By allusions to the rose garden and to the other moments of illumination that he has symbolized in the three poems so far, he suggests the common basis of such moments in their 'hints' of grace. He goes farther, and states that such 'hints' lead also to the central truth in his religious convictions:

> But to apprehend
> The point of intersection of the timeless
> With time, is an occupation for the saint—
> No occupation either, but something given
> And taken, in a lifetime's death in love,
> Ardour and selflessness and self-surrender.
> For most of us, there is only the unattended
> Moment, the moment in and out of time,
> The distraction fit, lost in a shaft of sunlight,
> The wild thyme unseen, or the winter lightning,
> Or the waterfall, or music heard so deeply
> That it is not heard at all, but you are the music
> While the music lasts. These are only hints and guesses,
> Hints followed by guesses; and the rest
> Is prayer, observance, discipline, thought and action.
> The hint half guessed, the gift half understood, is Incarnation.
> Here the impossible union
> Of spheres of existence is actual,
> Here the past and future
> Are conquered and reconciled. . .

The doctrine of Incarnation is the pivotal point on which Eliot's thought has swung well away from the nineteenth century's romantic heresies of Deification. The distinction between thinking of God become Man through the Saviour, or of Man becoming God through his own divine potentialities, can be at the root of political as well as of religious belief. Eliot has long affirmed that Deification, the reckless doctrine of every great man as a Messiah, has led ineluctably to Dictatorship. What he has urged in his *Idea of a Christian Society,* is a re-established social order in which both governors and governed find their completion in their common humility before God. The above passage, therefore, compresses, at the climax of 'The Dry Salvages' the core of Eliot's thought on time, on history, and on the destiny of man.

The content of 'Little Gidding' is most apparently under the shadow of the war. But it underlines what Eliot declared in an essay on 'Poetry in Wartime,' that the more permanently valuable poetry of 1914-18 was 'more of sadness and pity than of military glory.' [7] The secluded chapel enforces thoughts of pilgrimage and prayer, but a further reflection on history carries the poet to the realization that

> *We cannot restore old policies*
> *Or follow an antique drum.*

If 'history may be servitude, history may be freedom,' and

> *Here the intersection of the timeless moment*
> *Is England and nowhere. Never and always.*

In the final movement he resumes successively all his major themes, opening with 'The end is where we start from.' This leads into another passage on words and form, since 'every sentence is an end and a beginning,' 'every poem an epitaph.' Comparably, every action is a step towards death, but may likewise be a step towards redemption. Once again we have a recognition of the potentialities of history far more resolute than what was seen in the tired backward look in 'East Coker.' For now the poet affirms that

> *We shall not cease from exploration*
> *And the end of all our exploring*
> *Will be to arrive where we started*
> *And know the place for the first time.*

What we will know is adumbrated through allusions that take us back through the series, back to 'the source of the longest river,' back, indeed, to the moment of release that he evoked in 'New Hampshire,' to 'the children in the apple tree.' But the completion of that glimpsed vision, as was the case with Dante's childhood love for Beatrice, must be sought through full maturity, through

> *A condition of complete simplicity*
> *(Costing not less than everything).*

The value of Eliot's device of incremental repetition hinges most on this final section of 'Little Gidding,' since there is hardly a phrase that does not recall an earlier passage in the series. Some readers may object that this makes too much for a circular movement, with insufficient resolution at the close. In one sense this is true, but only in as much as the questions on which the poet is meditating are endless in their recurrent urgency. And such structural recurrence of themes, as Proust also found, is the chief device by which the writer can convey the recapture of time. The concluding lines mount to finality in their enunciation that all

> *shall be well*
> *When the tongues of flame are in-folded*
> *Into the crowned knot of fire*
> *And the fire and the rose are one.*

Out of their context these lines may seem to be merely a decorative allusion to Dante's paradise. But once you have observed the central role that fire plays, intermittently through the series and dominantly in 'Little Gidding,' the potential reconciliation of the flames of destruction with the rose of light is weighted with significance. A glance at Eliot's varied symbolic use of fire can also give us an opportunity to examine more closely than we have so far the texture of the poetry he has developed through the structures of his quartets.

The lyric at the opening of the second part of 'Little Gidding' recounts the successive death of the elements. It versifies, with amplification, a sentence of Heraclitus that dwells both on the ceaseless flux and on the reconciliation of opposites, 'Fire lives in the death of air, and air in the death of fire; water lives in the death of earth, and earth in the death of water.' We can observe again the lasting impression made on the poet's consciousness by this philosopher, concerning whom he recorded in his student's notebook of thirty years ago: 'By God he meant fire.' But the fire in this lyric, and in the terza rima lines which follow it, is not the fire of creation:

> *In the uncertain hour before the morning*
> *Near the ending of interminable night*
> *At the recurrent end of the unending*
> *After the dark dove with the flickering tongue*
> *Had passed below the horizon of his homing. . .*

The 'dark dove' is the bird that haunts now all our skies; its 'flickering tongue' is the airman's fire of destruction. The figures who meet 'between three districts when the smoke arose' and who tread 'the pavement in a dead patrol' need no annotation of their function. But Eliot is occupied here with other meetings as well. It is no usual fellow warden whom he encounters but 'a familiar compound ghost.' This 'ghost' is akin, as some phrases show, to Brunetto Latini, whose meeting with Dante in Hell is one of the passages which has impressed Eliot most. A characteristic of Eliot's poetic thought ever since *Ash Wednesday* has been to make free transitions from the *Inferno* to the *Purgatorio;* and the last words spoken in this 'disfigured street' as the day is breaking, are advice to the poet that he cannot escape from the 'exasperated spirit' of old age,

> *unless restored by that refining fire*
> *Where you must move in measure, like a dancer.*

And here, in the image of the dance—as Theodore Spencer has remarked to me—one also moves in anticipation beyond the searing flames of purgatory to the radiant spheres of paradise.

The other chief passage on fire in 'Little Gidding' is the fourth movement, as impressive a lyric as any Eliot has produced:

> *The dove descending breaks the air*
> *With flame of incandescent terror*
> *Of which the tongues declare*
> *The one discharge from sin and error.*
> *The only hope or else despair*
>> *Lies in the choice of pyre or pyre—*
>> *To be redeemed from fire by fire.*
>
> *Who then devised the torment? Love.*
> *Love is the unfamiliar Name*
> *Behind the hands that wove*
> *The intolerable shirt of flame*
> *Which human power cannot remove.*
>> *We only live, only suspire*
>> *Consumed by either fire or fire.*

The control of the range of meanings here is masterly. On one level, the choice in the first stanza is between destruction and destruction, for as 'the tongues' on both sides declare it is either 'we' or 'they,' the 'incandescent terror' must blot out either London or Berlin. But the descending dove is, more profoundly, that of annunciation, and 'the tongues' of prophecy declare the terms of our possible redemption. The poem reaches the heart of its meaning in the heavily stressed end-word of the opening line of the second stanza. That most familiar word is yet unfamiliar to mankind, which cannot bear very much reality.' We can hardly face the fact that love is essentially not release but suffering; and that the intolerable burden of our desires—our Nessus shirt—can be removed by nothing within our power, but solely through grace. All we have is the terms of our choice, the fire of our destructive lusts or the inscrutable terrible fire of divine Love.

The poetry of purgation, as Eliot has observed, is ordinarily less exciting than that of either damnation or beatitude, but this lyric transcends such limitation through its fervour. The encounter between the air-raid wardens is the other most dramatic passage in the poem. Since it marks Eliot's first experiment with terza rima, it carries further the long series of his debts to Dante. But its method follows more particularly the lesson of another master. The 'forgotten, half-recalled' figure is evoked by the device of multiple reference which Henry James used in his 'ghost' stories. The figure, 'too strange . . . for misunderstanding,' suggests not only Brunetto Latini or Arnaut Daniel. When he reminds Eliot how their common concern with speech impelled them 'to purify the dialect of the tribe,' he virtually translates from Mallarmé's 'Le Tombeau d'Edgar Poe' ('donner un sens plus pur aux mots de la tribu'),[8] and indicates that he may be thought of as any of Eliot's dead masters. When he proceeds to disclose 'the gifts reserved for age,' it is interesting to recall that Eliot's bitter 'Lines for an Old Man' contain in the manuscript the epigraph, 'to Stéphane Mallarmé.'

It may be objected that such a range of suggestion detracts from dramatic singleness. It is more certainly true—as we noted in relation to his plays—that Eliot, from the time of his earliest poems, has been more successful in posing a dramatic moment than in developing a sustained action. It may also be charged that he betrays a limitation of content in comparison with some of the other strange meetings that he recalls. Whereas the lines spoken by Brunetto Latini are, as Eliot himself has said, Dante's 'testimony of a loved master of arts'; and Wilfred Owen's hallucinated pitiful encounter was with no less than the enemy he had killed; the main burden that Eliot's 'ghost' has to convey is the impotent lacerations of growing old.

But to the charge that has been brought against Eliot that ever since his conversion his content has been tenuous, the range of reflection and feeling in the quartets should serve to give a persuasive refutation. The trouble has been that whereas Eliot's earlier poetry was difficult in form, his later work is difficult in thought. The reader of 'Gerontion' had to learn how to supply the missing connectives. The reader of the quartets finds a sufficiently straightforward logic, but is confronted with realms of discourse largely unfamiliar to a secular age. Sustained knowledge of the dark night of the soul is a rare phase of mystical experience in any age; and it is at that point that agnostic and atheist readers have been most severe in demanding whether Eliot's lines express anything more than mere literary allusions. The severity is desirable, but it should not be forgotten that authentic poetry often takes us into experiences equally remote from our ordinary hours, as in Oedipus' vision at Colonnos, in Rilke's *Duino Elegies,* or in almost the whole *Paradiso.* Misconceptions of Eliot's content may be avoided if we remain aware, at least, of what he is aiming to do. As our examination of the structures of his quartets has borne out, the greatest change from his earlier poems is that his intentions now are only intermittently dramatic. Or rather, he has tried to concentrate his desire for drama into his two plays; and what he has produced in his quartets is what in the seventeenth century would have been called meditations. Yet the most striking change in the texture of his verse is his abandonment of the devices that he learned from Donne and the other metaphysicals. The qualities for which he now aspires are those of a less popular seventeenth-century master, Lancelot Andrewes, whose 'spiritual discipline' he has contrasted with Donne's broken intensity. The three attributes of Andrewes' style that Eliot singled out for praise can belong to poetry as well as to prose: 'ordonnance, or arrangement and structure, precision in the use of words, and relevant intensity.' Those attributes seemed very far from the poetical aims of 'The Hollow Men' which he had written the year before his essay on Andrewes; but something comparable to the purely contemplative' emotion he found in Andrewes is what he now wants most to express.

The measure of an author's attraction for Eliot can always be read in what that author has taught him about the development of his medium; and it is notable that the passage which Eliot cited to show how Andrewes' spiritual reflections can force 'a concrete presence upon us,' provided him with the starting point of his own 'Journey of the Magi.' [9] Another sentence ('Let us then make this so accepted a time in itself twice acceptable by our accepting . . .'), which illustrated how Andrewes did 'not hesitate to hammer, to inflect, even to play upon a word for the sake of driving home its meaning,' gave Eliot a similar word-play in 'Burnt Norton' ('There they were as our guests, accepted and accepting'), and stimulated him to such an independent development as the startling

Distracted from distraction by distraction.

Those who demand that a poet's content should be immediately useful will take no satisfaction in Eliot's belief that the poet in wartime should as a man 'be no less devoted to his country than other men,' but that 'his first duty as a poet' is still to the preservation and development of his 'native language.' To the nationalist critics that will seem to beg the question of content altogether. But the cheapness of Van Wyck Brooks's opinion that Eliot is a poet of little hope, less faith, and no charity, should be substantially refuted by the lyric on the kinds of love alone. But such a lyric does not exist alone; it rises organically as the summation of one of Eliot's profoundest themes. And those who are suspicious of the inertness of the passages which urge the soul to wait in the dark without hope, should remember that the final declaration, even in 'East Coker,' is that

We must be still and still moving.

The reconciliation of opposites is as fundamental to Eliot as it was to Heraclitus. Only thus can he envisage a resolution of man's whole being. The 'heart of light' that he glimpsed in the opening movement of 'Burnt Norton' is at the opposite pole from the 'Heart of Darkness,' from which he took the epigraph for 'The Hollow Men.' Essential evil still constitutes more of Eliot's subject-matter than essential good, but the magnificent orchestration of his themes has prepared for that paradisal glimpse at the close, and thereby makes it no decorative allusion, but an integrated climax to the content no less than to the form. Such spiritual release and reconciliation are the chief reality for which he strives in a world that has seemed to him increasingly threatened with new dark ages.

NOTES

1. 'The Music of Poetry' was the W. P. Ker Memorial Lecture at Glasgow. It also appeared in *Partisan Review* (November 1942).

2. By including in 'Little Gidding' a refrain from Juliana of Norwich—

> *Sin is Behovely, but*
> *All shall be well, and*
> *All manner of thing shall be well—*

Eliot also aimed, as he has said, 'to escape any suggestion of historical sentimentality about the seventeenth century by this reiterated reference to the fourteenth century and therefore to get more bearing on the present than would be possible if the relation was merely between the present and one particular period of the past.'

3. This was also observed by Helen Gardner, in 'The Recent Poetry of T. S. Eliot' (*New Writing*, Summer 1942). The other most useful studies of Eliot's later work that I have seen are Philip Wheelwright's 'The *Burnt Norton* Trilogy' (*The Chimera*, Autumn 1942) and James J. Sweeney's examination of the sources of 'East Coker' (*The Southern Review*, Spring 1941).

4. I am indebted for this point and for other fertile suggestions to Mr. John L. Sweeney.

5. At pp. 89-90 above.

6. A detailed analysis has been made by Leonard Unger, 'T. S. Eliot's Rose Garden: A Persistent Theme' (*The Southern Review*, Spring 1942).

7. 'Poetry in Wartime' appeared in *Common Sense* (October 1942). Eliot also wrote a poem on the same subject, 'A Note on War Poetry,' which appeared in the anthology, *London Calling* (1942):

> *Not the expression of collective emotion*
> *Imperfectly reflected in the daily papers.*
> *Where is the point at which the merely individual*
> *Explosion breaks*
>
> *In the path of an action merely typical*
> *To create the universal, originate a symbol*
> *Out of the impact? this is a meeting*
> *On which we attend*
>
> *Of forces beyond control by experiment:*
> *Of Nature and the Spirit. Mostly, the individual*
> *Experience is too large, or too small. Our emotions*
> *Are only 'incidents'*
>
> *In the effort to keep day and night together.*
> *It seems just possible that a poem might happen*
> *To a very young man: but a poem is not poetry—*
> *That is a life.*
>
> *War is not a life: it is a situation,*
> *One which may neither be ignored nor accepted,*
> *A problem to be met with ambush and stratagem,*
> *Enveloped or scattered.*

The enduring is no substitute for the transient,
Neither one for the other. But the abstract conception
Of private experience at its greatest intensity
Becoming universal, which we call 'poetry,'
May be affirmed in verse.

8. This point has also been observed by Delmore Schwartz.

9. How prose may be transformed into poetry is illustrated by the comparison between the quotation from Andrewes and what Eliot made of it:

'It was no summer progress. A cold coming they had of it at this time of the year, just the worst time of the year to take a journey, and specially a long journey in. The ways deep, the weather sharp, the days short, the sun farthest off, *in solstitio brumali*, "the very dead of winter." '

> *'A cold coming we had of it,*
> *Just the worst time of the year*
> *For a journey, and such a long journey:*
> *The ways deep and the weather sharp,*
> *The very dead of winter.'*

IX

THE POWER OF DEVELOPMENT . . . IN A DIFFERENT WORLD

BY C. L. BARBER (1958)

. . . a man who is capable of experience finds himself in a different world in every decade of his life; as he sees it with different eyes, the material of his art is renewed.—Eliot, 'Yeats' (1940).

One of the greatest capacities of genius is the power of development. The volume of a man's work should correspond to this capacity in him: what he leaves behind should be no more and no less than what is needed to realise each definite stage of his development.—Eliot, Letter on Joyce to the Institute of Contemporary Arts (1949).

ELIOT'S work since *Four Quartets* constitutes a 'definite stage of his development'; he has shown the same power to go on which he has praised in Yeats and Joyce. With *The Cocktail Party,* in 1949, he solved the problem of making a viable verse drama with contemporary setting and idiom, the problem with which he had wrestled in *The Family Reunion.* Since *Four Quartets,* virtually all his verse has been written for the theater,[1] *The Confidential Clerk* appearing in 1953, and *The Elder Statesman* due to appear at the Edinburgh Festival in the summer of 1958. The two plays that have already appeared at this time deal with the same basic problem that has always concerned Eliot, the relation between religious experience and the rest of life. But ordinary life is presented and valued in a new way. The emphasis is placed, not alone on what is lacking in the secular world, but also on the religious tendencies latent in its misconceived or incomplete strivings. A drastic revision of his dramatic practice and theory has gone with this change in emphasis. One could say that after the experiments of the thirties, he has come

[198]

to write a neo-classical drama, more like that of Racine than anything else—but to isolate that one affinity oversimplifies, and suggests a direct derivation where in fact there has been a complex, independent development. Eliot describes in two recent essays, 'Poetry and Drama' and 'The Three Voices of Poetry,' how he has moved step by step from one experiment to another in the theater. His literary criticism, much of it brought together in 1956 in a new collection, *On Poetry and Poets,* also illuminates his creative work, as does his social criticism in *Notes towards a Definition of Culture.* The prose reflects in a variety of ways the shift in emphasis towards wider tolerance and equilibrium. After leading the revolution in poetry and taste which Matthiessen described when he was writing in 1934, Eliot in the second half of his career has been concerned to be inclusive and judicious.

1. THE CRITICISM

Eliot has now several times described his best earlier criticism as 'essays on poets and poetic dramatists who had influenced me . . . , a by-product of my private poetry workshop.' Already in 1942, he took occasion to note the inevitable partisanship of such criticism: 'the poet, at the back of his mind, if not as his ostensible purpose, is always trying to defend the kind of poetry he is writing, or to formulate the kind that he wants to write. . . He is not so much a judge as an advocate. . . What he writes about poetry, in short, must be assessed in relation to the poetry he writes.' Eliot's criticism since the later thirties has rarely been of this kind. He returns in several of his pieces to figures who have *not* been sympathetic to him, such as Byron, Milton, Kipling, doing justice, discovering qualities he had missed, with wonderful perceptivity but without the excitement of adding to a whole developing view of poetry. Where the best of the earlier essays were written, he tells us, about poets with whom 'I had become thoroughly familiar, long before I desired to write about them,' these later pieces often are produced after deliberately rereading the work in question. That almost all of the later pieces were written as lectures makes for a less dense and pointed texture. And there are places where the effort to do justice leads to banality, where he is almost becalmed on a dead center of judiciousness. In the lecture on Goethe delivered on the receipt of a prize in 1955, Eliot describes himself as undertaking the 'very valuable exercise' of studying an unsympathetic author, one whose work presents particular obstacles to 'anyone like myself, who combines a Catholic cast of mind, a Calvinist heritage, and a Puritan temperament.' He observes that 'antipathy overcome, when it is antipathy to any figure so great as that of Goethe, is an important liberation from a limitation of one's own mind.' This sort of effort at overcoming limitations is characteristic of the later essays. In the case of Goethe, Eliot perhaps asked too much of himself, for what we get from 'Goethe as the Sage' is much less Goethe than it is Eliot's conception of the nature of wisdom, of greatness, and of the role of major literary figures in shaping the European tradition.

One can, indeed, generalize and say that, in the criticism of *On Poetry and Poets,* it is not what he writes about individual figures which carries the greatest freight. Except in the cases of Virgil and Johnson, he is not telling how he found himself in finding individual writers, as he used to do; instead, the excitement of enlarging understanding is in his general discussions of the nature of poetry, of drama, and of the relation of poetry to culture and religion. The first four lectures in the volume, written between 1942 and 1945, especially 'The Social Function of Poetry' and 'The Music of Poetry,' take their place beside 'Tradition and the Individual Talent' as masterpieces of balanced generalization about the literary process. The contribution of poetry to a people's language becomes a key conception: 'our language goes on changing; our way of life changes, under the pressure of material changes in our environment in all sorts of ways; and unless we have those few men who combine an exceptional sensibility with an exceptional power over words, our own ability, not merely to express, but even to feel any but the crudest emotions, will degenerate.' It is characteristic of the tough-minded subtlety of these essays that Eliot does not leave this point without observing that 'it will be equally true that the quality of our poetry is dependent upon the way in which the people use their language: for a poet must take as his material his own language as it is actually spoken around him. If it is improving, he will profit; if it is deteriorating, he must make the best of it. Poetry can to some extent preserve, or even restore, the beauty of a language. . . But poetry, like every other element in that mysterious social personality which we call our "culture," must be dependent upon a great many circumstances which are beyond its control.'

Eliot observes several times that the situation of poetry has changed in his lifetime as we have moved from a period of innovation to one of development. He distinguishes between periods when 'the task is to catch up with the changes in colloquial speech, which are fundamentally changes in thought and sensibility,' and periods when 'the task is to explore the musical possibilities of an established convention of the relation of the idiom of verse to that of speech.' Reconsidering Milton in 1947, he placed 'Milton's consummate powers' as those of a period of development. He explained how, earlier, his generation's need to revolutionize diction led to neglect of Milton, and suggested that 'the poetry of the rest of this century' needs to 'avoid the danger of a *servitude* to colloquial speech and to current jargon' and 'might have much to learn from Milton's extended verse structure.' Eliot's study in 1944 of 'Johnson as Critic

[201]

and Poet' was clearly undertaken in order to explore the virtues characteristic of a figure who comes at the close of a period of development. 'Johnson could accept much as poetry, which seems to us merely competent and correct; we, on the other hand, are too ready to accept as poetry what is neither competent nor correct.' Eliot notes how, in comparison with Johnson's sensitivity to the finer variations within a settled form, our ears have become thickened in growing 'accustomed, during the last century and more, to such a riot of individual styles,' and observes that 'the absence of any common standard of poetic diction is a weakness both of modern verse and of our criticism of it.' There is no simplifying suggestion that we can return to the age of Johnson and enjoy its advantages and limitations. But our own age is put into a perspective which emphasizes the need to move as best we can towards 'definite meaning expressed in the properest words,' the direction Eliot's own verse has taken.

Most of Eliot's criticism is not directly concerned with religion; yet his comments on literature and culture always prove to be adjusted to religious actuality as he conceives it. In the first decade after he joined the church, he wrote for the most part directly in religious terms: *Ash Wednesday; After Strange Gods; The Rock; Murder in the Cathedral.* Since then, he has increasingly chosen as his ground not religion itself but what leads towards it, goes with it, comes from it. He does not deny himself religious terms in referring to it from outside; but he has avoided the limitations that go with being *just* inside, with being a church artist working for church members. In *Notes towards a Definition of Culture* (1948) Eliot's central point is that we must see 'the culture of a people as the incarnation of its religion.' But he does *not* mean by this that the only culture that matters is that of the devout persons in a nation. On the contrary, it is one of his fundamental assumptions that men cannot avoid worshiping something, whether they know it or not. Culture is shaped by *all* worship, and in very complex, indirect ways, even though ultimately the quality of a given culture will depend on the character of its religion. 'It is against a background of Christianity that all our thought has significance. . . Only a Christian culture could have produced a Voltaire or a Nietzsche.' One need not share Eliot's religious faith, nor his conviction that our culture can have a future only as a Christian culture, to be enlightened by his grasp of the actualities of religion and culture in the past and present.

The span or range of his social criticism is remarkable: while he holds on consistently to his conviction that religion is primary, he always keeps a clear eye and open mind for the varieties and contradictions of art and life. *Notes towards a Definition of Culture,* despite its finical-sounding title, is a remarkably positive book, for in insisting on 'the limits of the plannable,' it keeps pointing to the six-sevenths of the iceberg that is under the surface: Eliot is realistic in recognizing how little the will and the mind can do, yet he does not lose hold of consciousness and deliberation in considering what *can* be done. In his social criticism, he has been a pioneer in attending, with an anthropological eye, to the implications of the educated half-truth. His is a very tolerant Christian anthropology, which recognizes a mystery at the center of life—even including the mystery that valid cultures are centered in religions other than Christianity, and must be respected as we respect life, wherever we find it. We cannot give other peoples our culture without our religion, but we can learn, he observes, 'to respect every other culture as a whole, however inferior to our own it may appear, or however justly we may disapprove of some feature of it: the deliberate destruction of another culture as a whole is an irreparable wrong, almost as evil as to treat human beings as animals.' In considering the various strains within our own European culture, Eliot adopts a sociological point of view which recognizes the value for culture of a variety of religious sects, as well as the counter-claims of factors working for unity and continuity. This sort of respect for what is actual in an imperfect religious heritage is cognate to the respect which the recent plays express for the incomplete religious impulses of people in ordinary social life.

His interest in what is moving *towards* Christianity is nowhere clearer in the recent prose than in 'Virgil and the Christian World' (1951), where his thesis is that Virgil was indeed in a valid sense a prophet of Christianity. In considering the famous passage in the fourth *Ecologue,* Eliot of course rejects the notion of any conscious intention to 'predict' Christ; and he takes the occasion to make an observation about unconscious meaning which relates prophecy to much poetry, including some of his own:

A poet may believe that he is expressing only his private experience; his lines may be for him only a means of talking about himself without giving himself away; yet for his readers what he has written may come to be the expression both of their own secret feelings and of the exultation or despair of a generation. He need not know what his poetry will come to mean to others; and a prophet need not understand the meaning of his prophetic utterance.

The essay then considers the Christian affinities of Virgil's conceptions of labor, of piety, and of destiny. Eliot describes Aeneas as 'the prototype of the Christian hero' in a fashion which illuminates his own distinctive heroic ideal. Aeneas is 'a man guided by the deepest conviction of destiny, but he is a humble man who knows that this destiny is something not to be desired and not to be avoided.' His 'end is only a new beginning. . . He suffers for himself, he acts only in obedience.' The way Eliot develops Virgil's conception of destiny is illuminating for the even-handed dramatization of destinies in *The Cocktail Party*. Such a destiny as Aeneas' 'is an election which cannot be explained, a burden and responsibility rather than a reason for self-glorification. It merely happens to one man and not to others, to have the gifts necessary in some profound crisis, but he can take no credit to himself for the gifts and the responsibility assigned to him.' Eliot's reading of the Dido episode is also characteristic: he points out that although destiny requires Aeneas to leave her, following destiny does not relieve a man of moral responsibility. This represents a change of emphasis from the presentation of Harry in *The Family Reunion*, where as Professor Matthiessen notes, we miss precisely the remorse we should expect in the hero about the human consequences of his following his fate.

The study of Virgil is one clear case, among the recent lectures, where Eliot is describing the meaning he has found over the years in an author he came to know well long ago. He underscores the relation of the *imperium romanum* as Virgil conceived it, to the tradition of Christian Europe, for which he feels Virgil's kind of piety. He contributed to reconstruction after the war by delivering three broadcast talks to Germany on *Die Einheit der Europaeischen Kultur*. When he was awarded the Nobel Prize in 1947, his speech was an effective expression of piety for the European tradition of poetry. His acceptance began, characteristically, by dismissing his personal feelings and the claims of his individual talent: 'May I . . . ask that it be taken for granted, that I experienced, on learning of this award to myself, all the normal emotions of exaltation and vanity.' He went on to say that he found in the Nobel Award 'something more and something different' from recognition of merit. 'It seems to me more the election of an individual, . . . selected by something like an act of grace, to fill a peculiar role and become a peculiar symbol. A ceremony takes place, by which a man is suddenly endowed with some function which he did not fill before. So the question is not whether he was worthy to be so singled out, but whether or not he can perform the function which you have assigned to him: the function of serving as a representative, so far as any man can be, of something of far greater importance than the value of what he himself has written.' When Yeats received the same award twenty-five years before, he was much more richly human about it, not saying simply things like 'hardly any one of us is, more than others worthy,' but speaking instead of Lady Gregory and Synge: 'When your king gave me medal and diploma, two forms should have stood one at either side of me, an old woman sinking into the infirmity of age and a young man's ghost.' But Eliot's way of going beyond himself, beyond his ineradicable shyness, is moving too, and dramatic in his characteristic fashion. Instead of seeing the prize as part of a continuity in his own and other lives, his analogy to 'an act of grace' insists on the discontinuity by which something is created which did not exist before. Value is placed, by a dramatic shift, not on individual merit or endeavor, though such things continue to matter, but on 'something of far greater importance.' This is the sort of moment of recognition on which the recent plays turn—though what is recognized of course differs.

In studying the recent criticism, I have been more and more impressed with how affirmative it is, after all. Eliot has the uncynical disillusion of a tempered religious sensibility. He can envisage, perhaps half expects, a debacle of Western culture should the residual organizing power he sees in Christianity be finally exhausted. But he sees a great deal of strength in 'what is already living':

We are all, so far as we inherit the civilization of Europe, still citizens of the Roman Empire, and time has not yet proved Virgil wrong when he wrote *nec tempora pono: imperium sine fine dedi*. But, of course, the Roman Empire which Virgil imagined and for which Aeneas worked out his destiny was not exactly the same as the Roman Empire of the legionaries, the pro-consuls and governors, the business men and speculators, the demagogues and generals. It was something greater, but something which exists because Virgil imagined it. It remains an ideal, but one which Virgil passed on to Christianity to develop and cherish.

In the end, it seems to me that the place which Dante assigned to Virgil in the future life, and the role of guide and teacher as far as the barrier which Virgil was not allowed to pass, was not capable of passing, is an exact statement of Virgil's relation to the Christian world.

Speaking in the same year of his ideal for the drama, Eliot concluded by referring to this same moment in Dante: he would like the drama to lead *to* Christianity as Virgil does. He sees the Greek dramatists as leading also, in their way, in the same direction, as the experiment with the Eumenides in *The Family Reunion* attempted to show. When he was starting to work on that play, in 1937, he gave a lecture on 'Religious Drama, Mediaeval and Modern,' in which he observed that an 'essentially religious craving is latent in all serious lovers of the drama,' and that 'so far as the stage in general has ever been serious, it has dealt with moral problems, with problems which in the end required a religious solution—whether this necessity was present to the mind of the author or not. This is obviously true of Greek tragedy.' When we come to look at *The Cocktail Party* and *The Confidential Clerk* in relation to the tragi-comedies of Euripides which are their prototypes, we shall see how each of them modifies the Greek plot so as to suggest a religious solution for moral problems.

The revision in dramatic method and theory made since the war was the outgrowth of an evolution which Eliot describes in a remarkably genial and self-critical way in 'Poetry and Drama,' written after the success of *The Cocktail Party* and before *The Confidential Clerk*. He tells how he became dissatisfied with special audiences, whether of religious people or of poetry lovers, with special, 'poetic' idioms, with emphatically allusive symbols, with choruses or arias that suspend the action. This development reflects the practical demands of the theater, which Eliot has been determined to make the best of, as he has made the best of other institutions: he has enjoyed working on a production team, learning by the feed-back of trial and error.[2] But the change in his dramatic methods has also served the change in his sensibility and interests. Up through *The Family Reunion,* when it was the gulf dividing spiritual from material, the shock of discovering spiritual reality, which Eliot was chiefly concerned to dramatize, he set a 'doomed or sanctified' hero, Sweeney, Becket, Harry, over against characters who were 'material, literal-minded and visionless'; most of the poetry (except for choric accompaniments) was spoken by the protagonist, who talked over the heads of those around him, or exploded grenades of meaning in their faces. A different method is required to convey what has concerned him since the war, the latent presence of religion in the ordinary world. If he is to catch this reality, to bring it out, he must find it, without benefit of clergy, in contemporary speech and contemporary manners. By 'imposing a credible order upon ordinary reality,' he seeks to elicit 'some perception of an order *in* reality.'

Eliot stresses that the crucial problem was verse rhythm, 'to find a rhythm close to contemporary speech' instead of the rhythm of neo-Shakespearean blank verse, which implies 'an unreal world in which poetry is tolerated.' 'What we have to do is to bring poetry into the world in which the audience lives and to which it returns when it leaves the theater.' The audience 'should find, at the moment of aware-ness that it is hearing poetry, that it is saying to itself: "I could talk poetry too!" Then we should not be transported into an artificial world; on the contrary, our own sordid, dreary daily world would be suddenly illuminated and transfigured.' Eliot first worked out the verse idiom he needed in *The Family Reunion,* a half-way house in technical evolution. Here he developed the line of varying length, with a caesura and three stresses, which he has continued to employ, though he used it chiefly for his hero's hectoring the other characters. Certainly my own experience with that play is an unwilling confirmation of his judgment that its versification was a success: shortly after it appeared I wrote an essay about its failures to control its material; [3] yet many of the lines themselves have stayed with me over the years, singing in my head and proving to be landmarks for important areas of experience. The verse has a quality of *actuality* I have never found in the language of *Murder in the Cathedral.* Indeed, the central experience presented in Harry remains deeply meaningful and moving, despite the play's failures in placing and evaluating it (failures to which Eliot himself has given very short shrift). One can add that where the conversational verse fails in *The Family Reunion,* it is in the moments of relaxation, where the 'visionless' people speak. This failure is a confirmation of what Eliot says in 'Poetry and Drama' about the importance of 'unbroken transition between the most intense speech and the most relaxed dialogue,' and the need to 'avoid poetry which could not stand the test of strict dramatic relevance.' The trouble with Ivy's and Violet's inanities is that their only relevance is irrelevance.

Or one can put it that they are not created characters; for it is only when characters have been given an independent life that their language can have life, a life which must come from dramatic relevance. Perhaps it is true that where attention is focused entirely on one figure's relation with divinity, the other figures cannot have much character, since the heart of a character, at least for Eliot, is his relation to divinity. There are other created characters besides Harry in *The Family Reunion,* notably his aunt and his mother; they get almost all their reality by their relation to the hero. But the two more recent plays represent an enormous development in the power to create a variety of different characters, each speaking with a voice of his own, each endowed with an independent validity. These plays express the sort of 'understanding which comes from an affectionate observation of men and women.' Eliot wrote about learning to create other voices in his 1953 lecture, 'The Three Voices of Poetry.' He is much concerned there to make a distinction between the general meaning of 'dramatic' which fits dramatic monologue, and the meaning that fits voices fully differentiated from the poet's own voice. He insists that in presenting several characters in a verse play, you 'cannot afford to identify one of these characters with yourself, and give him (or her) all the "poetry" to speak. The poetry (I mean, the language at those moments when it reaches intensity) must be as widely distributed as characterization permits. . .' The limitations of *Sweeney Agonistes* and the other pre-war plays are obviously in mind here.

It has become apparent that it was only after Eliot had found his way to speaking in his *own* person in his meditative poetry that he was free to speak in *other* persons in his plays. The poetry before *Ash Wednesday* was written neither in his own voice (the 'first voice') nor in the 'third voice' of other persons; in a curious and very valuable way, it expressed, not a self, but the struggle to find a self, or do without a self. It cannot be equated with Pound's or Browning's dramatic monologues, because Eliot did not ordinarily 'identify a character with himself'—he was expressing the problem of being without a character. There is not only an old man in 'Gerontion,' but also other voices pressing from behind: 'I would meet you upon this honestly. . .' So too in *The Waste Land* the various identities, the various voices, are under pressure, are tested and found wanting, so as to express a need to which none of them is adequate. Pound's various personae, by contrast, are used to relish the exhilaration of appropriating identities. Eliot does not talk about his own early work in 'The Three Voices of Poetry,' but in locating the dramatic monologue in relation to drama, he provides tools for making distinctions such as these. The essay develops, or better, supersedes, his earlier reflections on the impersonality of poetry. A statement like 'poetry is not the expression of personality, but an escape from personality,' though there is a sense in which it is universally true, now appears as a rationale for the special (and very valuable) kind of poetry Eliot was writing around 1918.

In talking in 1953 about the way truly independent characters are created, Eliot does not hesitate to recognize connections between the personality of the author and his creations:

It seems to me that what happens, when an author creates a vital character, is a sort of give-and-take. The author may put into that character, besides its attributes, some trait of his own, some strength or weakness, some tendency to violence or to indecision, some eccentricity even, that he has found in himself. Something perhaps never realized in his own life, something of which those who know him best may be unaware, something not restricted in transmission to characters of the same temperament, the same age, and, least of all, the same sex. . . I believe that the author imparts something of himself to his characters, but I also believe that he is influenced by the characters he creates. It would be only too easy to lose oneself in a maze of speculation about the process by which an imaginary character can become as real for us as people we have known. I have penetrated into this maze so far only to indicate the difficulties, the limitations, the fascination, for a poet who is used to writing poetry in his own person, of the problem of making imaginary personages talk poetry. And the difference, the abyss, between writing for the first and for the third voice.

I find in copying out this passage that despite its interest, it is an example of the loose writing often present in the recent lectures, satisfactory for a lecture audience but disappointing to a reader. There is a tendency to multiply over-lapping instances, a certain deadness at the finger tips, in such places, though always the handling of the large move-ments of the discourse is masterful, and the reader is fre-quently delighted by finely made, tightly turned passages. The best writing, in recent years, has been reserved for the plays. Mr. William Wimsatt, in a long review of *The Cock-tail Party* which did perceptive justice to its artistic quali-ties, observes that 'a very distinct set of rhythms might be analyzed for each of the important characters.' [4] Whether or not one could pin them down, one can certainly hear them. And to listen to their interplay on the phonograph record-ing proves to be an experience which one can enjoy over and over again.

Although 'The Three Voices of Poetry' emphasizes that a dramatist can create characters only at the price of not iden-tifying one character altogether with himself, the essay also turns around to recognize that created characters can say things that the poet wants to say to the world (the second voice) and things that he wants to say to himself (the first voice). The ideal—what we get in Shakespeare—is a 'world in which the creator is everywhere present, and everywhere hidden.' The deepest communication, it is suggested at the close of 'Poetry and Drama,' is by the rhythm of the play as a whole. 'It seems to me that beyond the nameable, classi-fiable emotions and motives of our conscious life when di-rected towards action—the part of life which prose drama is wholly adequate to express—there is a fringe of indefinite extent, of feeling which we can only detect, so to speak, out of the corner of the eye and can never completely focus; of feeling of which we are only aware in a kind of temporary detachment from action.' That this sort of feeling is, in Eliot's view, essentially religious, or directed towards the religious, appears at the very end of the essay. He speaks of having before his eyes 'a kind of mirage of the perfection of verse drama, which would be a design of human action and of words, such as to present at once the two aspects of dramatic and of musical order.' Such drama, by 'eliciting some perception of an order *in* reality,' would 'bring us to a condition of serenity, stillness and reconciliation; and then leave us, as Virgil left Dante, to proceed towards a region where that guide can avail us no farther.'

2. THE CONFIDENTIAL CLERK

The Cocktail Party and *The Confidential Clerk* present failures of natural relations which lead to recognition of the need of the supernatural, and of the need to distinguish between the divine and the human. People are shown trying to find the divine in the human and have it on their own terms. In *The Cocktail Party,* it is the natural relation between lovers which fails to satisfy the need for something more than human; in *The Confidential Clerk,* it is the relation of parents to children. In each play, there are normal people who almost wreck their lives trying to get from human relationships what they cannot give; and there is one special person who discovers a destiny that is not primarily concerned with human relations at all, Celia in the earlier play, Colby in the later. Eliot does not attempt to deal directly with encounters with the supernatural; after the failure of the Eumenides in *The Family Reunion,* he has kept such encounters off stage. But we are led to feel the relation of the dedicated persons to the divine by what they do humanly, and by what they do *not* do, what they give up. Those who do not have a special destiny also sacrifice something—their claims on Celia or on Colby, claims they come to realize were impossible in any case. And they feel, in the lives that are taken from them, the brush of the wings of the Dove.

The Confidential Clerk was not nearly as successful on the stage as the earlier play: Eliot was not so fortunate in the choice of situations in modern life in which to show religious needs working themselves out dramatically. To make a religion of children is certainly one of our principal ways of looking for the divine in what Eliot sees as the wrong place. Eliot found a bold, explicit expression of this impulse in the *Ion*. Euripides presents the hunger for a child in Creusa and Xuthus and dramatizes how it turns into a jealous conflict over the graceful young hero, a temple servant of Apollo. Ion, who has not known his parents, actually *is* partly divine, born to Creusa after her rape by Apollo and exposed by her before her marriage, but rescued by the god's intervention. Euripides ends his play by a recognition scene in which Creusa finds her long lost child, the child of a god, so that he can become heir to the patrimony she and Xuthus share. Eliot sets out to do a very interesting thing—to make a modern version of this plot which ends with the recognition that one *cannot* have the child of a god for one's human child. Euripides' moral problem, as he sees it, requires a religious solution—the giving up of human claims on the dedicated person to free him to pursue his relation with divinity. So Eliot's Creusa, Lady Elizabeth Mulhammer, and his Xuthus, her husband Sir Claude, end by discovering that Colby is not the child of either one of them, and so must in effect be given back to the service of the god. The other half of their final recognition is that it is their natural children, whom they have been neglecting in their fascination with Colby, that they must recognize and learn to love. In this way, the last act of the play dramatizes very effectively a liberating recognition of the difference between the human and the divine. But to set up the ending involves an almost impossibly far-fetched plot.

To spell it out baldly makes the difficulties manifest, and is necessary in order to discuss the play intelligibly. Sir Charles Mulhammer, a successful financier, has engaged as his private secretary or confidential clerk a quiet, adroit young man, Colby Simpkins, for whose upbringing Sir Claude has paid on the assumption that he is his illegitimate son. Sir Claude hopes that his wife will come to like Colby so that he can tell her his parentage and they can adopt him as their son. Before her marriage, Lady Elizabeth wanted to inspire an artist, had an illegitimate child by a guardsman who wrote poems to her, lost track of the child when his father was killed hunting, and could not recall the name of the foster mother to whom he had entrusted it (the rape by Apollo and the exposure of Ion). The name was in fact 'Mrs. Guzzard of Teddington' (the priestess of Apollo), and Lady Elizabeth recalls it when she hears that that was the name of the woman who brought up Colby. So she concludes, in a rapture, that Colby is her son. Sir Claude, on his side, only *thought* he had a child by Mrs. Guzzard's sister. (Xuthus' escapade with the slave girl, from which he presumes that Ion resulted.) But in fact Mrs. Guzzard's sister died before her baby was born, Mrs. Guzzard's husband also died and left her with a new-born baby and without support, so she acquiesced in Sir Claude's misapprehension and allowed him to support her own son (no precedent in Euripides). To provide the natural children who are to be recognized instead of Ion, Eliot arranges that Sir Claude *does* have an illegitimate daughter, Lucasta, whom he has supported but has not recognized and has always felt as an embarrassment. And he has given a start in business to a young man, 'B.' Kaghan, engaged to marry Lucasta, a breezy, warm-hearted person whom Lady Mulhammer regards as 'rather worldly.' In the end Kaghan proves to be her 'mislaid' son: when her lover died and payment for his care stopped, he was adopted by neighbors who brought him up. His first name, which he never uses, is Barnabas—'child of consolation' or 'of exhortation.' Such he is indeed to Lady Elizabeth.

Now the plots of many fine plays seem impossibly complicated when summarized, and often involve situations which

are as out of the ordinary as all these illegitimate and mislaid children. The question, always, is whether plot pays off
in dramatic meaning. Eliot's handling of his story certainly
overloads the play with retrospective explanation. And there
is too little relation between the quality of the Mulhammers'
life in the present, where we see them, and the events re-
covered from their pasts: the problem is that these events
really only remotely relate to the present need of the characters to connect Colby to themselves. But if the machinery
of who's who is cumbersome, there is nevertheless a real and
effective action in the play. The movement consists of a suc-
cession of scenes in which people reach out for Colby; and
then one long finale when Mrs. Guzzard is summoned and
explodes the revelations which make them all let go of him
and turn to one another.

Each brings to Colby what he holds most dear and asks
Colby to share it with him and give himself to it. Kaghan
suggests they become business partners. Lucasta, a very appealing character, wants him to teach her to understand
music, which is what he cares for most—he has given up
hopes of a career as an organist when he realized that he
could never be first rate; but Lucasta wants, more deeply,
for him to share with her her sense that, despite the fact that
she is illegitimate, she has her own integrity (that she is
chaste, *casta*). She and Colby are perhaps on the way to falling in love when their developing relation is abruptly
stopped by her revealing that she is Sir Claude's daughter; she thinks that Colby is shocked by her being a bastard,
but what in fact shocks him is his belief that he is her half-
brother. This bar to their relation is a misconception; but
before it is removed by the final revelation, she has come to
see that the thing she wanted to reach in Colby could not
be the basis for love between a man and a woman—she will
marry Kaghan:

I've something to give him—
Something that he needs. Colby doesn't need me,
He doesn't need anybody.

She describes his special temperament, or destiny, from her vantage, by saying

you're terribly cold. Or else you've some fire
That warms you, that isn't the same kind of fire
That warms other people. You're either an egotist
Or something so different from the rest of us
That we can't judge you. That's you, Colby.

In the end it proves to be true that the relationship in which they can love one another is that of brother and sister, even though they are not literally related. They find their relationship in the process of finding what Colby's real destiny is—to be a priest, or something very like a priest, although the word is never mentioned. The reason why romantic love fails to develop between them is not handled in terms of sexual feeling (one thinks, by contrast, of the moment with the hyacinth girl in *The Waste Land*). Instead, the play keeps to its central theme by showing how their encounter reflects their sense of themselves in relation to parents, to being illegitimate and to being orphaned.

What Sir Claude wants to share with Colby is of course, ultimately, his name, his identity; immediately, it is his business, and nearer to home than business, the love of art. Sir Claude, to carry on his father's business, has accepted disappointment as an artist, which makes it seem right to him that Colby should do the same. The older man had wanted to be a potter, but found that he could never become a first-rate one, and so has resigned himself to collecting beautiful things which he keeps in a private room—as he expects Colby to resign himself to playing, when he is alone, on the very fine piano he has bought for him. He confides to the younger man what his collection means to him:

[217]

But when I am alone, and look at one thing long enough,
I sometimes have that sense of identification
With the maker of which I spoke—an agonizing ecstasy
Which makes life bearable. It's all I have.
I suppose it takes the place of religion:
Just as my wife's investigations
Into what she calls the life of the spirit
Is a kind of substitute for religion.
I dare say truly religious people—
I've never known any—can find some unity.
Then there are the men of genius.
There are others, it seems to me, who have at best to live
In two worlds—each a kind of make-believe.
That's you and me. Some day, perhaps,
I will show you my collection.

One's first response to such a passage, presented in isolation, may well be to wonder what use there is in watering down the thought of *Four Quartets* in this fashion. There certainly is a paucity of invention in *The Confidential Clerk:* Eliot re-uses motifs he has employed before, and draws on veins of well-bred talk and civilized aspiration which are fairly thin. But the *use* he makes of this material is not stale. The important meaning of such a speech as Sir Claude's is dramatic: in context, we feel it as a pressure in relation to the polite, kind, but firm resistance which Colby is putting up; we consider Sir Claude's assumption of the necessity of make-believe in relation to Colby's

But . . . something in me
Rebels against accepting such conditions.
It would be so much simpler if you weren't my father!

And Sir Claude's gesture towards Colby gains significance in relation to his wife's. The opening scene overdoes the build-up of Lady Elizabeth's ladylike lunacy, but when she comes on stage, just back from studying 'mind control' with a 'wonderful doctor in Zurich,' she provides some delightful comedy as she tries to take over Colby in her own way. She decides on the spot that his first name is his last name, and that she must decorate his apartment according to her taste:

> My husband
> *Does not understand the importance of colour*
> *For our spiritual life, Mr. Colby.*

When in her turn she has her serious conversation with Colby, her folly proves to have its own sort of wisdom. She is sure that their childhoods must have been alike—sharing unhappy childhoods being her equivalent for Sir Claude's sharing the disappointment of artistic hopes; each is a common way that people today express a spiritual need. And indeed their so different childhoods did have in common the fact that each was forced to make a fresh start, she because she loathed her titled parents, her governesses, and her innumerable carnivorous relatives—'Always killing things and eating them.'

> *Do you know, I actually* liked *to believe*
> *That I was a foundling—or do I mean 'changeling'?*

She recalls how she used to believe in reincarnation:

> *That was only a phase. But it made it all so simple!*
> *To be able to think that one's earthly parents*
> *Are only the means that we have to employ*
> *To become reincarnate. And that one's real ancestry*
> *Is one's previous existences. Of course, there's something in us,*
> *In all of us, which isn't just heredity,*
> *But something unique. Something we have been*
> *From eternity. Something . . . straight from God.*
> *That means that we are nearer to God than to anyone.*

Using notions picked up among the flotsam and jetsam of her society education, she nevertheless says a great deal about the kind of person Colby is: her childhood fantasy comes close to his actuality. (Eliot is becoming more and more expert at making do with inadequate words by put-

ting just the right English on them as he uses them: Lady
Elizabeth's 'foundling—or do I mean "changeling"?' is a
good example. This way of rescuing words depends on having
the power to use them dramatically, the power of making
characters, like Lady Elizabeth, whom we can feel saying the
words.) That Colby *is* a kind of foundling has appeared in
his responses to Sir Claude's appeals after Sir Claude has
spoken of his own relation to his father:

> *You spoke of atonement.*
> *Even your failure to understand him,*
> *Of which you spoke—that was a relationship*
> *Of father and son. It must often happen.*
> *And the reconcilement, after his death,*
> *That perfects the relation. You have always been his son*
> *And he is still your father. I only wish*
> *That I had something to atone for!*
> *There's something lacking, between you and me,*
> *That you had, and have, and always will have, with your father.*
> *I begin to see how I have always thought of you—*
> *As a kind protector, a generous provider:*
> *Rather as a patron than a father—*
> *The father who was missing in the years of childhood.*
> *Those years are gone forever. The empty years.*
> *Oh, I'm terribly sorry to be saying this;*
> *But it goes to explain what I said just now*
> *About rebelling against the terms*
> *That life has imposed.*

Because he is a kind of foundling, Colby is also a kind of
changeling (Lady Elizabeth has no syntax for the relation,
but she is feeling for it). Where we have a father, Colby tells
Sir Claude, we accept the compromises his example bids us
—we atone to him, as Sir Claude has told Colby that he has
all his life been atoning to his father. But where we do not,
then . . . The implication is that it is in such people, change-
lings for whom the natural sequence from parent to child
has been broken, that the need is most intense to atone with
a father behind fathers, and so to reject the compromises on

which continuities between particular lives are founded. This implication is not acted out or spelled out. Instead we are led up to it: the needs which the several characters bring to Colby create a field of force which defines a direction and starts a movement. It is a movement which cannot be fulfilled except by breaking the parent-child relationship which Sir Claude and Lady Elizabeth are seeking to establish.

Without realizing it, they want to have things both ways. By a fine comic irony, Lady Elizabeth has no sooner found kinship with Colby on the basis that we all come 'straight from God' than she hears about Mrs. Guzzard and leaps to the conclusion that Colby comes straight from *her*. The consequence is the summoning of Mrs. Guzzard. She is a wonderful comic invention—a fairy godmother from the suburbs, with defensive middle-class dignity but a downright, no-nonsense manner that soon turns the tables on all the grand people who are hanging on her words. Her clipped, oracular pronouncements deal out destinies as though she brought them up out of a battered leather shopping bag. Everything about her says that life is a hard business, where one does not get one's way for nothing, nor all of one's way for anything. Eliot uses the fairy-story feeling about the dangerousness of having wishes granted:

> *Whose son would you wish to be, Colby:*
> *Sir Claude's—or the son of some other man*
> *Obscure and silent? A dead man, Colby.*
> *Be careful what you say . . .*
>
> *You shall have your wish. And when you have your wish*
> *You will have to come to terms with it . . .*
>
> *Then I will say good-bye. You have all had your wish*
> *In one form or another. You and I, Sir Claude,*
> *Had our wishes twenty-five years ago;*
> *But we failed to observe, when we had our wishes,*
> *That there was a time-limit clause in the contract.*

The grim side of her role goes with the realistic tendency of Eliot's finale, as against the wish fulfillment of the classical recognition scene with which Euripides ends. Such scenes present as actually happening between human beings the total atonement we all feel a residual need for, because of the failures of our actual relations: Mrs. Guzzard's role as a grim fairy says that such things cannot happen, that a transcendent moment cannot fill up what Colby called so movingly 'The empty years.' (Of course it is also true that scenes of recognition and atonement can be handled in such a way that they are in effect types of atonement with the divine: Eliot saw the reunion in *Pericles* in this way, as his 'Marina' bears witness.)

But there is also a side of the Mrs. Guzzard business which is hilariously funny. For the first half of the scene, she is the center for farcical quick-changes which give a feeling that anybody can be anybody:

> *But, Mrs. Guzzard, this is where you can help us—*
> *Do you know any other Mrs. Guzzard?*

That everything hangs on her absurd name suggests that names are absurd; identities come to seem fortuitous:

SIR CLAUDE: *I believe, Elizabeth,*
That you have found your son.
EGGERSON: *Subject to confirmation.*
LADY ELIZABETH: *And to my being able to adjust myself to it.*
(Re-enter Colby, with Kaghan and Lucasta)
COLBY: *I have told them to be prepared for a surprise.*
LADY ELIZABETH: *Barnabas! Is your name Barnabas?*

On the stage this spree worked wonderfully. And the comic action itself is centrally meaningful, not a mere diversion. The farce of mistaken identities is blowing up the conception of paternity on which too much has come to depend. Lady Elizabeth, leaning so heavily on Colby's being her son, becomes the comic butt. Through the comic switches, we

[222]

feel the largeness of things, particular relations are tumbled about, life opens up. The finding of Kaghan prepares the way for the freeing—and losing—of Colby.

The tone changes, however, as this happens, for Sir Claude is more a figure for compassion than a comic butt. He has a role in relation to Colby that is parallel to that of the mother in relation to the hero in *The Family Reunion*. Eliot said in 'Poetry and Drama' that 'my sympathies now have come to be all with the mother . . . ; and my hero now strikes me as an insufferable prig.' Colby is not a prig— it is a triumph to have been able to create him in the negating role he has to play without his being priggish; Eliot has done it by creating a young man who has the diffidence, not of weakness, but of exceptional power that has not yet found itself, that is incommensurate with his situation. Sir Claude becomes a very moving character as he loses control in losing his son:

> *What's that? Oh. Good-bye, Mrs. Guzzard.*
> (Exit Mrs. Guzzard.)
> *What's happened? Have they gone? Is Colby coming back?*
> LADY ELIZABETH: *My poor Claude!*
> (Lucasta crosses to Sir Claude and kneels beside him.)

He says nothing while, in the short remainder of the scene, Kaghan reflects that 'we all made the same mistake,' that 'we wanted Colby to be something he wasn't,' while Lady Elizabeth says, 'Claude, we've got to try to understand our children,' and Kaghan answers for himself and Lucasta that they 'would like to mean something to you . . . if you'd let us.' Then just before the curtain, as Lucasta puts her arms around Sir Claude, the play ends with his saying

> *Don't leave me, Lucasta.*
> *Eggerson! Do you really believe her?*
> (Eggerson nods.)

[223]

It is a very moving recognition scene in its own kind—a double kind; the recognition of what they *can* have is given both poignancy and reality by the recognition of what they cannot have.

Eggerson, whose nod is final, is the one character I have difficulty with. He is Sir Claude's former confidential clerk, who comes back at moments of crisis from his retirement in the suburbs, a Christian adaptation of the Admirable Crichton. That is to say, he is a better man than his boss but never shows it because of the admirable class system. Eliot is reported to have told E. Martin Browne that 'Eggerson is the one fully *developed* Christian in the play' (a remark that is revealing as to his intention to present people *developing* towards Christianity). It is through Eggerson that the explicitly Christian destiny of Colby is suggested. When Mrs. Guzzard reveals that he is the son of a not very successful organist, he wishes to return to his vocation for the organ and Eggerson has a vacancy to propose. It is in his own parish, where he is sure Colby will be given a fair trial:

> *The Parochial Church Council will be only too pleased,*
> *And I have some influence. I am the Vicar's Warden.*

It helps—a *little*—that Eggerson has never used 'I' this way before. But it is all so beamish. And so eager not to give offense:

> *The stipend is small—*
> *Very small, I'm afraid. Not enough to live on.*
> *We'll have to think of other ways*
> *Of making up an income. Piano lessons?*
> *As a temporary measure; because, Mr. Simpkins—*
> *I hope you won't take this as an impertinence—*
> *I don't see you spending a lifetime as an organist.*
> *I think you'll come to find you've another vocation.*
> *We worked together every day, you know,*
> *For quite a little time, and I've watched you pretty closely.*
> *Mr. Simpkins! You'll be thinking of reading for orders.*

And you'll still have your music. Why, Mr. Simpkins,
Joshua Park may be only a stepping stone
To a precentorship! And a canonry!

Oh, Mr. Simpkins! Yes, Mr. Simper! It may be only my
American middle class prejudice against the whole English
lower middle class, but these lines seem to me to be silly.
It would perhaps be sillier still to say the same thing with
deep ecclesiastical pedal-point; no matter what local habita-
tion and name Eliot might decide to give religion, there
will be the difficulty that troubling social concomitants
come into play. The aim with Eggerson is to show how the
church transcends class lines, for this is the first moment
where Eggerson has stepped out of the role of perfectly disciplined, self-effacing helpfulness. So too, Eggerson's role
presents the one exception to the general tendency to take
over Colby. At the end the plan is for Colby to live with
Eggerson and his wife while getting started in Joshua Park;
but only while getting started: though he will have the room
left vacant by the loss of their son in the war, it is clear
that Eggerson wants to see him go about other business than
Eggerson's. (It is an achievement that nobody needs to say
'about his Father's business.' I wish that Eliot had denied
himself also the egregious pun about a hidden cleric which
keeps flapping out of the title.) Perhaps in Eggerson Eliot
has salvaged for his own purposes the stock role of perfect
servant. But even if one can forgive the simper, it is troubling to have Christian selflessness so nearly indistinguishable from servile selflessness.

In any case, the difficulty about naming Christianity is not
central; Eliot has made it secondary by conveying a gath-
ering sense of religious need through the expressions of the
actual make-shift religions by which those around Colby
live. This not only defines the direction in which Colby is
launched without depending on ecclesiastical definitions
which would assume too much; it also gives those who care

for Colby the opportunity for what is in effect a religious act without being called so—namely, the act of sacrificing Colby.

When the play was first produced in Boston, all but the last act misfired. After coming to know it well, my impression is that it is not undramatic, except for a few barren places, but that it is, until the last act, exceedingly difficult to act. The conversations in which people reach out for Colby do not give occasion for sharp dramatic turns; the only clear-cut dramatic change in a relation, before the question of who Colby is starts the second movement, is the rather forced misapprehension about incest which upsets Colby's communication with Lucasta. But for actors who knew what they were about, and an audience familiar with the play, there are opportunities in these interviews for interesting and moving modulations of feeling—in a paler way, the sort of opportunities the French classic theater offers. During the first run, there did not seem to be much comprehension on either side of the footlights; a revival might go much better. One prefers that a play should not need to be read in advance (Eliot says emphatically that that is his goal); but many fine works of art do require study, and are none the less alive in performance because of it. And after the restrained, searching first half, the play will reward the audience with the fun and pathos of the last act; once Mrs. Guzzard is on the stage, nothing can stop it.

3. THE COCKTAIL PARTY

In adapting the *Ion* Eliot cut out its fulfillment of the wish to have the divine in the human; in his handling of the *Alcestis* he has followed the same course. Euripides keeps the folk-tale sort of plot intact, while treating with troubling realism the human implications for a wife of dying for her husband, and for a husband, of letting his wife die for him. Since Admetus was a king hedged with divinity, Alcestis' act was after all on one side a religious sacrifice. Eliot's Celia is a woman who without knowing it has been trying to find, in an affair with an ordinary man, a way to dedicate herself to the divine. The action of the play, for her, begins with the discovery that Edward is only human, moves through the recognition, in the psychiatrist's consulting room, that what she has 'sought for in the wrong place' can be pursued in a dedicated life, and ends, we learn, in death at the hands of unconverted savages when she is serving as a member of a nursing order, caring for Christian natives in a plague-stricken jungle. So the action, on her side, moves from the religion of human love to religion—from her trying, in a misconceived way, to do what Alcestis did, to her giving herself to God.

Eliot 'saw two characters in Alcestis—the ordinary woman and the saint.' [5] Lavinia 'dies' too, in a way designed or at least abetted by her psychiatrist: she clears out, leaving Edward with a cocktail party on his hands (including the psychiatrist, incognito, as an uninvited guest). When she has come back next day, she explains that

> *I thought that if I died*
> *To you, I who had been only a ghost to you,*
> *You might be able to find the road back*
> *To a time when you were real . . .*

The action, for Edward and Lavinia, leads in the opposite direction from Celia's: it amounts to a process of disentanglement from their search for the divine in the human. Each has been having an affair: in maneuvering Peter Quilpe into a liaison that broke up before the play opens, Lavinia had been seeking to capture the love of a sweet, ardent nature, so that she could feel that she was lovable; Edward had accepted Celia's gift of herself so that he could have the reassurance of feeling that he could love. Lavinia's departure is enough to make Edward realize that he wants his wife back, that his relation with Celia can lead to nothing. But when Lavinia comes back, a hilarious scene of married bickering shows how each uses the other by blaming him. Eliot observed in *Notes towards a Definition of Culture*, by way of analogy to misunderstandings among cultures, that 'It is human, when we cannot understand another human being, and cannot ignore him, to exert an unconscious pressure on that person to turn him into something that we *can* understand: many husbands and wives exert this pressure on each other.' In the relation of Edward to Lavinia, he shows a man subject to such pressure, and acquiescing in it to make of his wife a kind of supernatural power:

> *And then you came back, you*
> *The angel of destruction—just as I felt sure.*
> *In.a moment, at your touch, there is nothing but ruin.*
> *O God, what have I done? The python. The octopus.*
> *Must I become after all what you would make me?*

Their recognition, in the consulting room, is, as Sir Henry Harcourt-Reilly puts it:

> *How much you have in common. The same isolation.*
> *A man who finds himself incapable of loving*
> *And a woman who finds that no man can love her.*
> LAVINIA: *It seems to me that what we have in common*
> *Might be just enough to make us loathe one another.*
> REILLY: *Rather see it as the bond that holds you together.*
> *While still in a state of unenlightenment,*
> *You could always say: 'He could not love any woman';*
> *You could always say: 'No man could love her.'*
> *You could accuse each other of your own faults,*
> *And so could avoid understanding each other.*
> *Now, you have only to reverse the propositions*
> *And put them together.*

It is characteristic of Eliot's method that he only implies the positive statements, which would go: 'Since I cannot love, you are unlovable—forgive me.' 'Since I am unlovable, you cannot love—forgive me.' But he conveys the change of heart very effectively by dramatic means, especially at the moment when instead of going on talking separately to the doctor, they reach out to each other:

> LAVINIA: *Then what can we do*
> *When we can go neither back nor forward? Edward!*
> *What can we do? . . .*
> EDWARD: *Lavinia, we must make the best of a bad job.*
> *That is what he means.*
> REILLY: *When you find, Mr. Chamberlayne,*
> *The best of a bad job is all any of us make of it—*
> *Except, of course, the saints—such as those who go*
> *To the sanatorium—you will forget this phrase,*
> *And in forgetting it will alter the condition.*

At the second cocktail party, two years later, the condition *has* been altered: the brief last act conveys convincingly, by gestures in themselves banal, that each has learned to love the other and blame himself. The two movements in the play have crossed: Edward and Lavinia have found their way to humanity; Celia has found her way to divinity.

Writing in 1940 of *The Idea of a Christian Society*, Eliot spoke of 'the natural end of man—virtue and well-being in community— . . . for all, and the supernatural end—beatitude—for those who have the eyes to see it.' As I said at the outset, *The Cocktail Party* is the first play of Eliot's to present the natural end of man as a valid consideration; in *The Family Reunion* the audience was asked to adopt the perspective of a protagonist for whom the natural has become a nightmare unreality. The difference comes out neatly if we contrast the way Harry and Celia use the cricket as a symbol for such unreality. In *The Family Reunion* Harry, leaving, says,

> *Let the cricket chirp. John shall be the master.*
> *All I have is his. No harm can come to him.*
> *What would destroy me will be life for John.*

[229]

Celia, as the scales fall from her eyes, has an almost Kafka-like vision of Edward:

> *I listened to your voice, that had always thrilled me,*
> *And it became another voice—no, not a voice:*
> *What I heard was only the noise of an insect,*
> *Dry, endless, meaningless, inhuman—*
> *You might have made it by scraping your legs together—*
> *Or however grasshoppers do it . . .*
> EDWARD: *Perhaps that is what I am.*
> *Tread on me, if you like.*
> CELIA: *No, I won't tread on you.*
> *That is not what you are. It is only what was left*
> *Of what I thought you were. I see another person,*
> *I see you as a person whom I never saw before.*
> *The man I saw before, he was only a projection—*
> *I see that now—of something that I wanted—*
> *No, not* wanted—*something I aspired to—*
> *Something that I desperately wanted to exist.*
> *It must happen somewhere—but what, and where is it?*
> *Edward, I see I have simply been making use of you,*
> *And I ask you to forgive me.*

Celia moves past the nightmare vision to a point of vantage beyond Harry's, from which she can see Edward as a human being again, divested of her illusion *and* her disillusion. For her, too, as well as Edward and Lavinia, it is only by giving up the search for the supernatural *in* the natural that the natural can be seen and respected for what it is.

The last act, in which this process of separating the human from the divine is completed, has been much criticized. Eliot has observed that it 'only just escapes, if it does escape, the accusation of being not a last act but an epilogue.' Others have objected that Celia's death off in 'Kinkanja' is too remote to be made real by a report, and that the report itself is wantonly shocking in the way it shifts from Colonial-office humor about monkeys and cannibals to Celia 'cruci-fied / Very near an ant hill.' My own response, when I saw it on the stage, was mixed: I saw relatively little point in

Alex's chatter about his colonial mission; I was moved by the news of Celia, but with a sense that I was somehow being imposed on. I now find the act much more satisfactory: it seems to me that something *does* happen, not just in the report, but to those hearing it. On reflection, Celia's mission does not seem irrelevant or arbitrary: Eliot has imagined her working in the sort of area where an English Christian might find the most challenging responsibility. He observes in *Notes towards a Definition of Culture* that it is a reversal of values to 'offer another people your culture first, and your religion second,' yet he sees how factitious it is to be prescriptive about the problems of the colonial regions, and concludes that it is only when 'we give our attention to . . . the limited area that we know best, and within which we have the most frequent opportunities for right action, that we can combat the feeling of hopelessness that invades us, when we linger too long upon perplexities so far beyond our measure.' Celia, speaking of ordinary love between a man and woman, says, 'If there's no other way . . . then I feel just hopeless.' Her dedication to another kind of love permits her to embrace and master in her nursing mission 'the hopelessness that invades us,' and by doing so she brings to the natives her religion first, her culture second. 'We found that the natives . . . had erected a sort of shrine for Celia.'

Alex's witty talk skates on very thin ice as he tells about the monkeys multiplying and so ruining the pagan natives who hold them in veneration, while the Christian native converts eat the monkeys and so prosper—until the pagan natives rebel and

> *instead of eating monkeys*
> They are eating Christians.
> JULIA: *Who have eaten monkeys.*
> ALEX: *The native is not, I fear, very logical.*
> JULIA: *I wondered where you were taking us, with your monkeys . . .*

EDWARD: *And have any English residents been murdered?*
ALEX: *Yes, but they are not usually eaten.*
When these people have done with a European
He is, as a rule, no longer fit to eat.

Under Alex's sangfroid we feel the precariousness of the general European situation. Of course, when we know the story, we think all this time of Celia: even hearing it for the first time, we are cued to wonder whether she was eaten as soon as we hear she was taken. Eliot has played before with this order of ideas, or better, impulses:

> SWEENEY: *I'll carry you off*
> *To a cannibal isle.*
> DORIS: *You'll be the cannibal!*
> SWEENEY: *You'll be the missionary!*
> *You'll be my little seven stone missionary!*
> *I'll gobble you up. I'll be the cannibal . . .*
> DORIS: *You wouldn't eat me!*
> SWEENEY: *Yes I'd eat you!*
> *In a nice little, white little, soft little, tender little,*
> *Juicy little, right little, missionary stew.*

The cannibal impulse, as it is encountered in *The Cocktail Party,* is still relevant to love and worship—as it is, of course, in the Lord's Supper, which in a Christian view is what the several sorts of primitive and primitivist aberrations point to. The pagan natives, worshiping monkeys and eating people, look for the divine in the animal as the Europeans tend to look for it in the human. Their taboos reverse ours, but after Julia's talk about a pet monkey we feel a Swiftean shock when Alex says blandly, 'The young monkeys are extremely palatable: I've cooked them myself. . .' (This, from Alex, connects the taboo feeling with the concern with eating, and for drinking ceremonially together, which runs through the play: everybody tries to feed Edward after Lavinia leaves him; Celia, after their break-up, looks 'absolutely famished.') Edward did *not,* however, 'gobble up'

Celia; she found a way to give herself that did mean becoming his 'missionary stew.' Alex's talk, by bringing alive for us the cannibal impulse and the dread of it, sets up a field of force, a tension, which the spiritual communion with Celia sublimates and resolves.

The disappointing effect of the last act in the phonograph recording, where almost everything is left out but the report and Sir Henry's comments on Celia's destiny,[6] makes one realize how much the meaning of her death depends on our experiencing its sudden impact on a lively group taken up with life. We get something similar to the realization of the presence of a dead person which Joyce expresses at the end of 'The Dead' (a passage that Eliot very much admires [7]). But where Joyce shows Nora Conroy held back from the adulterated possibilities of ordinary married life by her memory of the unrealized capacity for love in the boy who died for her, Eliot shows how the fulfillment in her death for God of Celia's capacity for love *frees* those she might have attached. It is crucial that those who hear the news together are a *group:* Eliot is presenting the curious moment of atonement and communion which comes when people share the experience of a death, especially when it is the death of a noble or devoted person, a death encountered through devotion. Peter Quilpe's response is particularly effective in showing how such a moment moves a person past self-concern. He thought his concern was all for Celia: he had planned to get her into films, now that he has had a success himself in them. But without his realizing it, his talk in telling of his grief for her is all about *his* plans, about himself:

And now it's all worthless. Celia's not alive.
LAVINIA: *No, it's not all worthless, Peter. You've only just begun.*
I mean, this only brings you to the point
At which you must *begin. You were saying just now*
That you never knew Celia. We none of us did.

[233]

What you've been living on is an image of Celia
Which you made up for yourself, to meet your own needs.

> *. . . perhaps what I've been saying*
Will seem less unkind if I can make you understand
That in fact I've been talking about myself.

Celia's selflessness provides a touchstone by which each is carried beyond his own egotism; or better, what they hear about her death forms a presence among them which makes them feel that their limitations matter less—a presence that frees them to acknowledge their limitations. To spell this out in moral terms makes the scene sound like moralistic highfalutin. But in fact the moral and religious insights spill over, so to speak, as an overflow from the dramatic development—they express new human relations developing before our eyes, including relations to Celia:

EDWARD: *Your responsibility is nothing to mine, Lavinia.*
LAVINIA: *I'm not sure about that. If I had understood you*
Then I might not have misunderstood Celia.
REILLY: *You will have to live with these memories and make*
  them
Into something new. Only by acceptance
Of the past will you alter its meaning.
JULIA: *Henry, I think it is time that I said something:*
So please don't interrupt . . .
Everyone makes a choice . . .

Out of context, such speeches may sound like a competition in being pollyanna; but they function not primarily to make moral points, but to convey a movement. It is a very beautiful scene, not for the residue of ideas, though there is that, but for the movement, which approaches 'a condition of serenity, stillness, and reconciliation'—and then comes back again to the beginning of a new cocktail party, conducted as cocktail parties are, but with a new relation established between that sort of moment and 'other kinds of experience which are possible.' [8]

In our encounter with a new work of art, we are conscious at first of its materials as we have come to see them in other contexts. But if the work has form, has meaning, of its own, the derivation of its materials comes to matter less and less. Many people whose judgment I respect are still put off by the materials of *The Cocktail Party,* especially the materials that derive from British parlor comedy. The standard practices of actors tend to suggest that what matters most about the West End world is the glamour of top-drawer exclusiveness. But this snobbery, though it can be distracting in a performance, chiefly on first encounter, largely disappears with 'the development or expansion of enjoyment' as one studies the play. So too with the objection many people felt to Eliot's 'smuggling in a priest in psychiatrist's clothing.' As we come to know the play, Sir Henry's role acquires its own identity, beyond its materials. In using the figure of the psychiatrist, complete with the glamour of the receiving room, the mystery of the closing office door, the excitement of conspiratorial advising with friends, Eliot took hold of materials which are highly charged for many people. But he developed the role so as to bring out the potentialities that concerned his whole purpose.

When we consider Sir Henry's part, along with his attendant spirits, Julia and Alex, we realize that *The Cocktail Party* is partly a fantasy. It is like *The Tempest* in presenting people who undergo events that are manipulated without their knowing it so as to bring about spiritual changes in them. Like Prospero, Sir Henry is a version of the immemorial magic doctor who can bring people back to life— Dr. Ball or whoever in the St. George plays, Hercules in the *Alcestis.* Of course Sir Henry goes beyond the doctor's proper sphere—'There never was a doctor like Mister Doctor Ball,' sing the plowhands of the Lutterworth play. But if his conduct is sometimes unprofessional—or para-professional —his attitude towards himself and his powers is more hu-

[235]

man, more humble, than that of many an actual profes-
sional man on whom we force the role of medicine man.

> *And when I say to one like her,*
> *'Work out your salvation with diligence,' I do not understand*
> *What I myself am saying.*

One can add that there are in fact psychiatrists who go far
outside the office situation to help people on a catch-as-catch-
can basis (Merrill Moore was one such); the role of a devoted mental doctor inevitably approaches in some respects
the role of a priest. And though Reilly and Co. can contrive
meetings, they cannot alter the human nature of his pa-
tients, any more than Prospero and Ariel can in *The Tempest:* that rule of the game gives reality to the fantasy, makes
it a kind of experiment on human potentialities.

The comedy of manipulation in *The Cocktail Party* gives
a feeling of things opening up, of something at work more
than meets the eye, of limits dissolving. In the first act, the
conspirators are spying on Edward without his knowing it—
a comic version of the horror of being watched dramatized
in *The Family Reunion:* 'Do you like to be stared at by eyes
through a window?' Harry asks in anguish; here we get such
gay mystification as Reilly's song about one-eyed Riley,
somehow matching Julia's one-eyed spectacles,[9] or such ex-
changes as

JULIA: *Well, my dears, I shall see you very soon.*
EDWARD: When *shall we see you?*
JULIA: *Did I say you'd see me?*

The several invasions of Edward's privacy, telephone, door-
bell, telephone, etc., are perhaps a little too deliberately
good theater craftsmanship, but they do express comically,
in the large, the process of opening up Edward when his
whole instinct is to resist. In the cruder world of the *Com-
media dell' Arte,* the doctor would have used his syringe. In

Sir Henry, as Mr. Heilman says, 'Eliot has been most successful in creating an air, if not of the inexplicable, at least of the unexplained, of the quizzically irregular, of the modestly elusive, of the herculean at once urbane and devoted; . . . Reilly tells Edward that he (i.e. Edward) has started "a train of events / Beyond your control," and Lavinia confesses (in terms Alcestis might have used), "Yet somebody, or something, compelled me to come." ' [10] A self-constituted missionary team like the 'Guardians' might be poisonous in real life. But so might Prospero be poisonous in real life. In the play, the manipulators are justified by the comic action over which they preside, an action which makes distinctions that set loose energies otherwise frustrated, energies that at bottom, after all, *are* mysterious. Eliot has, moreover, included sufficient traits of mere humanity in Julia, Alex, and even Sir Henry, to signify that apart from their role, they are not magical: Sir Henry comes, like Prospero, to a moment when he must say in effect: 'Bear with my weakness. My old brain is troubled.'

The masterful second act, in Sir Henry's consulting room, does not depend, and could not, on his being absolutely master; his art is only to *assist* nature, as Eliot remarked in an interview.[11] By a classic comic mechanism, he deftly switches Edward and Lavinia into a head-on collision; it is like the encounter in *The Jew of Malta* where Barabas, master puppeteer, arranges for his daughter's suitors to cut each other down:

LAVINIA: *No one can say my husband has an honest mind.*
EDWARD: *And I could not honestly say that of* you, *Lavinia.*
REILLY: *I congratulate you both on your perspicacity.*

Or again

LAVINIA: *You* are *cold-hearted, Edward.*
REILLY: *So you say, Mrs. Chamberlayne.*
And now, let us turn to your side of the problem.

They cut down each other's false pretenses: our hilarity as we watch the process is an experience of the weakness of such pretenses, blown away in laughter—after which Edward and Lavinia can start to make a new beginning. Because the process is positive, conveying the comic sense that life is larger than personalities, their encounter and change of heart makes an effective preliminary and foil to Celia's interview. The reversals of expectation in Celia's case are not for the most part laughable, but some of them are:

> REILLY: *You suffer from a sense of sin, Miss Coplestone?*
> *This is most unusual.*
> CELIA: *It seems to* me *abnormal.*

But her interview belongs to comedy, even when we are moved, perhaps to tears, by her expression of her plight, because it presents her situation being opened up by Reilly's redefinition of it—there is a turning of the tables which makes way for fulfillment.

> *We must find out what would be normal*
> *For* you, *before we use the term 'abnormal.'*

It is nothing new in Eliot to turn the tables on psychiatry by redefining what is 'normal': *The Waste Land,* written after treatment for a nervous crisis, comes to mind. In the 1956 lecture on 'The Frontiers of Criticism,' he went rather far out of his way to quote Aldous Huxley: 'The aim of Western psychiatry is to help the troubled individual to adjust himself to the society of less troubled individuals—individuals who are observed to be well adjusted to one another and the local institutions, but about whose adjustment to the fundamental Order of Things no inquiry is made . . .' Mr. Huxley ought really to say 'the aim of *most* Western psychiatry,' for 'adjustment' as a goal is widely replaced by various conceptions of creativity, some of them inclusive enough to accommodate Celia's work in Kinkanja. One should also observe that when Sir Henry makes game of Edward's notions of a 'nervous breakdown' and his expectations about his treatment, Eliot's psychiatrist is only saying what is quite commonly recognized by many in the profession.[12] Nevertheless, the reversals of expectation about the normal which Eliot presents in Celia's interview do not go stale, because they are drama, not journalism. Celia's account of her perplexity is very moving:

Well, there are two things I can't understand,
Which you might consider symptoms. But first I must tell you
That I should really like to think there's something wrong with
*   me—*
Because, if there isn't, then there's something wrong,
Or at least, very different from what it seemed to be,
With the world itself—and that's much more frightening.
That would be terrible.

So too she is very moving in her descriptions of what she had hoped for in her relation with Edward, and her recognition

that we had merely made use of each other
Each for his purpose. That's horrible. Can we only love
Something created by our own imagination?
Are we all in fact unloving and unlovable?
Then one is alone . . .

We have just seen Edward and Lavinia discover that they were 'unloving and unlovable,' and yet go back to the human condition. Eliot has constructed a dramatic situation which permits him to make crucial distinctions without imposing them; Sir Henry's comments come in response to a dramatized need for them:

A delusion is something that we must return from.
There are other states of mind, which we take to be delusion,
But which we have to accept and go on from. . .

Disillusion can become itself an illusion
If we rest in it. . .

There is another way, if you have the courage.
The first could be described in familiar term . . .
The second is unknown, and so requires faith—
The kind of faith which issues from despair.
The destination cannot be described . . .

Whichever way you choose will prescribe its own duty. . .

                    Neither way is better.
Both ways are necessary. It is also necessary
To make a choice between them. . .

Both ways avoid the final desolation
Of solitude in the phantasmal world
Of imagination, shuffling memories and desires.

Sir Henry's part, in its interplay with Celia's, is a fine achievement of simplicity without oversimplification; [13] the scene develops in a strong two-way rhythm:

                    Neither way is better.
          Both ways are necessary.

Celia's lines, eager, plangent, flow out to his decisive lines. By dividing the person who feels her way from the person who thinks his way, Eliot gives himself scope for a very beautiful 'design of human action and of words.'

   Nowhere in *The Cocktail Party* or in *The Confidential Clerk* do we hear a voice which has the urgency of anguish verging on anarchy, the pressure toward 'Hieronymo's mad againe' which was the deepest excitement of the poetry of *The Waste Land* period, and which was still present in the hero's role in *The Family Reunion,* striving toward an apocalyptic, inhumane domination. Nor do the recent plays have anything like the early range of materials, including the vulgar, the shocking, the sensual and perverse caught in a variety of social classes and types. But to condemn Eliot's late work because it is not like his earlier, as Mr. Spencer Brown [14] and others have done with gusto, is to be left behind by the poet's extraordinary power of development:

[240]

C'est à grands pas et en sueur
Que vous suivrez à peine ma piste.

The essay on Johnson remarks that in 'the perfection of any style it can be observed as in the maturing of an individual, that some potentialities have been brought to fruition only by the surrender of others.' It may be that in the poetry which Eliot wrote in his first two decades in England, the rhythms conveying the disruptive pressure of an unfulfilled need embody an interaction of American and British speech rhythms. At least one can say that when he found his way at last to writing for the 'third Voice' and creating entirely independent characters, their speech was entirely British. There are some speeches in the recent plays where I feel that the imitation of the cadences of English types verges on mimicry as opposed to full creation. These speeches are only occasional, limiting cases; but there are no speeches where we are swept wholly into the stream of passionate expression, or pressure for expression, as we are by passages in the poems. This is a real limitation: the plays lack one kind of intensity. They also lack the wonder and joy in the physical world and the physical powers which keeps return- ing in the poems, expressed in passages of lyric beauty that make the spiritual anguish the more poignant.

But the recent plays have intensity of another sort. Their force derives from the whole design, as the design develops, and contains, the parts of the several characters, and points beyond them. It is certainly true that the plays would be greater art if they realized natural life more fully in pre- senting the logic of sacrifice.[15] But Eliot does realize the part of natural life that is essential to his purpose—the *humanness* of his people. Because he has caught, in the accents of each character, an individual humanity, ordinary yet unique, reaching out beyond itself as best it can, he can make dra- matic designs which bring out 'a credible order' in 'ordinary reality.' The great moments are not climaxes of passion, but still points when we experience 'feeling which we can only detect, so to speak, out of the corner of the eye and can never completely focus . . . feeling of which we are only aware in a kind of temporary detachment from action.' Such experience is delicate, almost fugitive; yet we are brought to it by an action grounded in much common sense, in disillusion which has not destroyed wit and zest, in knowledge of the heart at once worldly and generous. The designs, as one comes to understand them, emerge as extraordinarily self-consistent and meaningful—expressions of wisdom. So what is delicate is also strong.

NOTES

1. 'The Cultivation of Christmas Trees,' a delicate, slight piece about the meaning of the remembered fragrance of Christmas celebrations, was published separately in 1956.

2. Eliot's team spirit in working on a production is described by E. Martin Browne in an interview with Burke Wilkinson, 'A Most Serious Comedy by Eliot,' *New York Times,* February 7, 1954, Sec. II, p. 1, col. 7. His willingness to learn from producers appears also in his own account of his experience in working on the film version of *Murder in the Cathedral, New York Times,* March 23, 1952, Sec. X, p. 5, col. 3.

3. Reprinted in *T. S. Eliot: a Selected Critique,* ed. Leonard Unger, New York, 1948, pp. 415-43.

4. *The Sewanee Review,* LVIII (1950), p. 671.

5. Mr. Robert Heilman makes this point and develops it with illuminating insights into the human qualities and relations Eliot and Euripides present, in '*Alcestis* and *The Cocktail Party,*' *Comparative Literature,* V (1953), p. 110. Mr. Heilman's article shows how richly Eliot's play rewards perceptive meditation.

6. Mr. Grover Smith, Jr., points out several relationships between Sir Henry's remarks and Charles Williams's novel, *Descent into Hell,* where some of the same lines from Shelley's *Prometheus Unbound* appear in the first chapter, in *T. S. Eliot's Poetry and*

Plays, Chicago, 1956, p. 226. Mr. Smith's study is remarkably helpful in exploring sources of all phases of Eliot's creative work.

7. Eliot discusses the story and quotes from it in *After Strange Gods,* New York, 1934, p. 40.

8. Mr. Heilman, in the article cited above in note 5, finds the final scene undramatic, 'tragedy *manqué.*' But he quotes a very apt remark from Mr. Dimitir Gotseff, one of his students, that the play is 'comedy with tragic relief' (p. 111).

9. Mr. Wimsatt, noting 'the one-eyed foolery' in his review, concludes: 'Teiresias, I shall venture, has suffered a split, into the male half and the female, each blind in one eye, but seeing mighty well in concert. (We may read this if we like as a joke, a flourish, an Eliot signature.)' (p. 676.) Mr. Smith assembles an astonishing range of possible parallels in his book, running back to Frazer, to *Dr. Faustus,* Eliot's 1923 review of Busby's book on Shakespeare's fools, etc. (op. cit., pp. 215-16).

10. Op. cit., p. 115.

11. Foster Hailey, 'An interview with T. S. Eliot,' *New York Times,* April 16, 1950, Sec. II, p. 1, col. 5.

12. Eliot's knowledge of psychoanalytic thinking was apparent in the treatment of the field in the *Criterion* in the years of his editorship; the magazine called attention, for example, to the work of the French physician Roland Dalbiez, in which the psychoanalytic method was deliberately separated out from Freudian metaphysical assumptions, in order to show that the method need not conflict with Catholic philosophy.

13. Mr. Wimsatt's review includes an effective discussion of the play's 'straight-shooting language' and its rhythm, 'a very marked thing throughout' (pp. 669-71).

14. 'T. S. Eliot's Latest Poetic Drama,' *Commentary,* XVII (April, 1954), 367-72.

15. Mr. William Arrowsmith argues that where Euripides, in dealing with supernatural events in a naturalistic manner, did justice to both planes, Eliot's comedies fail because they do not adequately realize the natural relations through which they seek to convey supernatural relations ('T. S. Eliot's Comedy,' in *English Stage Comedy,* ed. William Wimsatt, New York, 1956).

INDEX OF NAMES

INDEX OF NAMES

Sappho, 31
Schleiermacher, F., 96
Schwartz, D., ix, 197
Seneca, 13
Shakespeare, 11, 13, 15, 20, 32, 41, 45,
    48, 53, 68, 72, 75, 78, 80, 85, 86,
    88, 95, 97, 102, 103, 106, 111, 122,
    125, 127, 137-41, 150, 156-7, 158,
    161, 168-9, 171, 175, 243
Shaw, G. B., 103, 158
Shelley, 23, 28, 48, 59, 68, 75, 79, 108,
    242
Sidney, Sir Philip, 138
Sitwell, E., 151
Smith, Grover, Jr., 242
Smith, Henry Nash, xii
Sophocles, 126
Sorel, G., 91
Sparrow, J., 150-51
Speaight, Robert, 165
Spencer, H., 96
Spencer, T., 24, 26, 191
Spender, S., 155, 175
Spenser, 12, 39, 47, 49, 50, 68, 88
Spinoza, 14, 18
Stein, G., 107
Stendhal, 19
Stevens, Wallace, 184
Stevenson, 31
Strachey, John, 125-6
Strachey, Lytton, 72
Stravinsky, 134
Surrey, 69, 79-80
Sweeney, James J., 196
Sweeney, John L., 196
Sweezy, Paul M., xiii
Swift, 126
Swinburne, 7, 23, 28, 69, 77-8, 83, 87,
    160
Symons, A., 27-8

Tate, Allen, 108-9
Taupin, R., 27, 72
Taylor, Jeremy, 124

Tennyson, 7, 37, 48, 74-5, 80, 160,
    173-4
Theocritus, 47
Thomson, James, 80
Thoreau, 8, 42
Tolstoy, 126
Tottel, Richard, 79
Tourneur, 104, 169
Trollope, 42
Trotzky, 127
Turgenev, 24

Unger, Leonard, 196, **241**

Valéry, 58, 153
Vaughan, 15
Verlaine, 27-8, 46
Vermeer, 112-13
Villon, 19, 53
Virgil, 47, 204, 206-7, **213**
Voltaire, 203

Wardle, M., 153
Webster, 13, 21-2, 51, 88, 107, 136, 175
Weston, Jessie, 36-7, 49-50, 143-4, 153
Wheelwright, Philip, 184, 196
Whibley, C., 4
Whitman, 70
Wilkinson, Burke, 242
Williams, Charles, 242
Williamson, G., xii, 27, 29-30
Williamson, H. R., 54
Wilson, Edmund, 99, 121, 123-4
Wimsatt, William, 212, 243
Wordsworth, 5, 23, 48, 86, 113-14, 133,
    153
Wren, C., 124
Wyatt, 69, 79-80

Yeats, W. B., xxi, 20, 40, 90, 103, 117,
    155, 156, 175, 178, 198, 206

Zabel, Morton, 73-4

GALAXY BOOKS FOR THE DISCRIMINATING READER